MASTERMIND OF DUNKIRK AND D-DAY

The Vision of Admiral Sir Bertram Ramsay

BRIAN IZZARD

CASEMATE
Oxford & Philadelphia

For those men who did not return and for David, a D-Day veteran

Published in Great Britain and the United States of America in 2020 by
CASEMATE PUBLISHERS
The Old Music Hall, 106–108 Cowley Road, Oxford OX4 1JE, UK
and
1950 Lawrence Road, Havertown, PA 19083, US

Copyright 2020 © Brian Izzard

Hardback Edition: ISBN 978-1-61200-838-7
Digital Edition: ISBN 978-1-61200-839-4

A CIP record for this book is available from the British Library

Printed and bound in the Czech Republic by FINIDR s.r.o.

Typeset in India for Casemate Publishing Services. www.casematepublishingservices.com

For a complete list of Casemate titles, please contact:

CASEMATE PUBLISHERS (UK)
Telephone (01865) 241249
Email: casemate-uk@casematepublishers.co.uk
www.casematepublishers.co.uk

CASEMATE PUBLISHERS (US)
Telephone (610) 853-9131
Fax (610) 853-9146
Email: casemate@casematepublishers.com
www.casematepublishers.com

Contents

Acknowledgements

Admiral Ramsay's official reports, especially those for Operation *Dynamo* and Operation *Neptune*, proved invaluable.

The Dunkirk evacuation reports of Rear Admiral William Wake-Walker, Captain William Tennant and Commander Hugh Troup also provided much useful information, as did the experiences of many Royal Navy commanding officers and Merchant Navy captains.

It is fortunate that Admiral Ramsay left a wealth of material – letters, diaries and other papers – which is held at the Churchill Archives Centre, Cambridge. I am indebted to the centre's director, Allen Packwood, and his staff for their help with my research. Admiral Ramsay's family have been generous in allowing me to use the material.

I am grateful for the facilities provided by the Imperial War Museum, London. Interviews with Dunkirk and D-Day veterans were a rich source of material, in particular those given by Stanley Allen, Albert Barnes, Andrew Begg, Arthur Dench, Frederick Gooding, Charles de Groot, Frederick Hannaford, Reginald Heron, George Honour, Robin Hutchins, Alfred Leggatt, Charles Lightoller, Colin Madden, Lord Newborough, John Pearce, Harold Nelson Smith, John Tarbit, Arthur Turner, Harold Viner, Henry Faure Walker and Wilfred Walters.

I would also like to thank the following: the Air Accidents Investigation Branch, Aldershot, Hampshire; Squadron Leader Ross Clarke of the Military Aviation Authority, Bristol; the Collections Enquiry Team, Royal Air Force Museum, London; the Defence People Secretariat, Ministry of Defence, London; Robert Green of *After the Battle* magazine; The National Archives, Kew, London; Dave McCall of the Imperial War Museum's image licensing department; the National Maritime Museum, Greenwich, London; the Trustees of the Liddell Hart Centre for Military Archives and the Alanbrooke Trustees; Rear Admiral Bruce Williams, editor, *The Naval Review*; and Cathy Williams, archives services manager, King's College London.

Rear Admiral W. S. Chalmers's 1959 biography of Admiral Ramsay, *Full Cycle*, was a useful guide. As mentioned in my last chapter, the rear admiral had the advantage of being able to contact some of Admiral Ramsay's contemporaries, notably Field Marshal Lord Alanbrooke. He had the disadvantage, however, of not being able to use a significant amount of material in the forthright admiral's letters and diaries.

I am most grateful to the naval historian W. J. R. Gardner for reading the manuscript and for his comments.

Once again I have appreciated the guidance of my agent, Duncan McAra. And my thanks to Casemate's Ruth Sheppard, Isobel Fulton and Alison Boyd.

Author's Note

There is a tendency in official documents and letters to begin common nouns with an upper case letter. For style and consistency, lower case was generally preferred when quoting from them.

It is the publisher's style to refer to ships as it rather than the traditional she or her.

Foreword

Admiral Sir Bertram Ramsay must be the least known of the great military figures of World War II. This lack of recognition is partly due to his untimely death in an air crash in early 1945, only months after his outstanding achievement – Operation *Neptune* – the maritime element of the successful D-Day landings. He did not live to gain the rewards and decorations, or to write his memoirs like the other great Allied commanders.

Ramsay had been placed on the retired list in 1938 – he could have expected to go on further but he did not suffer fools gladly, even if they were senior to him. His intellect and administrative genius were understood and, although on the retired list, he was given a dormant appointment as the flag officer in Dover. He was re-engaged with the coming of war and would go on to mastermind the two greatest maritime amphibious operations of the war – leaving no doubt that he was one of the key leaders in World War II, up there with figures such as Churchill, Roosevelt, Alanbrooke, Eisenhower, Cunningham and Montgomery.

Ramsay, rightly, has been seen as the saviour of Dunkirk. The evacuation could so easily have been a disaster. It was a classic case of cometh the hour cometh the man. Ramsay galvanised the organisation in Dover and when the Allied armies were defeated in the Low Countries and cut off on the French coast near Dunkirk he was ordered to evacuate as many as possible. Ramsay's mastery of the Dunkirk evacuation cannot be underestimated. Churchill admitted at the time that he thought only 20,000 to 30,000 troops might be saved. The most optimistic estimate was 50,000. In the end more than 338,000 were brought to Britain. Around 850 vessels of all shapes and sizes took part in Operation *Dynamo* and nearly 240 were lost.

Though battered, the country still had the nucleus of an army that would fight another day. It took time for the tide to turn, and it was not until November 1942 that Britain, along with the United States, was ready to go on the offensive, with the invasion of French North Africa. Ramsay proved a mastermind of the amphibious operation – *Torch*.

Torch was an outstanding success and from the naval point of view went according to plan.

But there was no rest for Ramsay who became naval commander of the British assault forces for the invasion of Sicily. It was a triumph, with UK and US troops occupying the island by 17 August 1943.

Ramsay was then selected to mastermind Operation *Neptune*. How felicitous that the man who had masterminded the Allied withdrawal from Europe should similarly lead the return. The invasion involved the greatest amphibious operation in history, about 7,500 ships and craft. *Neptune* was Ramsay's crowning glory.

His work was still not done, and his efforts to ensure resupply of the Allied armies as they moved towards Germany and victory proved crucial.

Ramsay was not to see that victory. On 2 January 1945 he died in an unexplained air crash. He was 61.

In this book Brian Izzard allows us to understand Ramsay, a very private man who eschewed the cult of personality, and goes a long way towards correcting our nation's lack of knowledge of his achievements.

Admiral the Lord West of Spithead GCB DSC PC
First Sea Lord 2002–6

CHAPTER I

The Banished Warrior

It was, without doubt, a disappointing end to such a promising naval career. In July 1938, Rear Admiral Bertram Ramsay was given the news he feared. He was told that he would be placed on the retired list. Ramsay was paying a high price for having embarrassed a senior officer, a future First Sea Lord no less. For some, in the highest reaches of the service, Ramsay's actions amounted to a scandal; others had only sympathy for the rear admiral.

The Naval Secretary, Rear Admiral William Whitworth, informed Ramsay of the decision. After 40 years in the Royal Navy, he would be retired on 10 October, with the rank of vice admiral. Whitworth was sympathetic. 'It is a rotten job to have to be the purveyor of bad news to one's friends, and especially if I feel that this retirement will be a very distinct loss to the Service.'[1] Ramsay received many messages of support. One of his closest friends, Admiral of the Fleet Sir Reginald Tyrwhitt, wrote, 'I have always looked on you as a future First Sea Lord and I think you would have made a damned good one. We have been below par here for some time.'[2] Lady Tyrwhitt was 'livid with rage'. Vice Admiral Andrew Cunningham, who would play such a prominent role in the forthcoming war, told Ramsay he was a loss to the service and it was 'a bad business that you have never had a job to hoist your Flag in'. Someone serving in the battleship HMS *Iron Duke* wrote, 'I – like so many hundred others – deplore the loss of your vast technical and administrative experience at a time when the needs of the expanding Service are crying out so loudly for it.' Another supporter, who was 'mortified' to read about the retirement in *The Times*, told Ramsay, 'I don't understand this country. Just at this moment, surely, we can ill afford to spare people who may be counted as among our best.'[3]

Ramsay had not been in a post since December 1936 after falling out with the Commander-in-Chief of the Home Fleet, Admiral Sir Roger Backhouse.

They had been friends for many years, but Ramsay found it impossible to work effectively as Backhouse's chief of staff. The rear admiral, noted for his high standards and work ethic, was left deeply frustrated. In private, he likened Backhouse to Mussolini. Ramsay yearned for another appointment, but from those in authority there was little inclination to offer him one, certainly not a position that would advance his career. He would be left to wither on the vine.

The navy was casting aside someone who had shown total dedication since joining as a 15-year-old cadet in 1898. As he rose in rank, senior officers frequently praised him. His attention to detail could border on the obsessive. Whatever ship he was serving in, he expected it to be the smartest. This was an officer who could write many hundreds of words on how to paint a warship properly – 'Painting is an art and can only be attained with practice and experience. Paint is expensive. Therefore every drop of paint put on the ship must be put on to last its maximum time and look its best. The brush must not be overloaded: the strokes must be firm and put on horizontally first and vertically second, finishing off with the upward stroke.'[4]

During those 40 years in the navy, he had filled many appointments and commanded vessels ranging from a 540-ton monitor to a 30,450-ton battleship. He was a stickler for the right attitude, as one officer recalled after a Far East posting, 'He told me that officers were not to go ashore at Wei-hai-wei without headgear. If they had no hat, how could they raise it to him?'[5]

A magazine article painted this picture of Ramsay: 'The man himself is not easy to deal with. If he is on the hard side with his juniors, no consideration of his advancement has ever made him acquiesce in what he felt to be unjust treatment by his seniors; if he once makes up his mind that he has been unfairly treated, he will stick his toes in, regardless of the consequences to himself.

'Ramsay has always been able by force of ability to get the best out of men, although he is quite ruthless. Nobody is allowed to play tricks about his orders, or even his wishes for that matter. He has a personal disinclination to attend to detail, but he conquers it because he is acutely conscious of the necessity for meticulous attention to such matters. He will therefore show untiring patience in achieving his results. Moreover, he has a great aptitude for getting others to attend to detail and for supervising their work. It is not that he picks a good staff, but that he has a faculty for training any staff which is sent to him and for drawing out their qualities and initiative until he gets what he wants.' Ramsay was also described as shy, a bad mixer and highly strung, 'a most staunch friend, but by no means a friend to all the world'.[6]

A few months before Ramsay's retirement was announced, Admiral Sir William Fisher, under whom Ramsay served in the Mediterranean, had pointed out there was 'so much uncertainty in the world' that it might mean 'untold possibilities – so don't lose heart'.[7] Ramsay was well aware of the threat from Germany. In May 1938, he had asked to see Winston Churchill, whom he believed would a key figure in the growing crisis. By way of introduction, Ramsay reminded Churchill that he had served in his father's regiment, the 4th (Queen's Own) Hussars. The rear admiral said it was his duty to warn that the navy was unprepared for war. He also discussed his falling out with Backhouse. Churchill, out of office, gave him a sympathetic hearing but said he was unable at that time to take any action. The future prime minister remembered the interview during a visit to Dover in 1940 and remarked, 'You were right – in fact, you were proved right.'

But retirement did have one major consolation. Ramsay could spend more time with his wife Margaret and their young sons, David and Charles, at their home in Scotland; a haven of peace and tranquility, far away from the machinations of the Admiralty. He had been there a lot anyway since December 1936, with little to do as a naval officer after stepping down as Backhouse's chief of staff. Ramsay and his wife shared a love of the countryside and a passion for hunting, polo and racing. Both were expert riders. And Ramsay, though not physically imposing, had a reputation for being fearless when it came to horses. His father, the cavalry officer, had made sure from a young age that he took to riding.

As Admiral Fisher had predicted, 'untold possibilities' became a reality. Bizarrely, 13 days before he was officially due to head to retirement, Ramsay was told that he was being nominated as Flag Officer in Charge at Dover in the event of war. He was well qualified for the task because he had served in the Dover Patrol during World War I. And who should put him forward for the appointment? One Roger Backhouse, who had become the First Sea Lord. Perhaps Backhouse felt guilty about Ramsay's treatment.

Ramsay was assigned to the staff of Admiral Sir Edward Evans, the Commander-in-Chief, Nore, based at Chatham. Evans was a World War I hero who had made his name in a famous action as captain of the destroyer HMS *Broke*. Ramsay's task was to make preparations to establish his headquarters at Dover. When the Munich Agreement of September 1938 appeared to bring peace, Ramsay returned to Scotland as a retired vice admiral. The agreement, of course, soon unravelled, and by May 1939, Vice Admiral Ramsay – still officially retired – was back in Dover making further preparations. His temporary headquarters was the Brown House Hotel and he admitted that the 'organisation here is quite chaotic', with a lack of office facilities, no stationery, books or typists, a few tables but no chairs, and 'maddening communications'. He had 'some lovely destroyers, the very latest, and some sloops and very little else'.[8]

On 15 July, Backhouse died in London from a brain tumour, aged 60. He had resigned as First Sea Lord two months earlier because of poor health, having been in the post less than 10 months. Shortly before his death, he was promoted admiral of the fleet. Admiral Sir Dudley Pound succeeded him.

After Britain declared war on Germany on 3 September 1939, Ramsay wrote to his wife, who remained in Scotland, 'It's come, the war, and perhaps it's for the best. But what a wreck it will make of all the world.'[9] Destiny had called on Vice Admiral Bertram Ramsay.

CHAPTER 2

A Ramsay Who Riled Wellington

Bertram Home Ramsay, known as Bertie, was born in Hampton Court, Middlesex, on 20 January 1883. His father, Captain William Alexander Ramsay, a Scot, was in command of a detachment of the 4th (Queen's Own) Hussars based at barracks adjoining Hampton Court Palace, home to the ghosts of Henry VIII, Anne Boleyn and Cardinal Thomas Wolsey. Bertie's mother, Susan, was from Clontarf, County Dublin. Captain Ramsay, son of a Royal Artillery captain, had joined the 4th Hussars as a cornet in 1869 and spent the next 31 years with the regiment, which had fought at Talavera, Salamanca, Vitoria and Toulouse during Wellington's Peninsula campaign, and taken part in the Charge of the Light Brigade at the battle of Balaclava in 1854. Despite his many years with the regiment, Ramsay saw little action, with a long spell in India. Winston Churchill, a subaltern in the 4th Hussars, wrote to his mother, 'I am now getting on quite well with Colonel Ramsay who takes my advice in most matters.' Ramsay, a noted polo player, was given command of the 4th Hussars in 1896. When he retired from the army, he settled in Cheltenham, Gloucestershire, where his late parents had lived. In 1912, he was made an honorary brigadier.[1]

The family had a military hero in Major William Norman Ramsay, who was once placed under arrest on the orders of Wellington. William Ramsay, son of a Royal Navy captain, was commissioned in 1798 as a second lieutenant in the Royal Artillery. During the Peninsula campaign in 1810, he fought at Busaco with H Battery, Royal Horse Artillery. The following year, at the battle of Fuentes d'Onoro, the battery was cut off from the main British force and surrounded by French cavalry, but Ramsay led a daring counter attack, driving back the enemy – 'an English shout pealed high and clear, the mass was rent asunder, and Ramsay burst forth, sword in hand, at the head of his battery, his horses breathing fire, stretched like greyhounds along the plain, the guns bounded behind them like things of no weight, and the mounted gunners followed close, with heads bent low and pointed weapons in desperate career.'[2]

The battery took part in the battle of Salamanca in 1812 and for much of that year Ramsay was in command. In the aftermath of the battle of Vitoria on 21 June 1813, he was ordered to pursue the retreating French, but later Wellington told him to wait at a village for further orders. Because of a misunderstanding, Ramsay carried on with the pursuit. Wellington saw this as disobedience and ordered his arrest. Ramsay was soon released.

The episode intrigued the poet John Masefield, who wrote, 'Wellington personally ordered him to stay at a point with two guns until he, personally, ordered him away. The next day, Captain Ramsay's divisional general and one of Wellington's staff officers both ordered him elsewhere. He judged that the latter brought Wellington's personal order and obeyed it. Unfortunately, this was not the case, and as the roads were jammed with traffic, he could not quickly get back when the mistake was shown to him. Wellington is said to have been furious, and put him under close arrest (of course only for a few hours). Wellington seems to have been hard towards those who vexed him (perhaps most people are). He is said to have barred Ramsay's promotion thenceforward.'[3]

Ramsay resumed command of his battery in the middle of July and before the year was out he gained promotion to brevet major. A fellow officer pointed out that he was 'adored by his men, kind, generous, and manly, he is more than the friend of his soldiers'.[4] Ramsay had seen much fighting and there was more to come – Waterloo.

His battery was soon in action on 18 June 1815 and during the battle it was in position near the strategic Chateau d'Hougoumont. The fighting was fierce, with Guards' regiments repelling waves of French infantry. In late afternoon, a bullet passed through Ramsay's snuff box, entering his heart and fatally wounding him. He was buried near his guns during a lull in the battle. Later, the body was sent to Scotland and reinterred in the churchyard at the village of Inveresk, near Edinburgh. Wellington acknowledged afterwards that 'the success of the battle turned upon the closing of the gates of Hougoumont'. In honour of its courage at Waterloo, H Battery was given the title Ramsay's Troop.[5] Two brothers also died in army service.

Bertie was one of five children. There were two older brothers, Frank and Alexander (also known as Gerald), who both pursued army careers, and two younger sisters, Georgina (also known as Ina) and Elizabeth, who both married army officers. Frank proved a fine soldier during World War I, rising to the rank of major general. Twice wounded, he received the Distinguished Service Order and was Mentioned in Despatches seven times. Alexander's war was brief. A major, he was taken prisoner in 1914, the first year of the war, and spent the rest of the time incarcerated in Germany.

At some point, Bertie's father was posted to the Essex garrison town of Colchester, and his youngest son and Alexander were sent to Colchester Royal Grammar School, which can trace its history to 1128. Bertie was there for less than a year, leaving in the summer of 1892, 'too short a period to have made much of an academic impact'.[6] With such strong family links to the army, it seems surprising that he was pointed in the direction of a naval career. He may have welcomed the idea. In those days, families with limited funds often saw the Royal Navy as the right course for the youngest son (being cheaper than an army career). Bertie was sent to Stubbington House, a few miles from Portsmouth, which specialised in coaching pupils for naval cadetships. The school, founded by the Reverend William Foster in 1841, produced a number of admirals and several recipients of the Victoria Cross. Scott of the Antarctic was a pupil before joining the navy in 1881, aged 13.

From an early age, Bertie developed an independent streak. There was, perhaps, little choice. His father was given a posting to India in 1895 and he next saw his parents five years later. Holidays were spent with relatives or family friends in the countryside, riding, hunting and shooting, which suited Bertie. His father had insisted on his son making full use of the regimental riding school. Bertie also enjoyed sport, especially athletics.

In January 1898, the 15-year-old cadet joined the training ship HMS *Britannia* at Dartmouth, under the command of Captain Assheton Curzon-Howe, apparently 'the politest man in the navy'. In previous years, there had been complaints of bullying. Cadet Ramsay impressed his instructors and he left in May 1899, praised as 'zealous, promises well'. He went to the cruiser HMS *Crescent*, flagship of Vice Admiral Sir Frederick Bedford, Commander-in-Chief of the North American and West Indies Station. Ramsay was soon promoted to midshipman.[7]

In October 1901, he wrote to his mother about a visit to Halifax, Nova Scotia, where there was a large parade for the Duke and Duchess of York. 'We marched past the Duke [the future King George V] awfully well. He was very pleased indeed with us. The Royal Marines band played us past. The Duchess is awfully nice and I fell in love with her at Quebec the first time I saw her. I don't believe the Duke cares one bit for her.' The following month, he wrote to his mother pointing out a difficulty.

'It is awfully hard writing to you and father at the same time as there is not enough news to tell you both separately.' His father was in command of a cavalry brigade at the Curragh in County Kildare, Ireland, and his mother was at an address in Bournemouth.[8]

Ramsay spent three years in *Crescent* and, in later life, often remarked that he was fortunate to have served in such a happy ship, making lasting friendships. He also appreciated the cruiser's high standards. Ramsay continued to get excellent reports, gaining first-class certificates in seamanship and gunnery, though only a third in navigation. Promoted sub lieutenant, he joined the cruiser HMS *Hyacinth*, flagship of Rear Admiral George Atkinson-Willes, Commander-in-Chief of the East Indies Station. *Hyacinth* did not impress Ramsay. Writing to his mother from the Persian Gulf in November 1902, he remarked, 'We feed awfully well in the mess which is a comfort. Otherwise it is an uncomfortable ship in every way.' Mrs Ramsay appeared to be having difficulty getting domestic staff and her son sympathised. 'It would be awful to spend Xmas without servants.' Curiously, the 'loving son' signed the letter with the formal B. H. Ramsay.[9]

One year later, he found himself sailing to Bombay in the P&O liner SS *Arabia*. At Port Said, he wrote to his mother, who was having problems after hiring servants. 'I am awfully sorry the servants are giving such trouble. I should give them a rather bad character [reference]. I am getting awfully bored with this journey and shall be glad to finish it. We had a horrid passage from Marseilles. There are quite a lot of army officers on board, but I don't care much for them, bar one or two. We have a crusty old man in our cabin and he is very fat and takes up all the room. It is rather nasty.'[10]

Returning to *Hyacinth*, he faced action for the first time during the Somaliland campaign of 1902–4, one of Britain's small wars, which would see five awards of the Victoria Cross. Dervishes led by Mohammed Abdullah Hassan resented growing colonial influence in their part of Africa. After several engagements, Hassan was defeated at Jibdalli and forced to retreat. In April 1904, a combined naval and army force, including Royal Marines and men of the Hampshire Regiment, attacked the fortified port of Illig. Landing on an open beach in heavy surf, a soaked Ramsay rushed forward brandishing a cutlass in one hand and a pistol in the other. Under fire, he suddenly realised that the men he was leading were not showing the same enthusiasm and he checked his progress. Illig was eventually captured after fierce fighting. Three sailors were killed and 11 men wounded. The dervishes suffered 72 casualties. A *Hyacinth* midshipman, Arthur Onslow, who charged through a burning hut into concealed caves to bayonet snipers, was awarded the Conspicuous Service Cross. Ramsay earned his first campaign medal. It was an early experience of an amphibious assault.

Promotion to lieutenant and service in the cruisers HMS *Good Hope* and HMS *Terrible*, and the battleship HMS *Renown* followed, and he continued to win praise as a 'very promising officer' with 'good judgement'. Perhaps his most significant posting before World War I was to HMS *Dreadnought*, the battleship that revolutionised naval power. Ramsay joined *Dreadnought* in 1906; the year of its first commission. Brainchild of Admiral Sir John Fisher and built in Portsmouth in record time, the ship carried 10 12in guns, and Ramsay was placed in charge of one of the turrets. At that time, gunnery was seen as key to high rank, but after two and a half years in *Dreadnought*, he decided, with characteristic independence, to specialise in signals. He was an officer who liked to be immaculate and disliked getting his hands dirty. And he was interested in the bigger picture, the movement of fleets.[11]

In 1909, Ramsay spent four months at the signals school in Portsmouth, later that year joining the pre-dreadnought battleship HMS *Albemarle* as flag lieutenant to Rear Admiral Sir Colin Keppel in the Atlantic Fleet. The flag captain was Ernle Chatfield; the future First Sea Lord who would play such a crucial role in Ramsay's future in the thirties. Chatfield recalled how annoying Ramsay could be in *Albemarle*. 'He was a bright young lieutenant of great ability and keenness. He was, however, at that age lacking in tact. Yet, I liked him very much – the difficulty was he tried to run me through the admiral, such as coming on the bridge when we were about to unmoor in Oslo. We were the only ship present, and without consulting me he hoisted a signal for *Albemarle* to unmoor and weigh southern anchor first. Which, of course, I ignored as it was the wrong anchor! Then he ran against David Beatty, the captain of the *Queen*. In a squadron signal exercise off Dover, Ramsay made a signal – "the *Queen*'s signal men are a disgrace to the fleet". David Beatty came aboard the *Albemarle* at 9 o'clock the next morning in frock coat and sword, and made a furious complaint to poor Colin who, like me, knew nothing about it.'[12]

There was a more relaxing time for Ramsay in the Mediterranean as flag lieutenant to Rear Admiral Sir Douglas Gamble in the cruiser HMS *Bacchante*. In Malta, there was time to enjoy sport. Gamble, to Ramsay's delight, was keen on horse racing. The flag lieutenant was also able to train and lead a navy polo team that beat the army, the kind of success that would always go down well with a senior officer. In June 1912, he returned to Portsmouth to join the staff of the signals school. The following year saw an important career move. In the rank of lieutenant commander, he was accepted for the newly created war staff course in Portsmouth. He became one of the earliest naval officers to gain experience of the staff system. And with war looming, he had increasingly strong opinions on how a modern navy should be run.

CHAPTER 3

War Breaks Out

When war broke out in August 1914, Ramsay was back in *Dreadnought* as flag lieutenant to Sir Douglas Gamble, who had been promoted vice admiral and given command of the Fourth Battle Squadron of the Grand Fleet. There were three other dreadnoughts in the squadron, HMS *Bellerophon*, HMS *Temeraire* and HMS *Agincourt*. As ever, Ramsay was focused on efficiency and alertness. He was soon frustrated, writing in his diary, 'We are always last in everything and we are without exception the dullest flagship that ever existed. The reason is that the admiral will not listen to his staff and the flag captain is an absolute nonentity … One feels particularly bitter when one meets other staff officers and hear how different things are with them.'[1]

Ramsay came to the conclusion that peacetime training had been defective and gunnery officers were 'absolutely ignorant' of fleet tactics. In sunny Malta, with shared interests, such as horse racing, he had got on well with Admiral Gamble. In *Dreadnought*, a clash of personalities emerged. It was wartime and Ramsay saw himself as new navy, whereas Gamble was old navy. There was a showdown. Ramsay – still a lieutenant – wrote in his diary, 'The vice admiral and I had a set-to in his cabin about my shortness of manner at times and the war college training which he resents very much, or rather the way in which I display it. Anyhow it cleared the air and had to come … My faults are that I can't sit still and see things done in an antiquated and un-progressive way, and I must put my word in … He won't admit that a knowledge of war is the least necessary for any officers until they come to flag rank, but how they are to learn it then I don't know … Whatever the result of the war may be, it can but do good by washing out these old-fashioned ideas and bringing forward an up-to-date officers' training. At present the old school will not admit that any one junior to them can have any ideas at all.

'I never expected anybody to take my advice, but I do feel that the vice admiral might at least ask for my knowledge of things … My feelings of affection for him have not changed in any way, for indeed I am proud to think he is one of my greatest friends, but it is one thing serving with him in peace, when points don't arise, and in war when business is business.'[2]

On 25 August, the fleet, commanded by Admiral Sir John Jellicoe, was on exercise in the North Sea when there were reports of enemy submarines. Fortunately, there was no attack, but Ramsay had not been impressed with the response. 'Considering that we were in imminent danger of being torpedoed at any moment there was marvellously little excitement on board. People will not realise the danger, and everyone wants to leave his post and have a "look see".'[3]

Ramsay recorded another fiasco. 'The officer in charge of Y turret, which has a Maxim [machine gun] mounted on it, thought that the bugle he heard was "repel aircraft", so he rushed to his station and seeing an object in the sky immediately aimed at it and fired. On looking again, however, he saw that it was a kite being flown from the *Iron Duke* [Jellicoe's flagship] for trial.'[4]

The flag lieutenant had been right to be concerned about complacency. The German submarine menace became painfully clear on the morning of 22 September as the cruisers HMS *Aboukir*, HMS *Cressy* and HMS *Hogue* were on patrol in the North Sea, steaming in line abreast. Because of earlier bad weather, the ships were without a destroyer escort. They were spotted by *U9*, which had been sent to attack British transport vessels at Ostend. At 0620, the submarine fired a torpedo at *Aboukir*, hitting its starboard side and flooding the engine room. The other cruisers went to its aid. Only one boat was launched from *Aboukir* and it sank after half an hour. As the rescue was under way, *U9* fired two more torpedoes, hitting *Hogue*, which soon capsized. The submarine, under the command of Kapitanleutnant Otto Weddigen, briefly surfaced and *Cressy* opened fire and tried to ram it. *U9* dived and *Cressy* began picking up survivors. At about 0725, the first of two torpedoes hit the *Cressy*, which capsized and floated upside down before sinking. Steamers and trawlers answered distress calls but destroyers arrived at the scene only some four and a half hours after the first attack. Just 837 men were rescued. More than 1,450 sailors perished. Most of them were reservists. *U9* escaped. On 15 October, *U9* sank another cruiser, HMS *Hawke*, which had failed to take avoiding action. The lives of 524 sailors were lost.

The 22 September attack was a devastating blow for the Royal Navy. Early the next day, the Admiralty sent a signal to all ships stressing that a vessel torpedoed or mined 'must be left to its fate'. Other large ships needed to be clear of danger, with only small vessels giving help. The signal acknowledged that the captains of *Hogue* and *Cressy* were 'only complying with the dictates of humanity'.

The attack exasperated Ramsay, who wrote in his diary, 'From what we can gather yesterday morning one ship either *Hogue*, *Cressy* or *Aboukir* was sunk by a submarine and the other stupid ships went to her assistance and were simply asking to be sunk too. It does seem childish to think that it should be so but the evidence is rather strong. It just shows how utterly without imagination of war the majority of our senior naval officers are. About a month ago I remarked at lunch that I supposed it was recognised that if a ship of the fleet got hit by a submarine that she could expect no assistance from other ships and the VA [Vice Admiral Gamble] said that really I was too bloodthirsty and pessimistic for anything and why should I always be thinking of the worst side of things.'5

There was another major blow for the Royal Navy on 1 November, defeat at the battle of Coronel, in the southern Pacific Ocean, off the coast of Chile. A squadron of old ships led by Rear Admiral Sir Christopher Cradock engaged modern German vessels with disastrous results. Cradock's flagship, *Good Hope*, blew up with the loss of everyone on board. Another cruiser, HMS *Monmouth*, was also destroyed. A total of 1,600 were killed. There were no German losses.

Ramsay's attention was drawn to a parliamentary report in *The Times* later that month in which Lord Charles Beresford, who left the navy as an admiral in 1911, paid tribute to Cradock, 'one of the most brilliant of our sailors'. The report continued, 'It was impossible to overstate his pluck; he was a great leader of men and was most popular. He fought against a superior force; he had ineffective ships and reserve crews. It was said that he ought not to have engaged a superior force. The tradition of the navy was that you might go down yourself, but the enemy must not be allowed to get away unchallenged. Admiral Cradock had maintained that tradition, and anything said against him would be resented by the whole fleet.' Ramsay cut out the report and stuck it in his diary with the comment, 'It bears out my statements about many admirals being without up-to-date views on war.'6

It was not long before the navy took its revenge. On 8 December, the victor of Coronel, Admiral Maximilian von Spee, attempted to raid the supply base at Stanley in the Falkland Islands. Unknown to him, a large British squadron, including the battlecruisers HMS *Invincible* and HMS *Inflexible*, was there. Spee attempted to flee but his squadron was hunted down, losing six ships. The admiral and his two sons were among some 1,900 German dead. British losses were light.

Vice Admiral Gamble did not last long as commander of the Fourth Battle Squadron. In early 1915, Vice Admiral Sir Doveton Sturdee, who had defeated von Spee at the battle of the Falkland Islands, replaced him. Ramsay may not have been the only person who thought that Gamble was out of his depth in a new age of warfare. The vice admiral was offered command of the China Station, which he declined. After a 'special service' post, he retired at his own request in May 1917 with the rank of admiral.

After Gamble's departure, Ramsay was offered the post of flag lieutenant to Rear Admiral Sir Robert Arbuthnot, appointed commander of the First Cruiser Squadron, in HMS *Defence*. Arbuthnot was a keen rugby player, boxer and motorcyclist. He was probably the only officer of flag rank who kept a motorbike in his day cabin. He was also passionate about discipline, almost to the point of fanaticism, once producing 300 pages of instructions in addition to *King's Regulations*. Ramsay, of course, favoured the highest standards but Arbuthnot's reputation may have been too much even for him. He declined the post, a wise move in hindsight. At the battle of Jutland on 31 May 1916, Arbuthnot foolishly made his squadron an easy target for German cruisers. *Defence* was blown up, with the loss of Arbuthnot, his motorbike and everyone else on board – 903 men. The squadron was disbanded after the battle as three of its four ships had been sunk.

Arbuthnot's fanaticism aside, there was another factor in Ramsay's reluctance to remain a flag lieutenant. He wished to have his own command. After a spell at the Admiralty, making use of his specialisation in signals, he was granted his wish, command of the Dover Patrol monitor HMS *M25*. With a 9.2in gun, the vessel was designed for shore bombardment. *M25* supported the Allied armies in Flanders.

In June 1916, at the age of 33, Ramsay was promoted commander, and in October the following year, remaining with the Dover Patrol, he was given command of the destroyer *Broke*, which had taken part in the battle of Jutland. It was a career highlight, captain of a destroyer. But Ramsay did not like what he saw. *Broke*, in his view, was a fitting name. He produced a scathing report. It is worth quoting his points because they perfectly illustrate his attitude. There were five headings:

OFFICERS
(a) O. O. Ws [Officers of the watch] untrained in their duties. Never allowed to keep station or alter course. Officers who handled ship gave no consideration to their next astern.
(b) Assistant paymaster did nothing.
(c) Officers took no interest in their men, or their sport and amusements. Were not in touch with the men.

(d) O. O. D. [Officer of the day] in harbour did nothing.

(e) Officers did not correct faults when they found them, which was seldom owing to their slackness.

SHIP

(a) Ship from truck to keelson filthy, except E. R. department.

(b) Upper deck and mess decks, officers' quarters, magazines, and store rooms all equally neglected.

(c) Boats very dirty and neglected.

(d) Sick bay a disgrace to the name.

EFFICIENCY

(a) Ship's company untrained.

(b) Guns' crews badly drilled.

(c) Control arrangements execrable.

(d) Rangefinder never troubled about. Range taker never went near it.

(e) Dumaresq [a calculating machine] operator, who had been at his station one year, had no idea how to work his instrument.

(f) Training arcs of guns inaccurate.

(g) Voice pipe arrangement hopeless.

(h) Practice firing carried out once in previous 12 months.

(i) No effort made to get sights graduated, so as to make full elevation available on gun mountings.

(j) Guns in very dirty condition.

(k) Magazines in deplorable condition of dirt and disorder. Temperature records not bothered about.

(l) Collision mats rotten.

(m) Towing arrangements poor.

INTERNAL ECONOMY

(a) No standing orders.

(b) No records kept of letters and documents received, or sent.

(c) No trace of orders or memos received.

(d) No effort made at distribution of orders or promulgation.

(e) Confidential books kept in very slack method, many copies that should have been destroyed being still on board.

(f) All key memos in force, and complete list of private signals given to signalman, and kept on bridge.

(g) Books not seen weekly by captain.

(h) Signal books never mustered or arrangements made for this to be done.

(i) Ship's steward's accounts never supervised.

(j) No rounds other than 9 o'clock.

(k) Mess traps for ship's company neglected, some messes had traps for about 20% of their numbers.

DISCIPLINE

(a) Discipline bad. Much leave breaking. Leave breakers often not reported, and seldom punished. Open gangway during refit.

(b) Conduct books not properly kept, and never inspected by captain.

(c) No respect paid to captain or officers by ship's company. Ordinary remarks of respect such as standing to attention when officers pass, saluting, not shouting in presence of officers and enumerable small customs quite disregarded.

(d) Punishments not enforced, merely ordered.

(e) Liberty men not inspected before or after leave.

(f) No respect paid to after part of the ship.

(g) Gambling rife among ship's company.[7]

The report was marked private and confidential, and it is not clear if any senior officers saw it. But Ramsay's broadside was directed at a ship that had achieved heroic status. The previous captain, Edward Evans, was 'known throughout the Empire', as one newspaper put it, and many of his crew had been decorated.[8] Even King George V paid a special tribute to 'Evans of the *Broke*' and his men. Perhaps Ramsay was annoyed that in more than three years of war he had seen so little action and resented the acclaim. Perhaps, he thought the crew had become arrogant. One senior officer who took issue with Ramsay about *Broke* was Captain Wilfred Tomkinson, commanding the Sixth (Dover) Flotilla of Destroyers. Years later Ramsay's wife Margaret, whom he married in 1929, commented, 'My husband's efforts to alter these methods brought him the displeasure of Captain Tomkinson, who never lost a chance thereafter to find fault with my husband … Moreover Captain Tomkinson influenced Admiral Keyes, who in turn took a hard and unjust view of my husband.'[9]

On the night of 20 to 21 April 1917, Evans's *Broke* and the destroyer HMS *Swift* attacked six German destroyers in the Dover Strait near Goodwin Sands. The Germans had been shelling Calais and Dover. The British ships concentrated their fire on *G85*. Then *Broke* rammed *G42* so violently that its bow became embedded in the hull of the German destroyer. What happened next was reminiscent of the close-quarter fighting of Nelson's day:

'It is impossible to describe the sensations of those on board both these ships as the collision occurred – the *Broke*'s grimly triumphant; the Germans filled with terror-stricken amazement and horror. It was a dreadful moment; but worse was yet to come.

'Men were screaming and shouting for help as the *Broke*'s guns, at their maximum depression, pumped shell after shell at a few yards' range into the mass of men huddled on the deck of her stricken enemy. One of the German's torpedo tubes had stuck into the *Broke*'s side and was torn off its mounting. The anti-aircraft 2-pounders added to the din with their stuttering uproar, while the British seamen that remained alive in the forepart of the ship, with rifles and fixed bayonets, and revolvers and naked cutlasses, headed by Mr Midshipman Donald Gyles, R.N.R., already wounded by a shell splinter in the eye, swarmed forward on to the *Broke*'s forecastle to repel boarders. They were taking no chances. No quarter was given. Every German who clambered over the bows was shot or bayoneted. A deadly small-arm fire was poured from the forecastle into the terrified men on *G42*'s deck. Even the officers on the *Broke*'s bridge used their automatic pistols. Few of their enemies survived the storm of lead and nickel.'[10]

Broke was also taking punishment from the other enemy ships and was reduced to 'a smoking shambles'. *G85* and *G42* both sank. The remaining four enemy destroyers fled. *Broke*, with 21 killed and 36 wounded, was towed back to Dover. Commander Evans and Commander Ambrose Peck of the *Swift* both gained immediate promotion to captain and were awarded the Distinguished Service Order. Among other awards, 24 men of *Broke* and *Swift* received the Distinguished Service Medal, a remarkable number for a single action. Evans would rise to the rank of admiral, receiving a peerage in 1945.

There was more frustration for Ramsay in April 1918 when he missed the daring Zeebrugge and Ostend raids because *Broke* was having a refit. He did, however, take part in the second operation to block the port of Ostend the following month, leading a group of destroyers in support. It began badly for him. Before leaving harbour, *Broke* was damaged in a collision with one of the blockships (old vessels) but Ramsay carried on, fearing that he would be recalled. The destroyer bombarded shore batteries at Ostend. 'The Boches were evidently not awake, as it took them a good five minutes to reply,' Ramsay wrote later. 'Then a fierce barrage was put up, star shells falling all around us and burning in the water, while the heavy shells whistled overhead.'[11]

Ramsay's collision with the blockship incurred the displeasure of Vice Admiral Sir Roger Keyes, who had been appointed commander of the Dover

Patrol in the January. But worse was to come. On June 30, while on patrol, *Broke* and the destroyer HMS *Moorsom* attacked what they thought was an enemy submarine. It turned out to be HMS *E33*. The submarine was depth charged but returned to port undamaged.

A court of inquiry noted that the destroyers had challenged the submarine several times but received no reply. They considered it hostile but delayed action until the last possible moment in case it was British. 'We consider they were justified in doing so and that no blame is attributed to them.' The submarine had gone on patrol early and the captain should have realised that the destroyers were likely to be friendly in that area. With some irony, the court pointed out, 'We consider that the attack on *E33* through mistaken identity was admirably executed with prompt decision. It is to be observed that the only fault appears to have been that the Challenge was made with too weak a light, which could not be read and in fact misled *E33*. This however appears to be a common occurrence.'[12]

The inquiry cleared the two destroyer captains, but Keyes was having none of it. He rejected the findings. And Ramsay was furious. At the top of his copy of Keyes's comments he wrote, 'Hymn of Hate by Roger Keyes', and scrawled other comments, including 'wrong', 'absolutely unjustified' and 'purest hate and unfair'. The admiral stressed the destroyers should have used better signalling, and they knew a British submarine was leaving port that evening. *Moorsom* reminded *Broke* when passing. Keyes wrote, 'Under these conditions to attack a submarine in the area beyond the barrage which *Broke* must have known was allotted to British submarines is in my mind inexplicable.' The onus on establishing the identity of the submarine had rested with *Broke*. It was also inexplicable that Ramsay did not know it was a British submarine until he reached Dover the next night. Rubbing salt into the wound, Keyes noted, '*Moorsom* certainly delivered a good attack, and gave *Broke* an excellent lead which fortunately she failed to take advantage of.'[13]

Their lordships at the Admiralty also rejected the inquiry's findings, deciding that *Broke* was at fault for the poor signalling. But Keyes's staff were also criticised for telling *E33* that all surface ships in a certain area were to be regarded as hostile.[14]

It was not a good year for Ramsay. There was yet another reprimand in the December. On 5 November, *Broke* was in collision with the hospital ship *Princess Elisabeth* in Dover harbour. Ramsay had achieved only a third-class certificate in navigation, and one wonders if this had a bearing on these mishaps.

An inquiry pointed out, 'There was a difference of opinion as to which entrance was to be used, the captain of *Broke* thinking that the *Princess*

Elisabeth intended to enter by the western entrance, whereas the captain of the *Princess Elisabeth* always intended using the eastern entrance. *Broke* appears to have paid no attention to the signals flying, governing the entrances to the harbour, which on this occasion showed that the western entrance was closed to incoming vessels.'[15]

The blame was 'entirely attributable' to *Broke*.[16] And Ramsay was informed of their lordships' 'displeasure'.[17] But Ramsay's wife said her husband had told her that Admiral Keyes 'was overheard by one of his staff to say that Commander Ramsay was to be found guilty for the collision of 5 November, this before any evidence was heard. The finding of the inquiry on the incident of 30 June 1918 was also most unjust as the submarine was not reported in the area, and the fault lay with the admiral and his staff. Admiral Keyes also stopped my husband receiving the DSO [Distinguished Service Order].'[18]

The war ended on a happier note for Ramsay. *Broke* was chosen at short notice to take King George V, the Prince of Wales and Prince Albert to Boulogne. Perhaps the king, so impressed by the famous battle in the Dover Strait, had asked specially for the ship, not realising that 'Evans of the *Broke*' was no longer captain. It seems unlikely that Keyes would have put forward Ramsay and *Broke*. Ramsay rose to the occasion, hurriedly making sure the ship looked its best. There was a resourceful search for paint. Ramsay and *Broke* made a good impression and shortly after the trip it was announced that the captain would receive the MVO (Member of the Royal Victorian Order). Campaign medals and a Mention in Despatches (for Ostend) aside, it was his only British decoration during World War I. From other countries came the Crown of Italy (Officer), the French Legion of Honour (Chevalier) and the Belgian Croix de Guerre.

CHAPTER 4

New Horizons

Ramsay left *Broke* in January 1919. The perfectionist was satisfied. 'Am happy to think I shall pay off *Broke* a much improved ship in every way.' He had been tough on discipline but was able to record, 'Had a good send-off.' Captain Tomkinson, the flotilla commander, acknowledged that Ramsay was a zealous CO who kept his ship in 'very good order', but added, 'I do not consider him tactful or to posses good judgment. Vice Admiral Keyes concurs.'[1] Ramsay's new challenge was flag commander to Admiral Lord Jellicoe in the battlecruiser HMS *New Zealand*. Jellicoe, controversial commander of the Grand Fleet at Jutland, had been appointed First Sea Lord in 1916, only to be sacked a year later. In early 1919, he went on a world tour with *New Zealand* to advise Dominion governments on naval policy. India was the first official visit. It was not all work. There was polo and at Gwalior, as guests of a maharajah, Jellicoe and Ramsay went on a tiger shoot. The admiral shot three of the beasts and the commander one. At Simla, Ramsay attended a dinner dance, a 'very good show but poor class of beauty'.[2]

After a six-week stay in India, Jellicoe, promoted admiral of the fleet, headed to Australia, arriving at Albany on the southern tip of the west coast on 15 May. At a dinner party in Melbourne, Ramsay met an attractive Australian girl and a day later decided he was in love. It was a dilemma. 'Haven't felt like this about anyone for ages … how on earth can I persuade her to like me enough to love me?' Within a week he asked her to marry him. Time was short 'and I daren't put it off. I do hope I haven't spoilt my chances. I know she is the one.' At a dinner party, 36-year-old Ramsay's heart 'simply melted' and he 'felt more hope of gaining her love'.[3] But that night she succumbed to an influenza epidemic. Despite the best efforts of doctors and nurses she died days later.

After going on to Sydney Ramsay visited a cousin, Sir Herbert Ramsay, and his family in the Blue Mountains. 'Nice kids but dreadful accent,' he observed. Ramsay would not see his cousin again. Sir Herbert, who possessed 'a charming personality', was in poor health after working as a stock and station agent and he died in 1924, aged 56.[4]

New Zealand was the next country and again there was a warm welcome. Although there were many social engagements, Jellicoe focused on his mission, visiting ports throughout the country. His lengthy report would accurately stress the importance of a Pacific fleet with good docking facilities to counter a possible threat from Japan. The admiral was keen to become New Zealand's next governor general, seeing 'such an appointment as a dignified and happy way of erasing the hurt caused by the manner of his dismissal as First Sea Lord. Moreover, he admired New Zealand's staunchly loyal attitude to empire.' In September 1920, after the tour came to an end, his wish was granted.[5]

Jellicoe's chief of staff was Commodore Frederic Dreyer, who wrote of Ramsay, 'An excellent staff officer of very good judgment. Should do well in the higher ranks of the Service; active and plays games; rides very well; of excellent appearance and manners; cheerful and popular; strongly recommended for advancement.'[6]

Ramsay, still a commander, would have to wait until April 1921 for his next major appointment, executive officer of the Iron Duke-class battleship HMS *Benbow*, which had been recommissioned in the Mediterranean Fleet. *Benbow*'s commanding officer was James Somerville, who would play a key role in the Dunkirk evacuation. Ramsay wasted no time in making his presence felt. *Benbow* had to be the smartest, most efficient ship in the fleet, without question. Before joining it, the Jutland veteran was involved in operations supporting Greek forces during the Greco-Turkish War. In 1922, after a refit at Malta, *Benbow* took part in further operations against the Turks. Ramsay continued to insist on the highest standards even if the ship was involved in conflict. His efforts were rewarded. After an annual inspection in 1923, Rear Admiral John Kelly enthused, 'In all my experience I have not seen a cleaner or better kept ship. I carried out a very thorough inspection lasting three days. I would specially draw attention to the executive officer, Commander Bertram Home Ramsay, MVO, RN, who has been in the ship since she commissioned, as I am satisfied that these results could only have been achieved by means of unusual zeal, ability and personality, which qualities in this officer have impressed me as being quite exceptional.'[7]

On 30 June of that year, Ramsay was promoted captain and later given command of the cruiser HMS *Weymouth*. The perfectionist was not pleased with what he found. 'This ship has been scandalously neglected. Nothing refitted, weather-work not cleaned, paint slapped on over dirt anyhow, guns filthy, mess decks lousy.' It was scathing criticism, similar to the *Broke* broadside. *Weymouth*'s crew soon got the message. A week later Ramsay wrote in his diary, 'Thank God she is not in that state now.'[8]

The ship sailed from Portsmouth taking relief crews for ships at other bases, with Hong Kong the final destination. Before sailing the captain noted, 'I have no personal experience on the China Station but I was told out there that the climate generally speaking is a trying one which soon finds out the weak spots in people.' One of the problems was the 'greater liability to contract venereal disease compared to home waters'.[9]

There was drama soon after leaving Portsmouth. A Royal Air Force seaplane was spotted after ditching in rough sea with engine trouble. The engines were half submerged and the crew of five were on top of the fuselage. The exhausted men were rescued but salvage was not possible and Ramsay destroyed the plane 'with the ram', pointing out, 'It is probable that but for the timely appearance of *Weymouth*, the results of the incident would have been disastrous.' The ship headed, appropriately, to Weymouth Bay where the RAF men were transferred to another vessel. The cruiser then proceeded to Gibraltar. The next morning it was discovered that an able seaman, one Hubert Saul, was missing. It transpired that during the night the sailor had gone over the side in Weymouth Bay, swimming to the shore and then walking some 65 miles to Southampton, where his bride's parents lived. Saul had married in secret before *Weymouth* left Portsmouth and he felt the need to unburden his conscience. After his confession he reported to naval barracks.[10] On the voyage home from Hong Kong, Ramsay sent a letter to the Admiralty suggesting improvements to ships and barracks, as well as suitable tropical uniforms, to promote better health on the China Station.

He found himself back in Malta in March 1925, taking command of the cruiser HMS *Danae* in the First Cruiser Squadron of the Mediterranean Fleet. Unsurprisingly, the cruiser did not meet Ramsay's exacting standards. He complained that the men 'are not made to wake up and move. So I told them so. They moved much better after that.' He was not impressed with his executive officer and another officer was 'quite useless – if he shows no improvement he must go'. Ramsay decided that officer training was partly to blame because it was little changed from the days of sailing ships. Rear Admiral Guy Warren, who later joined *Danae* as executive officer, pointed out, 'He could not stand inefficiency in any shape or form, but he was absolutely fair and for this reason, if for no other, he was well liked by the ship's company. They had to go all out and did so.'[11]

In the April, *Danae* paid a visit to Athens. Ramsay wrote in his diary, 'I was not favourably impressed by the attitude of the British community; generally speaking the presence of the *Danae* in the bay, and of the officers and men on leave, was completely ignored by them. On the other hand, a more favourable impression was gained of the Greeks, who were both respectful and friendly. A football ground was placed at our disposal every day.'

Ramsay did not confine his quest for efficiency to *Danae*. Two months after taking command of the cruiser, he cast his net wider, producing a paper 'on probable future problems of the Royal Navy'. The paper went to Rear Admiral Arthur Waistell, commanding the First Cruiser Squadron, who was not impressed, commenting, 'All of the points raised have already been carefully considered at the Admiralty. Many of the suggestions are, in my opinion, unsound and would not have been put forward if the disadvantages attached to them had been fully realised.' In his view Ramsay, an experienced officer, did not yet have the advantage of seeing both sides. Waistell sent the paper with his comments to Ramsay's old foe, Admiral Keyes, who had been appointed Commander-in-Chief of the Mediterranean Fleet.[12]

Keyes noted that he welcomed opinions that led to progress but then sarcastically commented, 'In this present case no useful purpose would result from forwarding somewhat vague proposals of a general nature, but economy might result if Captain Ramsay in due course put forward definite proposals for a reduction of personnel in *Danae*, such proposals being in conformity with existing procedure as regards training etc.'[13]

Ramsay also produced a lengthy paper on how to keep a ship clean. It was directed at *Danae* but he no doubt thought that other captains would benefit from his observations. His thoughts on paintwork bordered on the obsessive. He stressed, 'The first essential is to have good groundwork. To this end the surface of all weather paintwork whether it is aloft, funnels, superstructure or the side should be made smooth by rubbing down with pumice stone, glass paper etc. Where there is rust showing, the source must be removed by the scraper and red lead. Three coats of the latter are necessary and they in turn must be smoothed before recoating. The aim must be to have a surface that will not hold dirt: glass is quickly and effectively cleaned because its surface will not hold dirt. Every little obstruction on the surface even those caused by bad painting must be removed, and care must be taken in repainting that they are not renewed.'[14]

It was essential to have the right mix of paint. 'In all mixtures of grey paint in this ship I wish there to be equal parts of white lead and zinc white. The reason for this is that zinc white is the best preservative of steel and it prevents rust which means that the paint does not assume the yellowish hue that is so commonly seen in light grey paint.'[15]

On cleaning, he stressed, 'After rain or other circumstances tending to dirty the paint, it must be cleaned at the first available opportunity. It is not economical to delay. There is just as much art in washing paintwork as there is in painting.' The paper listed eleven points, ending, 'It is no exaggeration to say that a clean and smart ship is kept clean and smart with less effort than a slovenly ship is kept slovenly.'[16]

Life in Malta was proving to be pleasant and Ramsay reflected on his good fortune – comfortable quarters, a good steward, valet and cook, plenty to read and three polo ponies. And relations with Admiral Keyes improved after the navy started winning polo matches.

In July 1925, *Danae* called at Villefranche in the South of France, and Ramsay took a stroll to nearby Nice where he saw 'a very dull lot' of people on the Promenade des Anglais and a couple of women with 'enormous sterns' on the beach.[17] Other goodwill visits followed. In December 1926, there was concern about the behaviour of sailors on leave in Malta, and Ramsay, assisted by several officers, carried out an investigation. It was found that seamen used a total of 172 pubs and bars in Valletta, Msida, Sliema and Senglea. The first week of the month was usually the worst. Pubs were often crammed at 2300, closing time, with large numbers of chief petty officers, petty officers and ratings drunk or under the influence of drink. Many headed to brothels, which were grouped in two districts, Strada Fontana in Valletta and Msida. Most of the prostitutes were married, with an average age of 34. About a third of the women were suffering from venereal disease. Sanitary conditions in Strada Fontana were 'beastly'. Ramsay's report warned, 'The state of affairs in Msida from 2300 onwards is disgraceful. It is the worst district used by servicemen. The main flow of traffic commences after about 2300, when the cabmen pick up drunken men emerging from the public houses and desiring drink or women. These men are frequently brought to Msida, where they can obtain both. The district is full of pimps and prostitutes who cooperate to rob the sailor.' The report made a number of recommendations to provide leisure facilities for sailors.[18]

Ramsay's peaceful existence was only broken in early 1927 when the First Cruiser Squadron was ordered to China. The civil war there was threatening British interests. *Danae* was given 48 hours to get ready and Ramsay managed 'two hurried gallops and took a sad and affectionate farewell of my beloved ponies … I'm glad to think the government have decided to do this thing properly. Ramsay MacDonald [the Labour leader] or the Liberals would, as before, try turning the other cheek and then send two men and a boy. I know full well that if it's up to me whether we evacuate a British concession or no, it will certainly be no! Give an Oriental an inch and he considers you a fool.'[19] The show of force had the desired effect and Ramsay was able to resume his polo playing in Hong Kong. His time in *Danae* was almost up and in March 1927 he sailed for Britain in the P&O liner SS *Mongolia*. He was appointed an instructor on the war course for senior officers at the Royal Naval College, Greenwich.

One of Ramsay's lectures was on the battle of Jutland, and he was no doubt surprised to receive a message from Jellicoe, created an earl after serving as New Zealand's governor general, who wanted to see a copy of it. Jellicoe, sensitive about criticism of his handling of the Grand Fleet, replied with several corrections, which included comments such as, 'Therefore our hopes of providing a surprise were almost nil', 'The battle orders were revised just before Jutland, but this revision had not been issued. It was issued a month or two after Jutland,' and 'I don't recollect this being reported to me in *Iron Duke*. It is the first I've heard about.'[20]

In 1929, Ramsay returned to China as flag captain and chief of staff to Admiral Sir Arthur Waistell, Commander-in-Chief of the China Station, someone he knew from his Malta days. He took command of the admiral's flagship, the cruiser HMS *Kent*, at Wei-hai-wei. As ever, Ramsay was strict. James Rivett-Carnac, who was *Kent*'s executive officer and a future vice admiral, recalled, 'At times he had an aura of vinegar … He was always well dressed in well-cut clothes and objected to laxity in officers' dress. I remember he told me that officers were not to go ashore at Wei-hai-wei without headgear. If they had no hat, how could they raise it to him?'[21] *Kent* returned to Britain in May 1931 and Ramsay became an instructor again, this time at the Imperial Defence College, near Buckingham Palace. The commandant of the college was Air Marshal Sir Robert Brooke-Popham, the first RAF officer to take the role. Brooke-Popham found Ramsay hardworking with sound judgement, noting, 'When speaking in public he tends towards a somewhat dogmatic type of delivery, but sitting round a table will readily discuss all points of view.'[22] After two years as an instructor, Ramsay was back at sea, in command of the battleship HMS *Royal Sovereign* in the First Battle Squadron of the Mediterranean Fleet.

It was in Malta in 1925 that 42-year-old Ramsay realised that someone was missing from his life. 'I now want a charming wife.' In the spring, he had met Helen Margaret Menzies, 21 years his junior, during a spell of leave in Berwickshire in the Scottish Borders, where he had family connections and friends. Ramsay and Margaret, as she was known, found they had a lot in common – a love of horses, hunting and the countryside. Margaret's father,

Colonel Charles Menzies, chairman of the well-known distribution business of John Menzies, and her mother Helen, 'a great judge of both horses and hounds', were excellent riders. As Margaret put it, 'I was brought up to love horses, dogs, gardening and the country way of life. Rather too much so, as my outlook was insular and narrow.'[23] Ramsay and Margaret became friends and arranged to correspond.

From early on, it became apparent that Ramsay was hoping that their friendship would develop into something more. They met again when he went to Berwickshire in the summer. Soon after returning to London on the night train, he wrote to Margaret. The letter began unpromisingly with 'Dear Girl' but then he revealed he had dreamed of her. He was optimistic. 'I do feel that yesterday for the first time we made real good progress and it was joy in itself to see you smile naturally towards the end of it, and drop that cloak of reserve or shyness or whatever it is you cling to so hard. It's a thousand pities that we could not have had one more week together now.' But Ramsay realised that he needed to be patient. 'I do think that you are quite right to go slow and had you allowed me to kiss you yesterday it would have been the match which would have set me on fire and fogged one's better judgment. All the same darling, it would have been lovely! Still, something withheld is something wanted more! I hope that you no longer dislike touching my hand as you did. That's quite a big advance! Possibly I've given you ideas to think on.' Towards the end of the letter, he wrote, 'If you ever love me, I want you to love me spontaneously – and I think you can!'[24]

Many of Ramsay's sailors might have been surprised at their captain's softer side. And he soon came to realise that patience was indeed required. As Margaret put it, 'Being a selfish, stupid ass with a wrong set of values I was reluctant to give up hunting and my way of life to embark on a naval one instead, but he was a constant and understanding friend and I a foolish young woman.'[25]

Ramsay's persistence finally paid off. He and Margaret were married at Christ Church, Duns, in the Scottish Borders, on 26 February 1929. It was during Ramsay's time at the Royal Naval College and his bride left her beloved countryside to be with him in London. On his next posting to Malta, she went too. They had a house overlooking the Grand harbour and Ramsay's command, *Royal Sovereign*. In 1933 their first son, David, was born.

Many years later, Margaret would reflect, 'The marriage was a very happy one. We shared many interests and he was always appreciative, kind, humorous, deeply affectionate and ageless in his outlook.'[26]

CHAPTER 5

Battle of the Admirals

When Ramsay was appointed captain of *Royal Sovereign* in November 1933, a familiar theme surfaced. He told his wife he wanted to make the ship the smartest and most successful in the fleet. He impressed the second in command of the Mediterranean Fleet, Vice Admiral Sir Roger Backhouse, who later recorded that the captain was 'an officer of character and personality. Aims at the highest standards. His ship has improved markedly in smartness and appearance and on drills in the six months he has been in command.' Importantly for Ramsay, Backhouse, who was also in command of the First Battle Squadron, stated he deserved promotion to flag rank. The admiral was due to return to Britain in April 1934, and Ramsay remarked that 'everyone out here is very sorry as he is popular'.[1]

Backhouse's endorsement became a reality for Ramsay in May 1935 when he did indeed achieve his long-held ambition of flag rank. He had known for several months that he was in line for promotion to rear admiral, and so did Backhouse, who was set to become Commander-in-Chief of the Home Fleet in the August, having been promoted full admiral. In early January, Backhouse had invited Ramsay to become his chief of staff, writing, 'I think you know me fairly well and at least some of my peculiarities but perhaps not all. I like doing a good deal myself, but I believe there would be enough to keep us both busy in normal times.' He added, 'If you think you'd like to come, I shall be very glad to have you – but if you'd sooner be on your own after promotion I shall quite understand.'[2]

Such an appointment held 'many attractions' for Ramsay. Backhouse was seen as a future First Sea Lord 'which, if all went well, would be advantageous to my future'. And the role of chief of staff of one of the main fleets would be a valuable experience. Ramsay accepted. Backhouse replied, 'I am very glad you will take on the job and hope you'll like it and find enough to interest and occupy yourself.'[3]

It was a decision that Ramsay would come to regret. But they had been friends for many years, since they were shipmates in *Dreadnought* during its first commission of 1907–9. The two lieutenants were admirers of the actress and singer Lily Elsie, making several trips to London to see her in Franz Lehar's operetta *The Merry Widow*. The fact that Backhouse, an imposing 6ft 4in tall, was newly married did not seem to be a drawback. When it came to the navy, the men had a similar special focus, and comments on their service records could have been interchangeable. Early in his career, Backhouse, for example, was described as 'zealous, hardworking and very promising' and 'a brilliant officer'.[4] Only four years older than Ramsay, he was able to climb the promotion ladder faster.

In retrospect, Ramsay should have been more alert to Backhouse's admission that 'I like to do a good deal myself'. Years later Ramsay stated, 'It was common knowledge that the staff regime in the First Battle Squadron was not a happy one on account of the habit Sir Roger had of centralising all the duties he possibly could in himself.'[5] Yet Ramsay had told his wife in 1933 that Backhouse was popular.

In the Home Fleet, Backhouse flew his flag in the battleship HMS *Nelson*, based at Portland. At first Ramsay found the admiral charming to work with. 'But after about a couple of weeks Sir Roger remarked to me one day in his cabin that his basket was empty and confessed that he seemed to get many fewer papers than he had expected. I said that personally I would have considered that a matter for congratulation as I had a never ending stream in mine. The next thing that happened was that Barrow, his secretary, came to me and said that Sir Roger had given orders cancelling the exiting staff procedures, whereby all correspondence arriving in the office were distributed to the staff for remarks and/or draft proposals before being sent into the commander-in-chief. Urgent papers had of course always been taken to him and myself in any case, but in future every paper, however trivial, was to be seen by him first and he would dictate the action to be taken, or refer it to the staff for remarks if he wanted them.

'Now it is difficult for anybody who has not been connected with the staff of a fleet flagship to have any conception of the amount of correspondence received in the ship daily. And if you imagine the ship to be at sea for several days or a week even and the amount of correspondence is multiplied accordingly. Every paper had now to go through the IN basket on the commander-in-chief's desk. Shortly after this order was promulgated, another of similar nature was brought to me by the flag lieutenant to the effect that all signals of any nature were to be taken at once to the commander-in-chief by him and that the commander-in-chief would take the necessary action regarding them. In effect, these instructions completely paralysed the existing normal staff organisation and rendered null and void the instructions issued by my predecessor for the conduct of staff business.'[6]

As expected, an avalanche of papers and signals descended on Backhouse, keeping him busy from early morning until midnight or later. There were other calls on his time, visits from senior officers, inspections of ships and bases, trips to the Admiralty and dinner parties. He rarely took any exercise and there was not time even to read a daily paper. His health began to suffer and he was 'habitually tired and nervy'. Relations with Ramsay visibly deteriorated.

'Our free and happy association no longer held and he took me less and less into his confidence,' Ramsay complained. 'On my part, I resented the position in which I found myself placed, chief of the staff in name only and with no compensating factors, blaming Sir Roger for being the cause and myself for having walked so stupidly right into the spider's web.'[7]

Ramsay tried to persuade Backhouse to take some exercise but without success. He had so little to do that he was able to spend afternoons playing golf 'but one never feels comfortable going ashore while RB [Roger Backhouse] stays and slogs away in his cabin. He does all I do as well as I myself, which is unnecessary duplication, but it is his way and he can't change it.'[8]

There was a growing crisis over Italy's aggression in Abyssinia [Ethiopia] and Ramsay believed that the Italians were 'itching' to commit a hostile act against the British. 'I'm certainly beginning to hate all Italians. I'd love to see them scuttling back to their kennels with their tails between their legs.' Two days later he wrote to his wife, 'If we have a war, and I surmise it, I have quite made up my mind to quit at the end of it. I must say that unless the Italians get cold feet everything points to the outbreak of hostilities.' The League of Nations, with its limited influence, did not impress him.[9]

On a routine visit to the Admiralty in the last week of September, Ramsay was asked by the First Sea Lord, Admiral of the Fleet Sir Ernle Chatfield, to attend a meeting on operations to be carried out by the Home and Mediterranean fleets in the event of hostilities with Italy. Ramsay had discussed the crisis with his staff officers in *Nelson* and considered himself well informed. The question of strategy was Backhouse's province, but he had shown little interest. Returning to the flagship, Ramsay briefed the admiral and prepared a paper on the options, explaining that the Admiralty would be sending a document with its proposals and a response was necessary. As the days passed, relations continued to deteriorate, and Ramsay and the captain of the fleet feared the commander-in-chief was on the verge of a breakdown.

Ramsay told his wife he could not face staying in his post longer than a year. 'The whole point of having an admiral as chief of the staff is that he can carry sufficient weight to carry out the commander-in-chief's intentions for him and issue orders and make decisions. I can't make any decisions or issue any orders because RB is jealous and insists on doing it all himself.'[10]

Matters were about to get worse. On 11 October, Backhouse flew to London in *Nelson's* plane. On the return journey, the aircraft crashed in Portland harbour. Backhouse was rescued but he was badly bruised and suffering from shock. After a couple of days in bed, he felt better and called for papers to be brought to him. In spite of protests, he insisted on working in bed and later in his cabin wearing pyjamas. 'There is not the slightest doubt that he was in no fit mental or physical condition to do this, and it delayed his recovery,' Ramsay noted.[11] Such was the concern of the admiral's doctor and Lady Backhouse that the First Sea Lord was contacted and he virtually ordered a spell of leave. Reluctantly, Backhouse went off for a break of several days, insisting on taking a large suitcase full of papers. When he returned to *Nelson*, his health was little improved and his outlook unchanged.

Ramsay complained to his wife that he was 'only doing head clerk's work'. There was another problem. 'Many thanks for my washing. Annoying thing happened – two odd stockings only arrived, meaning that the other two had fallen out, alas!!'[12]

He was still waiting for the Admiralty paper on the Italian crisis but then, to his 'utter amazement', he discovered that Backhouse had received it and drawn up a reply with points that showed 'an incomplete understanding of the situation'. Desperate to discuss the reply with Backhouse, the chief of staff tried to delay the letter but to no avail. Ramsay was fuming. 'I have to admit that this latest and most barefaced indication of Sir Roger's intention to prevent me from functioning as chief of the staff came as a nasty smack in the eye, and for the first time I began to feel cross.' Ramsay went to see him but the admiral was reluctant to offer any explanation. When it was pointed out that his staff found it equally difficult, Backhouse replied that he was not going to waste his time reading 'their trash'.[13]

Ramsay felt he was in an impossible position and suggested that he should be replaced 'as I was unable to conceal my dislike of a system which was opposed to every principle upon which I had been trained and which I had profound belief'.[14] Backhouse agreed it would be better to make an early change. That evening, however, he asked to see Ramsay and during a friendly conversation he said he was sorry about their disagreement. He was not feeling well and planned to take a weekend break. On his return, he hoped that they would come to an amicable agreement on the workload. That did not happen.

Before returning to *Nelson*, Backhouse went to see the Commander-in-Chief, Portsmouth, Admiral Sir John Kelly, and the main topic of conversation was Ramsay. It seems that Kelly quickly sided with Backhouse, who then wrote to the First Sea Lord complaining about his chief of staff. 'I am sorry to say that I am having trouble with my chief of staff who persists in trying to do all my work and even keeps papers from me. He seems to think that it is just my job to do the entertaining. He is a very efficient officer and would do well in command of a squadron of small ships. I have had to warn him that if he cannot do better in future, I shall have to make a change.'[15]

Ramsay learned of the letter many months later. 'Sir Roger was already stealing a march on me by preparing the ground and lodging a fictitious complaint with the First Sea Lord. It is not a nice thought that someone in the high position that Sir Roger then occupied should stoop to such deceit, though I have not the slightest doubt that he wrote the letter at the instigation of Sir John Kelly. I think this because Sir Roger is naturally a kind hearted man and it was not in his nature either to make false statements or fail to keep a promise.'[16]

The description of Backhouse as 'a kind hearted man' seems at odds with comments that Ramsay made to an old friend, Admiral Sir Geoffrey Arbuthnot, known as Buffy, in November. Backhouse was likened to Mussolini. 'Like Mussolini he has steadily accumulated into his hands the reins of everybody else's office until he now has become the absolute dictator and managing director of the whole concern.' Ramsay added, 'It is abundantly clear that he is by nature terribly jealous professionally of anyone whom he thinks may be in a position to compete with him. He must be the best informed person on board on any subject connected with the Service, and it is visible agony for him to hear a bit of surprise information discussed or broached to him.'[17]

Later that month, Ramsay told his wife that he was 'entirely superfluous'. But he had the support of his staff and they were 'most anxious that I should not chuck my hand in'.[18] Lord Jellicoe had died and Ramsay went to his funeral in London. Afterwards, he had a long conversation with a close friend, Admiral of the Fleet Sir Reginald Tyrwhitt, who urged him to remain in his post 'at all costs'. The Naval Secretary, Rear Admiral Guy Royle, gave similar advice. Ramsay returned to *Nelson*, only to find relations with Backhouse were becoming even more strained. 'He literally barked at me on the few occasions on which I had dealings with him, and it seemed as though he was determined to provoke me into committing myself in some way such as would provide him with the excuse he required to go to the First Sea Lord and, reminding him of the previous complaint, ask that I should be relieved from my appointment.'[19]

Nelson sailed from Portland to Portsmouth. There was more frustration. Plans for anti-aircraft gun trials involving a squadron of the Fleet Air Arm were ignored by Backhouse, who made other arrangements without consulting any of his staff. This resulted in the trials having to be cancelled. Ramsay gave himself 48 hours to consider his future, but the time 'merely served to strengthen my resolve to clear out whilst my record remained clean and good, rather than remain on and head for disaster'. On the night of 1 December, he wrote to Backhouse asking to be released from his position. Ramsay said the request would 'cause you no surprise', and the letter ended, 'I have never allowed myself to become a mere cipher in any appointment I have hitherto held in the Service, and now that I have reached the flag list I am even less inclined to accept that role.'[20]

The next day at lunch Backhouse ignored Ramsay but later asked to see him in his cabin that evening. 'He looked daggers at me and for a minute or so did not speak, but then he said, holding up my letter "Is this the only solution?" to which I replied that I was afraid it was.'[21] Backhouse agreed but pointed out that he would have to consult the First Sea Lord. After visiting the Admiralty the commander-in-chief asked to see Ramsay. He was friendly but to Ramsay's surprise he did not mention the First Sea Lord's decision, giving the impression that everyone at the Admiralty was busy with other matters.

Ramsay was left wondering if Backhouse was contemplating 'a peaceful solution of the situation, and nothing would have pleased me better'. He had sent a copy of his letter to the Naval Secretary and dashed off a request asking Rear Admiral Royle to keep it private 'pending action by Sir Roger'.[22]

Ramsay was in for a shock. Royle replied, 'The whole thing was brought to a head yesterday when RB saw the First Sea Lord. I managed to get in before RB came and put up your side of the question to the best of my ability. I am afraid that the First Sea Lord was not sympathetic. He pointed out that it was the duty of the chief of staff to get on with his commander-in-chief and serve him in the way he wanted ... RB had already decided that you should go on December 17 when you take your leave ... Frightfully sorry this has happened. We must do our best to prevent any idle gossip getting into the papers.'[23]

Ramsay concluded that Backhouse was a moral coward. And the First Sea Lord should have 'inquired into the matter sufficiently to judge for himself whether or not there was any justification for my action. My record was excellent and I was not a fool, so why should I deliberately prejudice my future.' In fact, Chatfield refused to see Ramsay, which angered him further. 'Under no circumstances could such a decision be held to be justified, for even an ordinary seaman on board ship has the right to see his commanding officer should he have a request to make or feel himself to be suffering an injustice.'[24] On 31 December 1935, Ramsay was placed on half pay.

After leaving *Nelson*, Ramsay was concerned that his name might have been put on the blacklist. With the First Sea Lord refusing to see him, he was anxious to offer an explanation for his unwillingness to continue serving under Backhouse. Chatfield and Ramsay had been friends while holding appointments as flag captain and flag lieutenant in the Atlantic Fleet. A letter of explanation was sent to the First Sea Lord in which Ramsay stated, 'I have always considered it essential from every point of view, and I am sure you will agree, that a commander-in-chief and his chief of staff should be able to work in the closest possible accord, and that when this could not be so, owing to widely differing views on important matters of principle, it was the duty of the chief of staff to clear out and make room for someone else whose views more closely coincided with those of the commander-in-chief.' Ramsay insisted he had acted from the 'highest motives'.[25]

Chatfield sent a two-sentence reply, thanking him for the letter and adding, 'I am sure you acted from the best motives, but I greatly regret your action and can but take a serious view of it.' Ramsay was puzzled that it was acknowledged he had acted from the best motives but such action was greatly regretted.[26] Clearly, the Admiralty was in no rush to offer him another post.

In the middle of March 1936, Ramsay visited the Kent home of his friend Admiral of the Fleet Tyrwhitt, who had written several letters of sympathy and advice, one of which described Backhouse as unbalanced. Tyrwhitt had been to see the First Sea Lord to press Ramsay's case. But he was taken aback when Chatfield said Ramsay had behaved very badly and then related 'a discreditable story'. It was claimed that during exercises Ramsay had argued with Backhouse on *Nelson*'s bridge and then stamped his feet and stormed off. Ramsay recalled, 'This account of my behaviour had upset Admiral Tyrwhitt very much for the reason that, had anything of the same nature happened to him when commander-in-chief, it would have driven him into a frenzy of rage, and he would probably have sacked his chief of staff on the spot. I was, however, able to reassure him that there was absolutely no truth whatever in the story.' It was also nonsense that he had tried 'to run Sir Roger and keep papers and information from him'. Ramsay was disgusted that Backhouse could 'stoop so low as to misrepresent the case to the extent he evidently had done, and that the First Sea Lord should have accepted a one sided presentation of it'.[27]

Tyrwhitt and his wife urged Ramsay to fight on. That month, he asked for a meeting with Chatfield, who agreed. Royle the Naval Secretary gave Ramsay a friendly warning. 'I must say I think you will have to be frightfully careful what you say to the First Sea Lord. I am afraid that if you attempt in any way to criticise RB or his methods things may become very difficult.'[28] On the day of the meeting, Ramsay saw Royle first and asked him if he knew who was behind the untrue story of a clash on *Nelson*'s bridge and without hesitation he replied, 'Joe Kelly.' It was the Commander-in-Chief, Portsmouth, Admiral Sir John (known as Joe) Kelly, to whom Backhouse had turned for advice about Ramsay months earlier. Ramsay was stunned that he was the source, though he knew him as 'this most artful and dangerous admiral'.[29] Kelly would die before the year was out, aged 65.

Chatfield received Ramsay politely and listened to his prepared case. The First Sea Lord accepted that there was no truth in the *Nelson* story. And, tellingly, he revealed he was weary of admirals' complaints, as Ramsay recalled, 'He said that in carrying out his job as First Sea Lord, he had found only one problem difficult to deal with, and that was the innumerable complaints made to him personally by senior admirals about other admirals. It was most difficult because he either had to accept their statements at their face value, or to ask for explanations from the other party, which simply lead to a wrangle. As a rule, he found it best to do nothing and things settled themselves.'[30]

No doubt Ramsay left the meeting a happier man. He had put his case to the First Sea Lord and it was not unrealistic to think that he still had a promising future in the navy. It was not good news in May, however, when Royle contacted him about his next proposed posting, Rear Admiral Yangtze from October 1937. As Royle put it, 'I have no idea what your reactions will be to the receipt of this news – you may be very disappointed, and if you are you must console yourself with the fact that there are a large number of good chaps who are not going to hoist their flag at all.'[31]

Clearly, Ramsay was very disappointed, and Royle had to tell him, 'I honestly don't think you will do yourself a bit of good by arguing with the First Sea Lord about the appointment.' Ramsay was reminded that there were 'crowds of chaps' who would be pleased to take the post. A number of senior figures still blamed him for the breakdown of relations with Backhouse, and the Naval Secretary warned, 'There really is not a hope of your getting the offer of any other job and I honestly think that any outside pressure which may be brought to bear would merely have a hardening effect. I know the First Sea Lord himself feels that he has done more for you than any advisers whom he consulted would have recommended, and so when he finds that you are dissatisfied it is bound to have an irritating effect.'[32]

Ramsay had plenty of time to think about the appointment. He spent a long spell at home with his wife and their son David in the seaside town of North Berwick. The couple indulged in their passion for country pursuits. In October that year a second son, Charles, was born. Later they would buy a Georgian country house, Bughtrig, in Berwickshire. Surprisingly, Ramsay did not have to give his formal response to the Yangtze appointment until March 1937. He was being rather hypocritical when he wrote to the First Sea Lord saying the role 'greatly appeals to me and in the ordinary course of events I would not hesitate to accept it'. Turning down the two-year appointment, he explained that he had two young children and the climate in China would be too harsh for them. He did not wish to leave them behind in England. Ramsay may well have reflected on the five-year separation he experienced as a child when his parents went off to India.[33]

Royle replied, 'Your letter to the First Sea Lord refusing the Yangtze was a very nice one and the First Sea Lord said so when he read it. To be quite candid I am very much afraid that you are not on a very good wicket for being offered any further appointment, but in this uncertain life I should not give up hope – something may turn up unexpectedly.'[34]

The unexpected was Ramsay's appointment as Flag Officer in Charge at Dover.

CHAPTER 6

King of the Castle

When war was declared on Germany, Ramsay was still living in Dover's Brown House Hotel. Soon afterwards, he requisitioned a flat near Dover Castle. There was plenty to do, in contrast to his time with Backhouse. 'I've seldom been so busy in my life,' he told his wife. 'I never get done because events turn up in unending succession to make things more difficult and complicate an already puzzling enough puzzle. In addition everybody wants advice, assistance, this that and the other, and along with all this I have to get on with preparations for things to come, of no easy nature.'[1] Over the war years, he would write many letters to Margaret, whom he called Mag, and she would be his confidante. Ramsay signed his letters Bert, not Bertie.

During World War I, three terraced houses on the town's Marine Parade had served as naval headquarters. The air offensive in the Spanish Civil War had shown that such a location for Ramsay's permanent headquarters was out of the question, something that would be emphasised by the Luftwaffe's onslaught on Poland. So many bombs were dropped on Dover during World War II that the port became known as Hellfire Corner. Ramsay needed somewhere the Luftwaffe or long-range artillery could not target. The solution overlooked the White Cliffs – Dover Castle or, more precisely, the tunnels deep beneath it.

Dover had been of strategic importance from the time of William the Conqueror. Building work on the castle began in the 1170s during the reign of Henry II, and in the great siege of 1216–17, military tunnels were dug in an attempt to thwart French forces. These tunnels were enlarged and extended by hundreds of civilian workers and soldiers during the Napoleonic Wars. Such was the need for accommodation that some of the larger tunnel areas served as barracks. Vertical shafts provided ventilation and fireplaces had flues. Fresh water came from a central well and latrines had drains that flowed to the sea. But the tunnels were dimly lit and usually cold and wet. After Wellington's victory at Waterloo in 1815, the number of soldiers living below fell sharply. Over the next century or so, the tunnels were used for stores and little else, being home to bats and rats. Ramsay chose the easternmost tunnel complex as his command centre – Admiralty Casemate. Workmen were kept busy installing better lighting and ventilation, as well as telephone and radio links. Some of the tunnels were partitioned for meeting rooms and offices, and Ramsay had his own 'cabin' with a view of the Dover Strait and his ships in the harbour.[2] France was just 22 miles away.

The castle and its tunnels proved to be a wise choice. The Germans clearly never realised their importance. Although the town and the harbour area were heavily bombed over the war years, the castle escaped virtually unscathed, although one bomb narrowly missed Constable's Tower. A civilian, George Barton, would recall being on duty at the top of the tower and seeing Messerschmitt fighters 'swooping on barrage balloons to shoot them down in flames through the murk. My job was to estimate the areas of the fall of the balloon for the fire station. All this while bullets were thudding into the walls of the tower below.'[3]

One of Ramsay's first orders involved the laying of minefields in the strait to deter German U-boats. Anti-submarine trawlers patrolled the minefields. Ramsay also ordered better anti-aircraft defences for Dover harbour. There was a war on, but he still concerned himself with matters at home. After telling his wife that he had been given an official car, hoping to get 'a pleasant and efficient Wren driver', he offered advice about her own cars. 'I am glad you are able to get petrol for both your cars as it ought to keep the Morris going quite well. Will you please get Wilson to blow up the tyres of both cars and see to their batteries and oil every week, specially the automatic oil supply in the Rover. Don't forget this, darling.' He added, 'How splendid of your mother to take over the hounds again, and what fun for you to be field master, even if there is no field!'[4]

There was something else on Ramsay's mind. Money. He told his wife – from the wealthy Menzies family – that their joint incomes would mean paying 'a big lump in super tax … we must try and put by all the spare cash that we can'. He planned to send her a case of sherry but feared the cost of alcohol would rise through higher taxation. 'Dear, dear, what a curse that man Hitler is. I do hope that he suffers hell on earth as a punishment for all this. It's small satisfaction to anyone that he should suffer later in hell. I do feel that Hitler has got himself into a most difficult position and one that will finally bring about his downfall. His alliance with Russia will lead to his ruin and suicide…'[5]

Ramsay was on the move again. This time, his address was No. 1 Castle Mess, Dover Castle. He told Mag, 'I like my new house and it will be a blessing when I get the servants to do things as I want them. The cook hasn't produced anything remarkable yet, but at least she serves up food to eat.' He added, 'I need some face towels but I will get you to buy these locally.'[6]

The minefields in the strait and the Royal Navy soon took a toll on Germany's U-boats, with four of them destroyed in October. *U16* ran aground on the Goodwin Sands after being depth charged by two warships. The infamous sands swallowed the crippled submarine. Later, the bodies of five of the crew were washed up between Hythe and Rye. The losses forced U-boats heading for the Atlantic to take the long voyage round northern Scotland, shortening their patrols. October also saw the Royal Navy suffering a major loss. The battleship HMS *Royal Oak* was torpedoed by *U47* at Scapa Flow in Orkney, with the loss of more than 800 sailors. Ramsay told his wife about the tragedy but hurriedly wrote to her again after realising he had breached security. 'In my last letter I said something about where the *Royal Oak* was sunk. Will you now please forget it and not mention it to anyone.'[7]

Although Ramsay was in charge at Dover, he answered to the Commander-in-Chief, Nore. He believed that his command should be completely independent, reporting only to the Admiralty. That was the case during World War I. He won the argument and was given the new title of Vice Admiral, Dover. The staff were reorganised and those who did not meet his high standards were let go. Captain Llewellyn Morgan, who had served with Ramsay during Jellicoe's world tour, was appointed chief of staff. It was a busy time with patrols in the strait and the safeguarding of convoys. Huge underground storage tanks were being constructed in the cliffs to hold fuel oil for the navy.

December showed that they were in for a harsh winter. Ramsay wrote to 'Darling Mag' and after thanking her for sending gingerbread – 'a reminder of home!' – complained, 'We've had simply frightful weather and the wind and rain simply crash past. The wretched ships in harbour are completely weather bound and lose anchors, collide with each other and are generally wretched. A soldier walking along the Admiralty pier was washed off it by a huge wave, which came over the top and overturned two trucks laden with stones.'[8]

But there was 'great news'. He explained, 'I've got rid of the chief steward and have a real family butler with vast experience and grand presence.'[9]

CHAPTER 7

The Troops Head to France

Dover had seen a lot of naval activity in the months before World War II. Now it was the turn of the army. Shortly before Neville Chamberlain's declaration of war on 3 September 1939, thousands of soldiers were sent to the port. There was not enough military accommodation and many of them were billeted with civilians. Army lorries and guards were everywhere. A Territorial Army anti-aircraft regiment set up its guns at various locations, including the seafront, to defend the town. And the pubs did a roaring trade.

An exodus of civilians was expected. Those who remained would have to get used to the sound of air raid sirens, blackouts, gas masks and Anderson shelters. Other precautions included removing the stained glass windows from the medieval Maison Dieu Hall and taking them to a place of safety. Footpaths near Dover Castle, popular with Sunday afternoon walkers, were closed.

Many of the soldiers in the town would soon be going across the Channel to support French forces. The Black Watch, led by pipers, marched from their barracks to the railway station.[1] The main troop convoys left Southampton and Portsmouth for Cherbourg and Le Havre. The ports of St Nazaire and Dieppe were other destinations. General Lord Gort, awarded the Victoria Cross during World War I, was given command of the British Expeditionary Force (BEF). Before the end of September, more than 150,000 troops and some 21,000 vehicles were transported. The build-up continued. The BEF took up defensive positions along the Franco-Belgian border, to the left of France's First Army. In October, the Germans began planning for the invasion of France and the Low Countries. But for the BEF, there would be many months of 'phoney war', with little action. Time was spent building defences and on training. Brothels at the ports and other places such as Lille and Tourcoing had become attractions, and Major General Bernard Montgomery was so concerned at the high rate of venereal disease that he issued a warning about 'horizontal refreshment' without the use of 'French letters'. His intervention upset senior commanders who viewed such bluntness as being 'obscene'.[2]

In January 1940, Ramsay had a visit from Winston Churchill, who was appointed First Lord of the Admiralty on the day war broke out. The vice admiral told his wife, 'Winston was very pleasant to me and he knows now who or what I am, and I feel that he will, or may be, quite a help if the opportunity necessitates.'[3] King George VI was another VIP visitor. He went to Dover on three occasions, making two trips to see the troops in France. March saw him arriving in Dover in a blizzard, and after inspecting men on the eastern breakwater, the frozen monarch was revived with tea and whisky. Later, he went to the castle tunnels, only for the lighting and heating to fail soon afterwards. Fortunately, as Ramsay recorded, the king remained 'charming to me'.[4]

The phoney war led Ramsay to think that perhaps the BEF might not be involved in any full-scale fighting after all. 'The war seems to have taken a particularly quiet spell except for submarine warfare and opinion seems to be that the Germans will refrain from any big offensive in the west. What we are to do with all the troops we are pouring into France I can't think. They will really be an awful embarrassment to the C-in-C, who will have a job to keep them quiet.'[5] In April, Germany invaded Denmark and Norway. But there were concerns at home. That month saw a 'pretty nasty' Budget. Ramsay complained to his wife that whisky would cost 16 shillings a bottle, and 'all our savings will go in super tax'.[6]

On 9 May, after the failure of Britain's intervention in Norway, Chamberlain resigned, to be replaced by Churchill. At 0435 on 10 May, Germany launched its invasion of France and the Low Countries, with Junkers Ju 87 dive-bombers (Stukas) and Panzer divisions creating havoc. As soon as he learned of the offensive, Ramsay ordered a planned operation. Four destroyers were sent from Dover with teams to demolish Dutch and Belgian harbour facilities. It is telling that British military planners had not expected much in the way of effective resistance from the Netherlands and Belgium, which were officially neutral. Indeed, the Dutch surrendered on 14 May. The capitulation was so quick that Ramsay was forced to recall transports and destroyers sent to evacuate part of the Dutch army. German forces had occupied Luxembourg virtually unopposed. The Germans attacked on two main fronts, in the north and through the forested Ardennes, which the French had decided would be impenetrable for a large force. The 'impregnable' Maginot Line, defending France's border with Germany, was simply outflanked. Allied units that had pushed into Belgium were soon in danger of being cut off.

On 16 May, Ramsay wrote to his wife, 'Life has been hectic, and in running the whole concern one has to keep one's concentration all the time. I shall have a story to tell at the end of this phase of the war. Things have gone well on the whole with my command, though my losses have been heavy, partly from enemy air action, partly from accident and partly from stupidity. Apart from the latter, the behaviour and success of the destroyers has been phenomenal in achieving the almost impossible.

'I have been very well, in spite of lack of sleep and exercise, until yesterday when the effect of many things began to take their course. Lack of sleep even when in bed is the worst, and the constant anxiety upsets my tummy. But I am much better this morning, having had a better night. We live hand to mouth in these times and one can only hope that right will prevail, and that all our endeavours and losses will not have been wasted.'[7]

Destroyers were acting in support of French troops in Belgium. HMS *Valentine* was bombed at the mouth of the Scheldt and wrecked after its boilers exploded. Stukas sank HMS *Whitley* off Nieuport. Only two of the six destroyers involved were undamaged. As well as bombarding airstrips and beaches, they had escorted transports and taken off refugees.

The Germans proved to be vastly superior in armour and air power, and French generals were slow to respond to blitzkrieg tactics, still wedded to the strategies of World War I. The commander-in-chief of the French forces, General Maurice Gamelin, had the ultimate responsibility for the Allies' military planning. Early in the battle of France, there were reports of his soldiers fleeing their positions. By 18 May, Panzer divisions were racing through north-west France. They reached the city of Amiens, 75 miles north of Paris, and were threatening to push on to the Channel coast. The Allied armies in Flanders were in danger of being separated from their bases. That day General Maxime Weygand replaced Gamelin, but it made little difference. The following day, Gort concluded that the BEF was in a hopeless position and evacuation would have to be considered. The French were suggesting a major counter offensive, but he thought it unrealistic. On 20 May, British divisions were beaten at Albert, Amiens and Abbeville, and Panzers closed in on the coast, cutting off the Allies in the north.

Ramsay had realised early on that a large-scale evacuation was likely to be necessary. At a meeting at Dover with War Office and Ministry of Shipping representatives, he pressed for a fleet of merchant vessels and small craft to be ready to join a Royal Navy rescue operation.

Ramsay wrote to his wife, 'Just a few lines to say that things are getting even more hectic, and more and more tasks are being thrown at me. The situation is really grave, and I just cannot visualise what it will be in even four or five days' time. There must have been something very wrong with the French defence organisation to have permitted this frightful breakthrough. It puts the BEF in a terrible position, and I see little prospect of their being able to continue to function. But where there is life there is hope. Our time in England has not yet come, but that it will come from bombers, parachutists etc there can be no doubt. We've all just got to hold on and face whatever comes bravely.'[8]

As the Panzers advanced on Calais and Boulogne, Ramsay sent demolition parties to the ports. The destroyer HMS *Venomous* took one party and the crew were well aware of the risks, as Chief Petty Officer Hugh McGeeney recalled, with some humour, 'We were ordered to take a group of Royal Marines and Royal Engineers together with all their stores, explosives and demolition gear to Calais. They were to blow up the locks and docks, cranes and port facilities in general, and make their return as and when, on completion. The quarterdeck and after 4.7 inch gun deck were loaded with explosives and ammunition and many felt one hit would mark the end. The cross-Channel dash was made at high speed and in daylight. We entered the port area without incident, in an uneasy quiet, and tied up to a quayside lined with railway trucks. Gangways out, and there were plenty of volunteers to help move everything ashore. Then the bombs started falling from high-flying planes, silhouetted silver in the sun. Some men took refuge under the railway trucks and the captain, using the bridge megaphone, encouraged those unloading to greater effort – they needed no encouragement.'[9]

On 22 May, steamers brought some 1,500 men of the Irish and Welsh Guards and other troops to Boulogne as reinforcements. The Guards Brigade was holding the perimeter. Machine-gun fire from the surrounding heights was devastating. In the dock area, there were scenes of chaos as Allied non-combatants and refugees scrambled to board ships. Some French sailors and civilians were drunk after breaking into a naval storeroom and looting alcohol. The destroyer HMS *Vimy* arrived with a force of sailors and marines to help control the quayside. Rain was pouring down. The Irish Guards would later record, 'The quay was a scene of squalid confusion. It looked as if thousands of suitcases had been emptied on the ground by manic customs officers, and trampling over this sodden mass of clothes, bedding and filthy refuse was a horde of panic-stricken refugees and stray soldiers waiting to rush the ships.'[10]

The next day, with the enemy closing in, it was decided to evacuate the port, and Ramsay ensured that enough destroyers were available. One of the first soldiers to leave was Lieutenant General Sir Douglas Brownrigg, adjutant general of the BEF. In the afternoon, HMS *Keith* and HMS *Whitshed* tied up at the quayside as other destroyers remained off the coast bombarding enemy positions. The 'rabble' rushed *Keith* and unwanted passengers had to be cleared from the decks. Captain David Simson refused to take any French civilians. *Whitshed* sailed with 70 stretcher cases and 150 walking wounded. As a parting shot, *Whitshed* opened up with its 4.7in guns, demolishing a warehouse where machine-gun fire was pining down men of the Irish Guards, who responded with loud cheering. *Vimy* joined *Keith* at the quayside and troops poured on to the ships, which were attacked soon afterwards by the Luftwaffe. RAF planes intervened but fire was also coming from German ground forces and Captain Simson was fatally wounded on *Keith*'s bridge. Despite casualties and damage, both destroyers managed to leave the harbour. *Keith* sailed for England but *Whitshed* remained off Boulogne to control shipping. Later, with air support, *Whitshed* returned to the quayside with HMS *Vimiera* to pick up as many soldiers as possible. Preference was given to the Irish and Welsh Guards who had shown fighting spirit and excellent discipline, unlike other soldiers, some of whom were drunk.[11] The ships sailed with about 1,000 men. The destroyers HMS *Wild Swan* and *Venomous* took their place. Panzers opened up at a third destroyer, HMS *Venetia*, as it sailed in. The ship was hit and set on fire but survived. The evacuation ended early on 24 May. *Vimiera*, on its second trip, was the last ship to leave, packed with 1,400 Allied soldiers. A total of more than 4,300 men, women and children had been taken to safety. But soldiers were left behind.

Ramsay told his wife, 'Things are desperately serious ... No bed for any of us last night and probably not for many nights. I'm so sleepy I can hardly keep my eyes open, and we are all the same. The office is now the HQ of the "Brownie" [Lieutenant General Brownrigg] staff as well as mine and we've been in close conference since daylight. We've been on the telephone to everyone from the PM downwards, and the situation only becomes more and more difficult from hour to hour. Heavens what a mess we've been put in by the French. I can't pretend to see the future 24 hours ahead, events move so fast. It's hateful having to order ships to do things and go to places where one knows they are going to get bombed to blazes and to send troops into what I know to be an inferno.' He ended the letter, 'Thank you so much for the lovely box of asparagus and the gingerbread. They are good. Tons of love, darling.'[12]

Ramsay was now focusing on Calais, which was seen as key to delaying an assault on Dunkirk. On 22 May, his destroyers had escorted transports to Calais carrying reinforcements, which included the 3rd Royal Tank Regiment (3 RTR) and the Queen Victoria's Rifles, a Territorial Army unit from London. After they had landed, Brownrigg arrived in a destroyer and told 3 RTR's commander, Lieutenant Colonel Reginald Keller, to take his tanks to Boulogne. Brownrigg then departed, but as the tanks were being prepared, Gort's headquarters gave Keller a different order. He was to head in another direction, inland to St Omer. Later Brownrigg repeated his Boulogne order. But a confused Keller decided to go to St Omer. He had not gone far when he encountered German armour. After a bruising clash, he retreated to Calais with casualties and the loss of seven of his tanks. Brigadier Claude Nicholson, who had taken over as the British commander in the port, was sent two more infantry battalions to help with the defences. Early on 24 May, the War Office informed Nicholson that Calais might be abandoned and to prepare for evacuation. This did not go down well with the French commander in the port. But his own sailors soon undermined him when they left their coastal guns and headed to the harbour to be taken off by French ships. During the day, the Royal Navy bombarded the coast as destroyers and trawlers rescued some of the troops. There was the inevitable cost. Stukas sank HMS *Wessex* and two other destroyers were badly damaged. A large force of Panzers attacked Calais. Nicholson knew that he could not hold out against such a superior enemy. Calais was surrounded. That night, however, the War Office told Nicholson to fight on.

'We've been through and are going through an indescribable time,' Ramsay wrote to his wife. 'Days and nights are all one and we are dealing with a situation as complex as it is unsavoury. Always trying to save a situation by trying to do the impossible and then having to get out when the situation is lost. It's been my lot to operate the naval part of this, and anything more difficult and unpleasing I've never been faced with. At this very moment, we are racked with anxiety about the situation in Calais. I can't tell you of it or of the anxieties with which I am confronted – I can only say that the latter increase with each hour, and we are helpless to retrieve the position. We are also working in several dimensions at the same time, and the offices are a veritable beehive of officers. A connected and realistic story of this will be impossible because it is impossible to keep any record.

'What we are experiencing is nothing of course to what the poor devils are going through in Calais. Billy Fox-Pitt commanded the Guards Brigade that was put into Boulogne and which I had to get out. He had a bad time and was lucky to escape. Poor Captain D [Simson] was killed in the *Keith* there by a sniper or machine-gun bullet on his bridge, and I lost the captains of two other destroyers. I get new destroyers daily and throw them into the fray where they remain until they are so damaged they have to be sent away.'[13]

Although Ramsay did his best to ensure that supplies continued to reach Calais, he still worked on plans to evacuate defenders if the order came. A rescue fleet of trawlers, yachts and drifters was ready to cross the Channel. Vice Admiral Sir James Somerville, who had been sent to help him with the planning at Dover, decided to go to Calais to 'see for myself'. Early on 25 May, Somerville arrived in the destroyer HMS *Verity*. A battery opened fire but the ship took no hits and found a safe mooring. The vice admiral was taken to Nicholson's headquarters in a cellar under the town's railway station. The cellar was 'lit with a few candles and filled with exhausted officers and men fast asleep except for the staff officers and telephonists actually on duty'. Somerville recorded, 'I woke Nicholson who at once asked if we had come to bring them off. I had to inform him that this was not the case but that I had received a telephone message from the prime minister before leaving Dover that it was essential that the garrison at Calais should fight to the last in order to hold up the advance of the Germans which was threatening to cut off the BEF from their last remaining base at Dunkirk. Nicholson appeared to be quite unperturbed saying that he anticipated that he might get these orders and then showed me on the map what he proposed to do ie to retire if possible to the Citadel [a fortification completed in 1596] and hold out there as long as possible. I told Nicholson that in my opinion it was essential that I should order *Verity* and *Wolfhound*, another destroyer in harbour, to sail as otherwise they would certainly be knocked out by the German batteries at daylight. Nicholson said this would remove his only wireless communication with Dover but I pointed out that I had seen a wireless van in the station which had not been knocked out and I was fortunately able to give him the wavelength on which Dover was working as I had happened to pass the wireless van at Dover on my way to *Verity*.'[14]

Somerville returned to *Verity*'s jetty only to find that the ship had gone. He sailed in *Wolfhound* at 0300, arriving back in Dover at 0430. After reporting the situation at Calais to the Admiralty and to Ramsay, he slept for a couple of hours. Then he went to the RAF base at Hawkinge, a few miles west of Dover, where a wireless intercepting station had been set up to read the plain language messages made by the enemy's aircraft and tanks. He finally got to bed at midnight. Half an hour later he was woken by a heavy air raid on Dover.[15]

Early on 25 May, the fleet of yachts, trawlers and drifters reached Calais and some non-fighting personnel were taken off, as well as the remnants of a detachment of Royal Marines that had lost all of its officers. The day saw fierce fighting and Nicholson refused German offers to surrender.

At 0500 on 26 May, German artillery opened up and later that morning some 100 Stukas joined the attack. Much of the town was in ruins. British troops were exhausted and short of water, and all their tanks had been knocked out. The cruisers HMS *Arethusa* and HMS *Galatea* bombarded enemy positions, but German infantry continued to advance through the town. Hospital carriers trying to enter the harbour were fired on. During the afternoon, it was learned that the French commander had surrendered. Soon afterwards Nicholson was captured. His soldiers still fighting were ordered to form small groups and to try to escape from Calais. Most of them ended up as prisoners.

At Dover that morning, Somerville had relieved Ramsay for a few hours. Then he went to London to give a personal report to the First Lord of the Admiralty, A. V. Alexander, who was 'very depressed' and said that the BEF would have to be evacuated. Somerville also saw the First Sea Lord, Admiral of the Fleet Sir Dudley Pound. Somerville was about to play a bigger role, recording, 'As I knew Admiral Ramsay was feeling the strain of being continually on duty I suggested I should go to Dover to lend him a hand. This was agreed and I finally left at 9.30pm with a Wren driving my car. Unfortunately as it got dark I found she could not see in the dark and as I was too sleepy to drive myself we had to put up at a roadhouse until daylight at 4.30am.'[16]

On the evening of 26 May, Churchill was unaware of the fall of Calais. He had dinner at the Admiralty with the Secretary of State for War, Anthony Eden, and the Chief of the Imperial General Staff, General Sir Edmund Ironside. At 9pm, they reluctantly agreed to send a message telling Nicholson that he must fight on. There would be no evacuation. Eden found it a particularly painful decision because it involved the King's Royal Rifle Corps, in which he had served. It was, of course, all too late, and Nicholson probably never received the message anyway.'[17]

The motor yacht *Gulzar* was the last vessel to leave Calais. On Ramsay's orders, it had been painted with red crosses and sent from Dover. Shortly after midnight, *Gulzar* approached the harbour. Under fire, a group of soldiers jumped on board as it sailed close to the end of the eastern jetty. *Gulzar* returned safely to Dover, where the flames rising above Calais could be seen. Estimates of the number of people evacuated from the port have ranged from 440 to at least 1,000.

In his famous speech to the House of Commons on 4 June 1940 on the evacuation of the BEF, Churchill referred to the 'desperate fighting' in Boulogne and Calais: 'The Guards defended Boulogne for a while and were then withdrawn by orders from this country. The Rifle Brigade, the 60th Rifles

[King's Royal Rifle Corps] and the Queen Victoria's Rifles, with a battalion of British tanks and 1,000 Frenchmen, in all about 4,000 strong, defended Calais to the last. The British brigadier [Nicholson] was given an hour to surrender. He spurned the offer, and four days of intense street fighting passed before silence reigned over Calais, which marked the end of a memorable resistance. Only 30 unwounded survivors were brought off by the navy, and we do not know the fate of their comrades. Their sacrifice, however, was not in vain. At least two armoured divisions, which otherwise would have been turned against the British Expeditionary Force, had to be sent to overcome them. They have added another page to the glories of the light divisions, and the time gained enabled the Gravelines water lines to be flooded and to be held by the French troops. Thus it was that the port of Dunkirk was kept open.'[18]

Brigadier Nicholson was awarded the Companion of the Order of the Bath (CB) for his actions in Calais. He committed suicide while a prisoner in Germany in June 1943, apparently suffering from depression.

CHAPTER 8

Operation *Dynamo*

A meeting at the War Office on 19 May was the 'genesis' for Operation *Dynamo*; the evacuation of the British Expeditionary Force from Dunkirk. Ramsay did not attend the meeting, but he was represented. There was little optimism. A large-scale evacuation did not seem possible. It was agreed that the Vice Admiral, Dover, would be in charge of the operation, with all available shipping. There were further meetings on 20 and 21 May and liaison officers from the War Office and the Ministry of Shipping were attached to Ramsay's staff. The question of air cover was raised and it was decided that the vice admiral would have a direct link to RAF Fighter Command.

It was planned to rescue troops from the beaches at Dunkirk and to the east of the port. The gradual shoaling of the beaches was a problem, and a large number of small boats would be needed to ferry soldiers to ships offshore. It was also hoped to rescue men from the port itself. The operation would have been easier if the ports of Boulogne and Calais had remained open. The planning was immense. For several days, phones were constantly ringing between Ramsay's headquarters and the Admiralty, the Ministry of Shipping and the staff of the Commander-in-Chief, Nore; the splendidly named Admiral the Hon. Sir Reginald Plunkett-Ernle-Erle-Drax.[1]

Early on Sunday 26 May, it was clear that the position of the Allies was deteriorating rapidly. General Gort and General Georges Blanchard, who had taken command of the French First Army Group after the death of General Gaston-Henri Billotte in a car accident, drew up plans for withdrawal to the coast. The First Army Group, holding an important defensive line south of Lille, was in 'dire peril' of being cut off, along with four British divisions, which were quickly pulled back. The BEF had been on half rations for three days and it was desperately short of ammunition, petrol and water. At 1857, the Admiralty ordered Ramsay to launch Operation *Dynamo* with 'the greatest vigour'. The Admiralty's most optimistic assessment was that up to 45,000 troops might be saved over two days, when enemy action was likely to end the evacuation.

At the time the Admiralty gave its order, the BEF and its Allies were bottled up in an area that stretched roughly 68 miles along the coast from Zeebrugge in the east to Gravelines in the west and about the same distance from Dunkirk to Marchiennes in the south. German forces were advancing from all three directions. The Allies set up defensive lines using canals to slow the movement of the Panzers. After capturing Boulogne and Calais, the enemy was expected to press on to Dunkirk. But General Gort had a stroke of good fortune. Generaloberst Gerd von Rundstedt issued an order halting the Panzers, which was supported by Hitler. They were concerned that, amid mounting losses, the tanks were moving too fast without adequate infantry support. Panzergruppe Kleist had started out with nearly 2,500 tanks. It was estimated that 30 per cent had been put out of action and a further 20 per cent needed repair. The head of the Luftwaffe, Hermann Goring, saw a chance of glory. He persuaded Hitler that an air offensive would destroy the BEF. Yet the Luftwaffe, too, had suffered heavy losses and it needed reasonable weather to carry out effective raids.

Although the order for the evacuation of Dunkirk was given at 1857, requisitioned merchant ships, mainly ferries, had been bringing back wounded men for several days, using the ports of Dover, Folkestone and Newhaven. Ships were also taking supplies and soldiers to help with the organisation of Dunkirk. One of the first ships to make a successful round trip was the *Mona's Queen* of the Isle of Man Steam Packet Company, with its civilian crew. Near the French coast the ship came under attack, as its captain, Radcliffe Duggan, reported, 'We were shelled from the shore by single guns and also by salvoes from shore batteries. Shells were flying all around us, the first salvo went over us, the second astern of us. I thought the next salvo would hit us, but fortunately it dropped short, right under our stern. The ship was riddled with shrapnel, mostly all on the boat and promenade decks. Then we were attacked from the air. A Junker bomber made a power dive towards us and dropped five bombs, but he was off the mark too, I should say about 150ft from us. All this while we were still being shelled, although we were getting out of range. The Junker that bombed us was shot down and crashed into the water just ahead of us (no survivors). Then another Junker attacked us, but before he reached us he was brought down in flames. Then the tension eased a little.

'Owing to the bombardment, I could see that the nerves of some of my men were badly shaken. I did not feel too well myself, but I mustered the crew and told them that Dunkirk was being bombed and was on fire. On being asked if they would volunteer to go in they did so to a man and I am glad to say we took off as many as *Mona's Queen* could carry. Coming back from Dunkirk, I made a route for myself and am glad to say we arrived safely at Dover in the early hours of Monday.'[2] Some 1,300 personnel were landed.

The hospital carriers *Isle of Guernsey* and *Worthing* survived an air attack on the way over. Captain Ernest Hill of the *Isle of Guernsey* recalled, 'Arriving off Dunkirk, which was under an even heavier pall of thick black smoke than Calais, we manoeuvred our way inside through the various wrecks of vessels which had been struck by bombs and the *Worthing*, having been made fast to the quay, we moored alongside her. A few moments after our arrival streams of ambulances arrived threading their way through the columns of troops who were not so seriously wounded and were able to walk. Loading was commenced immediately and every member of the ship's crew assisted in stretcher bearing. By 9.55pm both hospital carriers were loaded with as many as they could take, the *Isle of Guernsey* having 346 cases on board and, as her number of cots is only 203, many of these cases were accommodated in between the cots, on the deck, along corridors, in fact wherever it was possible to put a stretcher.'[3]

The Channel ferry *Maid of Orleans*, which had taken men of the 3rd Royal Tank Regiment to Calais days earlier, brought over 6,000 two-gallon cans of water and embarked 988 troops. Another ferry, *Canterbury*, took off 1,340. Naval vessels also were kept busy, embarking soldiers, bombarding enemy positions and escorting merchant shipping.

Meanwhile, the Belgian army was on the verge of collapse on the Menin–Nivelle front, and Lieutenant General Ronald Adam was given the task of organising the Dunkirk bridgehead. In London, the Admiralty asked home bases to report on how many cutters and whalers they could make available for immediate service under Ramsay.

On Monday, 27 May, the first full day of the evacuation, Ramsay and his staff were concentrating on sending merchant ships, known as personnel vessels, to Dunkirk at the rate of two every three and a half hours. But after a promising early start, five of the ships were attacked and returned to England before reaching France. Ramsay decided it was impracticable to send vessels on the shortest route in daylight because of fire from shore batteries extending from Les Hemmes to Gravelines. The Zuydcoote Pass had to be used instead, but this increased the distance for a round trip from 80 miles to 172 miles.

Work began on sweeping mines from another route, which cut the distance to 108 miles. Sandbars off the French coast were another hazard for shipping. That afternoon, Captain William Tennant, appointed Senior Naval Officer Dunkirk, sailed to France in the destroyer *Wolfhound* with a party of 12 officers and 160 ratings. Stukas attacked *Wolfhound* on several occasions, but Tennant and his men arrived safely to begin the challenging task of trying to get an orderly evacuation. Five merchant ships made the round trip, bringing back a total of 3,952 troops, and 17 drifters from Dover later rescued 2,000.

Ramsay had wanted to keep a destroyer at Dunkirk as a communications link, but Captain Tennant decided the conditions there made it impossible. He sent a 'most immediate' message, 'Port consistently bombed all day and on fire. Embarkation possible only from beaches east of harbour A B C D. Send all ships and passenger ships there to anchor. Am ordering *Wolfhound* to load there and sail.'[4]

Tennant headed to the Allied headquarters, Bastion 32, a 19th-century fortification near the beaches. 'The town was heavily on fire, the streets being littered with wreckage of all kinds, and every window was smashed,' he reported. 'Great palls of smoke from the oil depots and refineries enveloped the docks and town itself. On our way up to the Bastion we had to take shelter from two more raids by enemy bombers, the bombs from the last of which fell unpleasantly close. There were a number of British troops in the town and we passed a good few dead and wounded in the streets – evidently the victims of these raids.'[5]

With some of his party, Tennant spent several hours checking the port and beaches. On the east side of the outer harbour, there was a long mole, cement piles with a wooden framework on top, which had been built as a breakwater. It had not been used to berth ships, but the water was deep enough and Tennant realised the mole's potential. It would be a quicker to put troops on ships at the mole than from the beaches.

Wolfhound was attacked on its way to Dover. Leading Seaman John Pearce had picked up a large number of troops from the beaches using the destroyer's motorboat with a whaler in tow. Soldiers were in such a hurry to disembark at Dover that they forgot to take personal belongings and equipment. 'They left behind chaos, bits of equipment, souvenirs, tin helmets, wallets, packets of letters, all sorts,' said Pearce. 'The mess deck, normally spotlessly clean, was a real mess. There was blood all over the tables and lockers. Of course, the order came through, get it cleaned up. We cleaned the ship from top to bottom. I did hear that five people had died in the mess deck, they were so badly wounded.'[6]

Ramsay had been sent six more destroyers from other commands. The naval officer in charge at Ramsgate was told by Ramsay to take responsibility for the refuelling and sending of small powerboats. The Commander-in-Chief, Nore, was also asked to send every available shallow-draught powerboat capable of ferrying troops from the beaches to waiting ships and stocked with fuel and provisions for two days.

That evening Dover received a message from Gort's headquarters warning that part of the BEF was in danger of being cut off from Dunkirk. Ramsay noted, 'This report appeared to confirm the results of air reconnaissance, which indicated that German armoured units were operating to the south of Dunkirk. Since it appeared that evacuation might well be strictly limited, both in regard to numbers and time available for the operation, it was decided to concentrate every effort in sending over as many craft as possible to the beaches without delay.'[7] A fleet of nine destroyers, four minesweepers, the cruiser HMS *Calcutta*, two transports, 17 drifters and several skoots (Dutch barges) gathered off the beaches. The vessels were told to use their own boats for ferrying as the inshore flotilla had not arrived from England.[8] The beaches where troops were gathering stretched from Dunkirk to La Panne; a distance of about ten miles. Surf did not help, as it overturned some of the boats.

It must have been a disappointing day for Ramsay, who no doubt had hoped that more men would have been evacuated. Shortly after midnight he wrote to his wife, 'I can't begin to tell you stories of the horrible time I've been through and am at this moment experiencing. The situation is past belief, frightful and one wonders how the British public will take it when the full implications are realised. It's all too horrible to contemplate.

'You wouldn't recognise my offices now from what they were. We are crammed with naval and military officers. James Somerville is here helping me and I couldn't wish for anyone better. We number five captains instead of one. All my staff officers have been duplicated and I have a commander as my personal assistant. [His staff officer operations was Commander (later Captain) Frederic Walker, who would become the legendary U-boat hunter in the battle of the Atlantic.] This is, in fact, the biggest staff of any admiral ashore or afloat. And the Admiralty have given me everyone asked for! I have on at the moment (it's 1am) one of the most difficult and hazardous operations ever conceived, and unless the bon Dieu is very kind, there will be many tragedies attached to it. I hardly dare think about it or what the day is going to bring. Really, for 17 days now I have conducted a series of heart-breaking operations. How I would like to cast off the mantle of responsibility which is mine and become just peaceful and retired again. Heaven knows when that will be possible.

'All my staff are in fact completely worn out and yet I see no prospect at all of any let up or opportunity to relax. As for my ships they have not a moments rest unless they are damaged badly. And every day adds to the list and sees new vessels join to replace those out of action. But enough of this. I am quite well but very sleepy. James Somerville and I share the night and go up for meals in turn. I expect him down about 2 or 3 o'clock when I will go to bed leaving everything to him. It is grand being able divest oneself of responsibility in this way and not to be wakened by the telephone through the night.'[9]

As Ramsay was writing his letter, Belgium's King Leopold III, as head of his country's armed forces, had already decided on an unconditional surrender.

CHAPTER 9

Tuesday 28 May

General Gort was at Bastion 32 in Dunkirk when he learned of King Leopold's surrender. It left him with an immediate problem. With the Belgian army no longer offering resistance, it meant there was a gap of some 20 miles between Ypres and the sea through which German armour could pour. For several hours, the general struggled to get back to his headquarters at Houtkerque, near the Belgian border. The roads were clogged with retreating soldiers, weary refugees and vehicles, military and civilian, many of which had been abandoned. When he eventually reached his headquarters, Gort was relieved to find that Lieutenant General Adam and Brigadier Frederick Lawson had helped to close the gap. Adam was the architect of Dunkirk's strong perimeter.

Churchill had appointed Admiral of the Fleet Sir Roger Keyes as liaison officer to King Leopold. In a message to the admiral on 27 May, the prime minister stressed that it was important Belgium should continue in the war. That evening they spoke on the phone, and Churchill pointed out that there were 200,000 Belgians of military age in France, and Belgium had greater resources than in 1914. Keyes was given the task of trying to persuade the king to change his mind because surrender would have disastrous consequences for the Allies.[1]

The king refused to reconsider and turned down an offer of sanctuary in Britain, saying he intended to stay with his army and his people. As far as he was concerned, the Allies' cause was lost.

On 28 May, Churchill addressed the House of Commons on King Leopold's capitulation, 'The House will be aware that the King of the Belgians yesterday sent a plenipotentiary to the German command asking for a suspension of arms on the Belgian front. The British and French governments instructed their generals immediately to disassociate themselves from this procedure and to persevere in the operations in which they are now engaged. However, the

German command has agreed to the Belgian proposals and the Belgian army ceased to resist the enemy's will at four o'clock this morning.

'I have no intention of suggesting to the House that we should attempt at this moment to pass judgment upon the action of the King of the Belgians in his capacity as commander-in-chief of the Belgian army. This army has fought very bravely and has both suffered and inflicted heavy losses. The Belgian government has disassociated itself from the action of the king and, declaring itself to be the only legal government of Belgium, has formally announced its resolve to continue the war at the side of the Allies.'[2]

France's premier, Paul Reynaud, denounced the surrender, and Churchill was more forceful about it when he spoke to MPs on 4 June, pointing out that the Belgians 'guarded our eastern flank and thus kept open our only line of retreat to the sea. Suddenly, without prior consultation, with the least possible notice, without the advice of his ministers and upon his own personal act, he [the king] sent a plenipotentiary to the German command, surrendered his army and exposed our whole flank and means of retreat.'[3]

At Dunkirk, Captain Tennant began using the eastern mole to evacuate soldiers. On the morning of 28 May, the ferry *Queen of the Channel* sailed with 950 troops. Soon afterwards, it was attacked by a dive-bomber and seriously damaged. The coaster *Dorrien Rose* was nearby and in 30 minutes rescued the soldiers and crew, who were taken to Dover. The ferry sank and Ramsay decided to restrict the larger merchant vessels to night operations. Throughout the day, destroyers embarked men from the mole, and small boats continued to work the beaches. Enemy air action over the mole was light due to RAF sorties and the fact that there was a heavy pall of smoke from the burning town. During the morning, three shells from an enemy battery south-west of Dunkirk landed near the embarkation point, but there were no injuries or damage. In the afternoon, however, there was heavy bombing at Bray-Dunes and Tennant ordered more troops to head to Dunkirk. An estimated 12,000 soldiers were taken off the mole in daylight.[4]

Tennant's party of sailors had been spread out, some helping at the mole, others trying to organise evacuation from the long stretch of beaches and acting, in effect, as naval police. Leading Seaman Harold Viner was one of the men involved. He had arrived in the destroyer HMS *Esk* and was told to report to the first naval officer he saw. 'We landed on the beach and this naval officer was walking towards me,' Viner recalled. 'He said your job is to organise columns of fifty because everything at the moment is chaos. Some of them are in a terrible condition.' The sailor, armed with a revolver, was told to go to Bray-Dunes and shoot anyone who tried to jump the queue. 'I said what do you mean shoot and he said, "Shoot to kill, son". We all looked aghast. Here I was a 23-year-old sailor being given carte blanche to shoot somebody if they didn't obey.' The officer, a lieutenant, pointed to a sergeant major and a sergeant, and said, 'They're 6ft and they're big and they're crying.'[5]

Viner had trouble with one army captain. 'There was this shouting going on in the water. I went forward and there was this captain shouting, "I'm a captain, I've got to get to the front." I said stay where you are. He said, "Who the hell do you think you're talking to?" Alongside this captain was this big

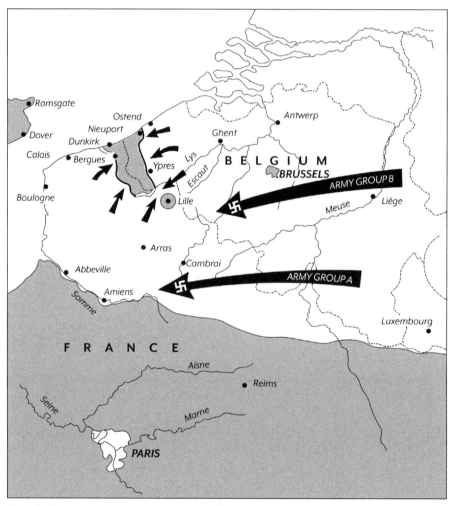

How the German pincer movement squeezed British and French forces into the Dunkirk pocket by 28 May 1940.

sergeant and he said, "Do as he bloody well tells you, sir, or you will die." I'd got the revolver out. The captain went back in.' Viner spent six days on the beaches helping to organise soldiers as boats took them off. There was little food or water, and he had been issued only with chocolate.[6]

After Ramsay had stressed that it was necessary to make the maximum rescue effort at night because of the danger of air attacks, the Admiralty instructed the Commander-in-Chief, Western Approaches, and the Commander-in-Chief, Portsmouth, to send every available destroyer to Dover. Patrols of motor torpedo boats (MTBs) and anti-submarine trawlers were ordered to cover the north-east flank of the evacuation area against attack by enemy craft.

For the night of 28 May, it was planned to use three hospital carriers, seven steamers and two destroyers at the mole. To cover the beaches, there would be some 20 destroyers, 19 paddle and fleet sweepers, 17 drifters, 20 to 40 skoots, five coasters, 12 motorboats, two tugs, 28 cutters and lifeboats. The cruiser *Calcutta* was told to take up a position opposite La Panne and to use its own boats for rescue work. All these vessels needed to be clear of the danger area by 0630.[7] Around 7,000 troops were still at Bray-Dunes and more were arriving all the time.

During the afternoon, Gort had ordered a general withdrawal to the Dunkirk bridgehead, which covered Gravelines, Bergues, Furnes and Nieuport. Shortly after midnight, *Calcutta* learned that III Corps of the BEF was at La Panne, where Gort had set up a new headquarters at a beachside villa.

CHAPTER 10

Wednesday 29 May

It was, without doubt, a black day for Ramsay and Operation *Dynamo*. A major loss came as early as 0045 on 29 May. At short notice, the destroyer HMS *Wakeful* had been ordered to sail from Plymouth to Dover on 27 May. The next day, it embarked 639 troops at the Dunkirk mole in about 25 minutes and they were landed at Dover. On the destroyer's return to France, nine German aircraft attacked it, dropping between 40 and 50 bombs, one of which fell close, making a hole in the engine room above the waterline. *Wakeful* anchored off Bray-Dunes and over eight hours picked up 640 soldiers from the beaches using the ship's boats. A sub lieutenant had been in charge of marshalling the troops, and at one point, he threatened them with his revolver.

Wakeful's captain, Commander Ralph Fisher, reported, 'All mess tables and stools and other available timber was placed on the upper deck for life-saving purposes and the troops were stowed as low in the ship as possible to preserve sufficient stability for rapid manoeuvring in case of air attack.'[1]

The destroyer sailed at 2300 on 28 May, using the long Route Y and heading for the Zuydcoote Pass and North Channel. When aircraft were heard, it reduced speed to show less wake. Fisher thought there might be an attack as they neared the Kwinte Whistle Buoy, north-east of Dunkirk, and five miles before reaching it he increased speed to 20 knots on a zig-zag course. All gun crews and bridge personnel were 'keyed up'.

At 0045 on 29 May, not far from the buoy, two torpedo tracks, very bright with phosphorescence, were spotted. The wheel was put hard a port and the ship swung enough for one of the torpedoes to miss, but the other hit the forward boiler room, breaking the ship in half. Fifteen seconds later both the bow and the stern were rising about 60ft above the water. *Wakeful* had been attacked by an E-boat based at Antwerp. 'Most of the guns' crews floated clear and 30 men and an officer remained on the stern portion,' Fisher recorded. 'All the troops were asleep below and went down with the ship except one, and all HMS *Wakeful*'s engine room department except one or two were lost. I floated clear of the bridge.'[2]

After about half an hour, the drifters *Nautilus* and *Comfort* arrived and saved 22 men in the water, including Fisher. Then the minesweeper HMS *Gossamer* joined the rescue, lowering boats and picking up a further 15. The tide swept men away and *Comfort* searched the area, before Fisher decided to return to the wreck to take off the men clinging to the stern. The destroyer HMS *Grafton* and the minesweeper HMS *Lydd* were there. *Comfort* went alongside *Grafton*, and Fisher warned the vessel it was in danger of being torpedoed.

'At that moment (0250) a torpedo hit her in the wardroom,' Fisher recalled, 'and the *Comfort* was lifted in the air, then momentarily swamped and as she bobbed to the surface again I was washed overboard. I was able to grab a rope's end, but as the *Comfort* was going full speed ahead with no one on deck I soon had to let go.

'The *Comfort* then came round in a wide circle and suddenly both HMS *Lydd* and HMS *Grafton* opened a heavy fire on her with Lewis guns and, I think, 4in. I realised that they very naturally thought she was enemy and kept under water as much as possible when the bullets were coming near me. The firing ceased and I swam to the *Comfort*, which had stopped engines and was drifting towards me slowly. As I reached her bow and was feeling for a rope's end HMS *Lydd* bore down on her at full speed and rammed her amidships on the opposite side, cutting her in half. I was submerged but came to the surface after an interval and swam about till about 0515 when I was picked up by a boat from the Norwegian ship *Hird* carrying 3,000 troops from Dunkirk.'[3]

Only one of *Comfort*'s crew and four of *Wakeful*'s survivors on board survived. *Grafton*, taking around 850 troops back to England, was torpedoed by *U62*. The destroyer's captain, Commander Cecil Robinson, was one of the 16 crew killed. Lieutenant Hugh McRea told of the moment two torpedoes struck. 'One of the lookouts on the port side of the bridge reported, "Torpedo port side". This was followed almost immediately by a violent explosion. A second explosion, which seemed of the same intensity, followed a few seconds later. I rushed to the after end of the bridge to try and find out what damage had been done. I sent a messenger down to the engineer officer to make a report to the bridge as to the extent of the damage, and tried to get as many seamen as possible to keep the soldiers quiet and stationary. After about five minutes I went back to the compass platform to report to the captain. I found that the compass platform had been wrecked. The whole of the fore screen had been blown in, and the asdic control and both binnacles smashed. The sides of the bridge were left standing. The bodies of Commander Robinson,

Lieutenant H. C. C. Tanner and a signalman were buried under the wreckage and a leading signalman had been blown onto B deck. All four must have been killed instantaneously.'[4]

Grafton remained afloat on an even keel, despite having its stern blown off. All compartments below decks were evacuated and 'the behaviour of the soldiers was now all that could be desired'. An E-boat was spotted approaching at high speed and *Grafton* opened fire. There was no attack. At about 0400, the steamer *Malines* came alongside and took off the troops, except for those wounded because the deck was too high. By this time, *Grafton* was listing to starboard. Shortly afterwards, five destroyers were seen approaching from the direction of Dover and one of them, HMS *Ivanhoe*, took off the wounded.

With *Grafton* sinking, the order to abandon ship was given and the remaining crew transferred to *Ivanhoe*. From a range of about 500 yards, *Ivanhoe* fired three shells to hasten *Grafton*'s end and then continued to Dunkirk.[5]

The attack on *Grafton* would have likely reminded Ramsay of the tragic loss of the cruisers *Aboukir*, *Cressy* and *Hogue* in the North Sea in September 1914. He had been staggered that after a U-boat torpedoed *Aboukir* the other 'stupid' ships went to its aid, only to suffer the same fate. And Ramsay would have remembered the rebuke he received from Vice Admiral Gamble for saying that 'if a ship of the fleet got hit by a submarine she could expect no assistance from other ships'.

As the steamer *Mona's Queen* approached Dunkirk in the early hours, it hit a magnetic mine. The master of the passenger ship *Killarney*, Captain Richard Hughes, saw the vessel coming. 'Whilst we were watching her, trying to ascertain who she was, there was a terrific explosion, and the centre part of her disappeared in a cloud of smoke,' Hughes recounted. 'When the smoke cleared away, her stern portion from the mainmast aft had vanished, and in about two minutes the forward part heeled over and sank.'[6] Twenty-four of the crew were lost.

Ramsay was keen to explore ways of speeding up the Dunkirk evacuation. 'Much consideration had been given to the practicability of building piers on the beaches using lines of barges,' he noted. 'Reports from ships that worked off the beaches showed, however, that owing to the very gradual shoaling of the water at all states of the tide such a barge pier, to be effective, would have to be of very great length, beyond the resources available.'[7]

Captain Tennant reported that surf was continuing to hamper operations off the beaches and asked if all the ships there could join the rescue effort at the mole. Ramsay refused, saying there would be too much of a bottleneck at the harbour. Also, it was feared that so many ships at the mole would invite intensive air attacks. And the RAF would not be able to provide continuous cover.[8]

At the mole on the morning of 29 May, Tennant was thankful that the enemy 'is leaving us alone', with embarkation proceeding at a rate of 3,000 to 4,000 an hour. He reported, 'Troops were now consisting mainly of the fighting corps, all the non-combatant troops in the area having been evacuated. The display of this corps troops was noticeably superior – previous detachments had reached the embarkation point in a straggling manner with scarcely any semblance of order. The corps troops marched in formation along the beaches, quickly scattering during an air raid, and reforming and continuing afterwards. It was this order which enabled such a high rate of embarkation to be maintained.'[9] Food and stores were urgently needed.

Later, the Luftwaffe launched many dive-bombing attacks on vessels heading to Dunkirk, at the mole and off the beaches. As Ramsay pointed out later, 'These attacks were to have a disastrous result on the evacuation arrangements at Dunkirk.'[10]

At 6,787 tons, the cargo ship *Clan Macalister* was the largest merchant vessel to take part in Operation *Dynamo*. Its size made it a magnet for the Luftwaffe. That afternoon, *Clan Macalister* arrived off Malo-les-Bains with a valuable cargo, eight assault landing craft, each capable of carrying 50 men and ideal for use in shallow water. The ship's cranes had unloaded six of the landing craft when the first attack came at about 1545. There were direct hits on the *Clan Macalister*, which started several fires, and the gyro compass and telemotor were put out of action. The destroyer HMS *Malcolm* came alongside and took off wounded crewmen and soldiers who had been picked up. *Malcolm* cast off as enemy planes launched another attack.

The master of the *Clan Macalister*, Captain R. W. Mackie, recorded, 'As it seemed to me that we could not get to sea and steer through the sandbanks and that we seemed to be a ship marked for destruction by the enemy who were dive-bombing at us frequently, we signalled a destroyer which was embarking troops inshore from us that we wanted assistance. He did not answer, but HMS *Pangbourne*, a minesweeper, which was entering the roads, came alongside and, when I told the commander that the telemotor was broken and that I could not get clear, he agreed to take us on board.'[11] Nineteen of the crew, all Indian merchant seamen, died. The *Clan Macalister* was burning fiercely aft and it eventually sank on an even keel, giving the impression that it was afloat and active. It continued to be a target for the Luftwaffe, reducing attacks on other ships.

In the late afternoon, five ships and six smaller vessels were berthed at the mole. The steamer *Fenella* was on the east side, with the special service vessel HMS *Crested Eagle* astern. On the west side were the other ships, including the destroyers HMS *Grenade* and HMS *Jaguar*, the ferry *Canterbury* and a French destroyer. The *Fenella* had between 600 and 700 troops on board. Stukas dived and there was a direct hit on the ship's promenade deck. The jetty was also bombed and concrete smashed through the steamer's port side below the waterline and into the engine room. Another bomb did further damage. *Fenella* began listing badly. After an inspection the master, Captain William Cubbon, decided it could not be saved and ordered an evacuation of the troops. 'As the jetty abreast of gangways had been blown away, the only method of disembarkation was to climb over the rails of the forecastle head which fortunately was level with the jetty,' Cubbon reported. 'The enemy was particularly active at this time and several times his bombing and machine-gunning held up the disembarking of the troops.'[12] The soldiers and *Fenella*'s crew embarked on *Crested Eagle*.

During the attack at the mole, *Canterbury*, accompanied by *Jaguar*, succeeded in leaving the harbour, but they were both dive-bombed and hit. The destroyer's engines and steering were badly damaged, and water began flowing into number one and two boiler rooms. The ship developed a list to port. 'An additional handicap was the extra load of 70 tons of troops who hampered all movement above and below decks,' the captain, Lieutenant Commander John Hine, reported. 'Under these circumstances it was decided to jettison torpedoes and depth charges.' But the stop valves of at least four of the torpedoes had not been closed and they ran onto the beach at Bray-Dunes 'where it was hoped they burnt themselves out'.[13] After all the air attacks it was probably the last thing soldiers wanted to see, Royal Navy torpedoes hurtling towards them.

As *Jaguar* drifted towards a wreck, the destroyer HMS *Express* came to its aid, arranging a tow. Most of the troops on board *Jaguar* were transferred to *Express*. Ramsay's headquarters was asked to send a tug, but by 1950, *Jaguar*'s engines had been repaired and it was gradually able to work up to a speed of 20 knots. Less than half an hour later a bomber attacked and a stick of bombs fell close to the stern. There were two further attacks but the destroyer's zig-zag course took it safely away and it reached Dover at 2350.[14] *Canterbury*, though badly damaged, also made it, disembarking 1,950 troops.

Grenade was a major casualty at the mole. The previous evening, it had taken 900 troops to Dover, returning that morning. The destroyer did not embark any more soldiers because Captain Tennant wanted it to remain at the mole. The first serious attack came at about 1500 when two bombs fell about 20 to 25 yards from the starboard bow, killing a rating and wounding another on the forecastle, damaging A gun and wounding a sailor on the searchlight platform. Several ratings in trawlers were killed. Less than three hours later, 12 enemy planes circled over the mole and two of them dive-bombed the destroyer, blowing a hole in the starboard side and starting a mess deck fire. Another bomb tore through the sick bay and almost reached the bottom of the ship before exploding. *Grenade*'s port side and the mole were also damaged.

The captain, Commander Richard Boyle, reported, 'As soon as I heard the attack commencing I gave orders for fire to be opened and for those not engaged to take cover. I did not actually see the bombs falling, but I realised from their noise that they were getting very close. When they hit, all the bridge personnel were lying down. The force of the explosion blew everyone three to four feet in the air; I personally noticed that I was level with the top of the screen at the back of the bridge before I fell. Almost immediately a large quantity of water and oil fuel started to fall on the bridge until it was one and a half feet deep.'[15]

Boyle saw that several of the crew had jumped over the side and he told them to swim back. *Grenade*'s stern was swinging away from the mole and the ship was in danger of blocking the harbour. The engines were out of action and there was a serious fire in number one boiler room. Other fires were reported. A lieutenant went to the chart house, placed two rockets and fired Very lights to destroy the charts. 'I then decided to give the order to abandon ship,' said Boyle. 'In the meantime *Grenade* had swung still further round and many officers and men were able to step on board the trawler *Polly Johnson*. I walked aft and tried to get into the after lobby to see about my confidential books. While I was doing this more bombs were dropped in the vicinity and as I found that I could not get the clips off the doors, which had been hammered up to bottle up the fire in the after lobby, I decided that I could do no more good on board. I walked forrard on the port side and stepped into the water from the deck which was practically level with the water, and was hauled on board the only remaining trawler.' After arranging for a tug to tow *Grenade* clear of the harbour, Boyle went on board *Crested Eagle*. The destroyer later blew up.[16]

A military policeman, Corporal Arthur Turner, told how one of the bombs hit the ship's provision store and 'spuds, carrots, meat' went flying everywhere. One of the badly wounded men was an army motor mechanic. He was on fire and screaming. 'We rushed to get a bucket of water and chucked it over him,' said Turner. 'As we put this bucket down, he was putting his arms in the water, but all his skin came off. Then the whole place was on fire.' An officer told Turner and others 'to swim for it'. The corporal recalled, 'My full pack hit me under the chin as I dived and I smashed a couple of my teeth, but I started to swim and managed to get off my battle dress jacket. I had khaki trousers and braces on and as I was swimming the braces were coming down. I swam for the shore and gradually got rid of my trousers and even my boots. I swam and swam. Then I managed to stand upright and walk to the shore. I was in vest and pants and nothing else except socks.'[17]

Earlier that day Leading Seaman Harold Viner, helping to organise troops on the beaches, had spotted *Grenade* off Bray-Dunes. His brother was one of the crew and Viner was given permission to visit him. After the attack on *Grenade*, Viner's brother transferred to *Crested Eagle*, and he died when the vessel was attacked.

It is something of a mystery why *Grenade* spent so many hours at the mole. Commander Boyle said in his report on the ship's loss, 'No troops were put into *Grenade* as the Senior Naval Officer [Captain Tennant] stated that he wished a destroyer to remain alongside.'[18] Perhaps Tennant wanted it there because of the need for reliable communications with Ramsay. But he had already told the vice admiral that it was too dangerous for a destroyer to remain just for that purpose. In his official report on the evacuation, Tennant commented on the air attacks on the mole on 29 May, stating, 'These resulted in HMS *Grenade* being bombed while embarking troops.' This was not true. The attack only cost the lives of 18 of the crew.

On the mole, Commander James Clouston, acting as a pier master, ordered the captain of the *Crested Eagle*, Lieutenant Commander Bernard Booth, to sail with all the survivors. But *Crested Eagle* had not gone far when enemy planes dropped five bombs, four of which hit the target. Booth said, 'As the engines were still functioning I held on my course for a little while, but I soon discovered that the ship was on fire, certainly from amidships right aft. The deck was up four or five feet and the sides were in.' The engineer, badly burned, reported on the bridge that the ship would not be able to go much further, and Booth decided to beach her. *Crested Eagle* was soon on fire from fore and aft. Booth reported, 'It is difficult to estimate the number of men on board, under the conditions that they were embarked, I should say round about 600. As the lower decks were filled first, casualties from the bomb explosions must have been severe. After beaching I advised all hands to take to the water as their only chance, and probably 200 men could be sighted at one time in the water. I regret to say that they were badly machine-gunned.

'In less than half an hour owing to the ship being all wood, with the exception of her hull, she was blazing furiously fore and aft and I feel that I can safely say that any gear or instruments left on board would never withstand the heat and be recognisable afterwards. The crew throughout behaved wonderfully well, the guns were kept going right up to the last.'[19]

The destroyer *Verity* arrived at the mole during the bombing raid and survived being straddled for 35 minutes. It headed to Bray-Dunes, joining other ships in rescue work. The attacks continued. A steamer carrying troops was on fire and *Verity* tried to get alongside to take them off. But the stricken vessel was unable to stop and the captain decided to beach her.

Verity had two captains during *Dynamo*. Lieutenant Commander Arthur Black was seriously wounded after shore batteries opened fire on the ship on 27 May and Lieutenant Eric Jones assumed command.[20]

HMS *King Orry*, a steamer commissioned as an armed boarding vessel, was attacked at about 1800 as it neared the mole, where there were only burning and sinking ships. *King Orry's* steering gear was put out of action and it hit the pier, causing considerable damage.

That evening, Ramsay, unaware of the extent of the day's toll on shipping, signalled that the evacuation must continue at 'maximum speed'. If there were not enough personnel vessels to take troops from the mole, destroyers would be sent. All other vessels except hospital carriers would embark from the beaches, which were divided into three equal parts – La Panne, Bray-Dunes and Malo-les-Bains. But the vice admiral would soon suffer a major setback. Because of the navy's heavy losses that day – three destroyers sunk and six others damaged – the First Sea Lord, Admiral of the Fleet Sir Dudley Pound, decided to withdraw the remaining seven newer and larger destroyers. That left Ramsay with a total of only 15 destroyers, most of them World War I veterans with limited space.[21]

At the Admiralty on the afternoon of 29 May, Vice Admiral Tom Phillips asked Rear Admiral William Wake-Walker if he would like to go to Dunkirk to help with organising the evacuation. Wake-Walker said he would be delighted. It was not intended that he should replace Tennant. His title would be Rear Admiral Dover in charge of the beach operations, with Tennant remaining at Dunkirk harbour as Senior Naval Officer. According to Phillips, 70,000 had been embarked already and 'a great effort' was needed to get off many more.

Wake-Walker recalled, 'Before leaving I saw the First Sea Lord who told me that it was thought that the French were not doing their full share and that I was to stress this on my arrival so that pressure could be brought to bear on them to send more ships. There was also the difficult question whether French troops were to be refused embarkation; it was obvious that our own troops had first call but it would be difficult to discriminate against Frenchmen.

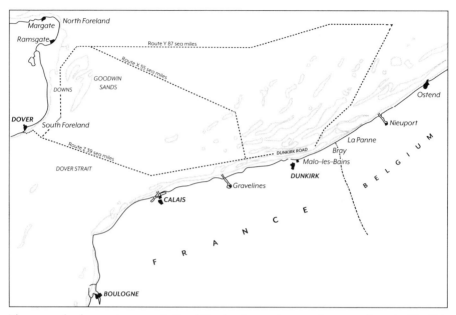

These were the three main routes, X, Y and Z, taken by vessels evacuating troops from the Dunkirk area. Sandbanks and sandbars were two of the natural hazards.

Actually it was not until Friday, 31 May, that a signal was made stating the government's policy to give equal opportunities to British and French troops.'[22]

Churchill had been giving thought to the question of evacuating French troops. He told Eden and the Chief of the Imperial General Staff, General Sir John Dill, who had replaced General Ironside, that it was essential to include the French, stressing the importance of cooperation.[23] The prime minister sent a similar message to Major General Edward Spears, his personal representative to France's Premier Reynaud in Paris. Churchill was in fighting mood, already looking ahead to build up a new BEF from St Nazaire.

After meeting the First Sea Lord, Wake-Walker was driven to Dover Castle where he saw Ramsay, who briefed him about the beaches at La Panne, Bray-Dunes and Malo-les-Bains. 'I was also shown the three approaches to Dunkirk. One of them from the east [Route Y] could no longer be used at night as enemy MTBs had sunk a destroyer there. The western one [Route Z] was being shelled from the shore in daylight and the centre one [Route X] was none too easy to make for navigational reasons.'[24] Two destroyers were ready to sail to Dunkirk with beach parties. Wake-Waker was told that in the early stages of the evacuation many of the troops had become a rabble, some throwing away their rifles, others lying on the beaches refusing to get into boats. The beach parties would restore order, but when Walke-Walker arrived, he found that discipline had much improved. He sailed from Dover in *Esk* with two other senior officers, Commodore Gilbert Stephenson and Commodore Theodore Hallett, who were going to supervise beach evacuations at La Panne and Bray-Dunes respectively, with Wake-Walker focusing on Malo-les-Bains.[25] Stephenson and Hallett were both retired vice admirals.

Ramsay summed up 29 May, 'The day closed with a formidable list of ships lost or damaged, a marked reduction in the number of destroyers available and with failure to achieve the high rate of evacuation hoped for. Some 38,000 were landed in England during the 24 hours, but the effect of the day's occurrences was to be more marked next day when, instead of some 50,000 to 60,000 which had been calculated as the probable achievement, only 48,000 odd were in fact transported.'[26]

Ramsay wrote to his wife that the tempo was frightful. 'Everyone is stretched to the nth degree, doing magnificently but flesh and blood can't stand it much longer … No one can forsee what tomorrow will be like. Perhaps it's as well. But we must all keep a brave heart and trust that we shall be able to stabilise and retain our position against what is to come.

'The Belgian collapse has added to the critical position of the BEF, already more than critical.'[27]

Vice Admiral Somerville sent a similar message to his wife. 'Things are very strenuous here [Dover] and one doesn't get much sleep … The news is of course damn black but we're doing our best to make it less so.'[28]

Retreating British and French troops, in frequently chaotic scenes, had been pouring through the Dunkirk perimeter all day. It was crucial that the defenders held on at such key positions as Nieuport and Furnes in the east, Canal de la Basse Colme and Bergues in the centre, and Saint-Pol-sur-Mer in the west.

CHAPTER 11

Thursday 30 May

Communications between Ramsay's headquarters and Dunkirk were often difficult. This led to confusion in the early hours of 30 May. There was little enemy activity and Captain Tennant saw it as a good opportunity to embark troops at the mole. But he was puzzled that no destroyers had arrived. Dover, it emerged, was acting on a warning from a naval officer at La Panne that Dunkirk harbour was blocked when, in fact, it was still accessible. A 'great opportunity' was missed, Tennant noted, believing that 15,000 soldiers could have been sent off before daylight if the ships had been there. During that time only four trawlers and a yacht arrived.[1]

The badly damaged *King Orry* was still at the mole and Tennant told the captain, Commander Jeffrey Elliott, to either beach the ship or try to sail to England with a trawler as escort. *King Orry* sailed at around 0300. Elliott reported, 'I found, however, that she was not at all handy on her propellers, and whilst endeavouring to point her for the channel she began to develop a list to starboard which developed seriously. Water was reported entering the stokehold and I sent the first lieutenant to investigate. Almost immediately, however, it became obvious that the ship was sinking, and I ordered abandonment. Our one remaining boat on starboard side was turned out previous to this but was submerged as the ship heeled over. As we had two Carley floats and a large number of rafts this was not a serious loss.' Elliott was on the bridge with other officers when the ship turned completely on its starboard side 'and I stepped into the water being afloat near the forward starboard boat, now submerged'. Several ships, including the destroyer HMS *Vivacious*, later picked up survivors but nine men were lost. Elliott was taken to Ramsgate and 24 hours later reported for pier duty, assisting in the handling of craft arriving with troops.[2]

When *Vivacious*'s captain, Lieutenant Commander Frank Parish, returned to England he found that his sight and judgement 'had become impaired to such a degree that, observing the importance of the operations, it was no longer safe for me to retain command'.[3] Ramsay was sympathetic and he was placed on sick leave. Parish also said that his ship's company was in great need of a rest. A commander in the Royal Australian Navy, Emile Dechaineux, replaced him and the destroyer went on to rescue a total of 4,000 troops. Dechaineux was later killed in the Pacific while in command of the cruiser HMAS *Australia*. A Japanese plane hit the ship during the Leyte Gulf landings of October 1944 in what is believed to have been the first kamikaze attack.

The destroyer HMS *Vanquisher* was off Malo-les-Bains when Ramsay's headquarters asked it to check on the state of Dunkirk harbour. The vice admiral would not have been pleased to discover that the entrance was, after all, 'practicable'. At 0500, he must have gritted his teeth again when he learned that the seven modern destroyers he so desperately needed had sailed for Sheerness following Pound's decision to remove them from danger. The First Sea Lord had made it clear that he needed as many ships as possible for the defence of Britain and the Atlantic convoys.

It was not until 0920 that the first merchant ship arrived at the mole. Fortunately, the previous day's sunshine had given way to mist. Tennant signalled Ramsay, 'Troops are concentrated in unlimited numbers just east of Dunkirk beach, on Bray beaches and at La Panne. Please do your best to distribute. I am getting along splendidly here. Send two hospital ships now. If mist persists I will bring them in on arrival.' After a promising start, few ships arrived during the misty morning and 'a great opportunity was again lost'.[4] There were more than 1,000 wounded waiting to be taken off but hospital ships did not appear until the afternoon.

In the early hours, Rear Admiral Wake-Walker had transferred from *Esk* to the minesweeper HMS *Hebe* off Bray-Dunes. On board was Captain Eric Bush, a veteran of the Gallipoli campaign, who had been standing in for him. Bush 'spoke of the ghastly sight of the shore black with men standing in the water up to their waists. He had had to watch the terribly slow progress of embarkation which I had not seen, but I did not feel that I could accept the note of despair which I seemed to detect in his voice.'[5] As dawn broke, Wake-Walker could see men all over the beaches. The sloop HMS *Bideford* was grounded with its stern blown off. The decks had been packed with soldiers when it was bombed. Many were left dead or wounded. Despite the damage, it was thought that *Bideford* could be saved. After picking up 620 British and French troops, the flat-bottomed gunboat HMS *Locust* went to *Bideford*'s assistance, passing a tow. An hour later, the sloop was pulled free but the tow parted several times during an epic voyage to Dover. They finally reached the port at 1200 on 31 May. *Locust* continued to play a role in the evacuation, surviving without any casualties. Despite being attacked, the only damage was sustained during *Bideford's* tow.

Ramsay was concerned that they were still not getting enough men away, a total of around 43,000 a day. He wanted at least 55,000 a day. Ramsay and Vice Admiral Somerville made urgent representations to the First Sea Lord. It was imperative that the withdrawn destroyers were returned. And Pound agreed. Orders were given for six of the ships, HMS *Harvester*, HMS *Havant*, HMS *Ivanhoe*, HMS *Impulsive*, HMS *Icarus* and HMS *Intrepid* to sail to Dunkirk immediately.[6] Such was the naval effort that the bases at Portsmouth, Chatham and Plymouth reported that they did not have any vessels left that could help in the evacuation.

That morning, Ramsay held a conference at Dover with senior army officers representing General Gort. Daylight on Saturday, 1 June, was given as the latest reasonable time when the BEF might be expected to hold Dunkirk's eastern perimeter. It would involve some 4,000 soldiers. Ramsay planned to keep ocean-going tugs, ships' lifeboats and other vessels in reserve for 'the climax of this critical operation'. The rearguard of 4,000, along with naval beach parties, would be lifted between 0130 and 0300 on 1 June.[7]

At Bray-Dunes, there were many boats of 'one sort and another' in the water and on the beach. Ships' motorboats were towing whalers, but it was difficult to get close in. Surf was continuing to be a problem. Soldiers were paddling pontoon craft and these were often abandoned after a rescue vessel was reached. When a destroyer or sloop was full, they took their boats, the boats' crews were guns' crews and no one wanted to be without them'. Wake-Walker asked for more ships and stressed the need for boats. Then he sailed in *Hebe* to Dunkirk harbour to confer with Tennant. The French were starting to use the harbour's west quay for embarkation, leaving the mole for British use.

Wake-Walker became aware of a problem at the mole. 'The tide had a big rise and fall and at low tide it was a 15-foot drop. A lot of ladders were sent over and secured to the sides of the pier, but it took time to get soldiers with their rifles and packs down these ladders.'[8] He had planned to keep *Hebe* as his headquarters but then felt he could not refuse to embark troops at the harbour and was soon filled up with around 700 men, some of them wounded. Wake-Walker began a balancing act, trying to make sure there were enough vessels and off the beaches at the right times. Later, he learned that General Gort was anxious to see him. He transferred his staff to the destroyer HMS *Windsor* and headed back to Dunkirk in MTB *102*, intending to drive from there to Gort's headquarters. But at some point, Wake-Walker changed his mind, deciding instead to rendezvous with the destroyer *Keith*, which was approaching Dunkirk. An element of farce ensued. That evening *Keith*'s skipper, Captain Edward Berthon, reported that he was 'unable to sight the admiral' and entered the harbour 'to gain more information'.[9] Berthon was told that Wake-Walker was still afloat in the MTB. *Keith* left and went in search of him but without success. Berthon decided that helping with the evacuation was the best course and returned to the mole, embarking a remarkable 1,400 troops. At high speed the destroyer returned to Dover, arriving at 0045 on 31 May.

It emerged that Wake-Walker had decided after all to head to Gort's headquarters in the minesweeper *Gossamer* and then the destroyer HMS *Worcester*. A whaler from the destroyer took him to the shore at La Panne and he got wet to the waist landing. Captain Tennant, who had driven to Gort's headquarters after being told he was needed for a conference, and Brigadier Oliver Leese met him on the beach. The admiral was taken to 'a pretentious house' where Gort and his staff were about to have dinner. The general was charming and insisted on Wake-Walker joining them. The admiral sat at the table with his trousers still soaked but he had the consolation of helping to finish Gort's last bottle of champagne. The final dish was fruit salad served from a tin. After dinner, Gort, Wake-Walker, Leese and Tennant discussed the evacuation. There was tension. 'It became obvious to me that they felt that they had successfully fallen back more or less intact on the sea in the face of great odds and that it was now up to the navy to get them off but that the navy were not making any real effort in the matter,' Wake-Walker recorded.[10] This did indeed seem an unfair assessment, and he stressed the difficulty in getting men off the beaches, suggesting that it would be easier if they went to the Dunkirk mole.

Leese referred to the 'ineptitude of the navy'. The brigadier was clearly unaware of the overall operation, with its many losses, and Wake-Walker took offence, saying he had 'no business or justification to talk like that'. Gort stressed that he wanted to withdraw his rearguard of 5,000 troops, 'some of the best', by midnight the next day so that they could get away.[11] The general had spoken to the First Sea Lord, who said the navy would make a supreme effort. The figure of 5,000 was 1,000 higher than the estimate Ramsay had been given that morning.

Wake-Walker admitted, 'I must confess I felt daunted at the prospect and the seeming impossibility of the task. Apart from the rearguard there were tens of thousands of others to come off beforehand, and the thought of that rearguard falling back in the dark and being embarked with an enemy active in pursuit raised unpleasant pictures.'[12] It was arranged that Gort would leave France in

Worcester the next morning. At 2200, in darkness, Wake-Walker made his way to the beach with Tennant, Leese and his flag lieutenant to join the destroyer. An enemy plane flew over and a Bofors gun opened fire at it. Tennant asked if the admiral had a boat ready to take him to the ship and Wake-Walker laughed, pointing out that boats were too precious to be kept hanging about. The tide was out and there were, in fact, a number of stranded boats.

There was an abortive attempt to leave the beach, as Wake-Walker related. 'A number of men of the 12th Lancers were trying to get pontoons afloat, and it was good to see them taking action to help themselves. Lying unused was a pontoon boat about eight feet by four – flat-bottomed with sides about 18 inches high. I called over some soldiers and we got round it and carried it to the water's edge. I then placed four of them each side and told them to wade out with it and get in when I told them. As we waded out the sea was calm, but a small swell was coming in and as the water got deeper I got them into the boat two by two until only flags and I were still wading at the stern and the water was well over our knees.

'Finally we got in together and I started the soldiers paddling by numbers, rather like a racing boat's crew. They soon picked it up but I noticed there was already a good deal of water in the boat – the freeboard was about three inches and the wavelets were washing up on my stern as I sat on the gunwhale. I decided we should not get far before we were swamped, and finding by means of my paddle that we were still in fairly shallow water I told my crew to jump out. Out we all got and returned with our boat to the beach and emptied it. Tennant and General Lees [Brigadier Leese] had been standing all this time watching and as we came ashore I could not resist the temptation of saying to the latter, "Another example of naval ineptitude."' The rear admiral reluctantly reduced his crew and they set off again, paddling 'in fine style' and eventually reaching *Worcester*.[13]

Gort was reluctant to return to England but he had no choice, as Churchill reminded him. In a message sent by the War Office at 1400 that day, the prime minister reminded the general that he had no personal discretion in the matter. If Gort were captured, it would be a propaganda coup for the enemy. He was told to appoint a corps commander to take his place. That officer would continue the defence of Dunkirk until the fight became pointless and then, in consultation with the French, he was authorised to surrender to avoid 'useless slaughter'.[14] Gort chose Major General Harold Alexander (later Earl Alexander of Tunis).

At Bray-Dunes, Lieutenant John Wells, one of the naval officers helping to evacuate troops, found that the main difficulty was the lack of ratings to take charge of boats going out to ships. Soldiers detailed to return boats usually ignored the order, and it became necessary to swim or wade out to retrieve them. Wells asked for more ratings but none arrived. Another handicap was the inadequate communication between ships and the beach. 'A motor cycle headlamp is a poor substitute for an Aldis lamp,' the lieutenant observed. Derelict lorries abandoned below the high-tide mark proved a serious danger to boats, and he saw three come to grief on the submerged wrecks. But the conduct of troops under shell fire impressed him, 'a fine example to the sailors, who soon picked up the idea of lying flat on the stomach and singing *Roll Out The Barrel* to pass away the time'.[15]

Lieutenant Geoffrey Vavasour was another naval officer involved in the evacuation at Bray-Dunes. A destroyer took him within sight of the beach and he reached it in one of the whalers. There were no signs of soldiers. Two minutes later an estimated 5,000 left their cover in the sand dunes. Only junior army officers were present and Vavasour noted that they had little or no control over the men. When naval ratings gave orders about queuing for boats, they were obeyed 'implicitly', but the arrival of stragglers made the task much more difficult.

'The morale of the soldiers was very good,' Vavasour acknowledged. 'They had experienced bitter disappointment in that some of them had been waiting as long as two days to be evacuated, and there had been only a few boats at very long intervals. Considerable discontent was felt against the French – not only to their fighting ability, which the British soldiers described most fluently – but as they were mingling with our soldiers waiting for evacuation. A few wholesome lies to the French soldiers as to the position of their own ships soon cleared the area.'[16]

The French probably had the last laugh because collapsible boats abandoned by British soldiers after reaching ships drifted east and came ashore where they had gathered. They did not hesitate to use them to go out to British ships.

The role of the French army after Germany launched its invasion has remained controversial, and Stanley Allen, a young seaman on board the destroyer *Windsor*, provided two telling examples. Allen recounted, 'When we got alongside [the mole] a file of Scottish soldiers wearing khaki aprons over their kilts came alongside led by an officer who had his arm in a sling. He called out to the bridge, "What part of France are you taking us to?" And one of the officers called back, "We're taking you back to Dover." And he said, "We're bloody not coming." And they went back to continue their war with the Germans. It was remarkable.' On another trip they found a lot of French soldiers. 'They all had their marching equipment in perfect order and it didn't look as though they'd ever fought,' said Allen. 'Everything was spot on. There were no wounded amongst them. They looked well fed, well shaved and clean. We were absolutely surprised. They didn't understand us when there were some derogatory remarks.'[17]

The minesweeper HMS *Ross* had embarked 353 troops at the mole on 28 May and taken them to Margate. The following day, the ship swept channels for mines. Early on 29 May, nearing Dunkirk, *Ross* took off 53 survivors, including troops, from the steamer *Normania*, which had been bombed and was sinking by the stern. *Normania's* funnels and mast would remain visible, with flags still flying in defiance. Off Bray-Dunes, the minesweeper picked up 410 soldiers, later returning to Margate.[18] The captain was Commander John Apps, and Wilfred Walters, a signaller on board *Ross*, said, 'There was one thing our captain was very justified in doing. A skiff came with three high-ranking army officers. The captain said, "I'm not taking you aboard this ship, go back on the beaches and take charge of your men." They didn't want to. The captain said, "If you don't I'll put a couple of rifle bullets through the skiff and let you get on with it. Your place is on the beaches, not trying to get away."' On another occasion, off La Panne, the minesweeper was picking up soldiers who were using lorry inner tubes to stay afloat. 'Just as one got alongside the inner tube suddenly deflated,' said Walters. 'He had all his kit. One of our stokers, a navy champion swimmer funnily enough, went straight over the side and who should it be but his own brother, a regular soldier, and they hadn't met for over four years.' According to Walters, the crew saw little of the RAF, despite the heavy air attacks. 'We used to say, "Where is the Brylcreem Boys? Where is the Brylcreem Boys?"'[19] (Brylcreem was a popular hair cream, much favoured by RAF pilots.)

On the morning of 30 May, at La Panne and Bray-Dunes, soldiers, including men of the Royal Engineers, built piers by driving lorries into the sea, with tyres deflated to help stability. Planks were placed on top. Ramsay thought it an excellent piece of work, although the makeshift piers proved to be suitable only for small boats. The continuing mist and a large black cloud over Dunkirk helped to limit attacks on ships.

France, so far, had not played a major role in the evacuation, but on 30 May, a number of its vessels arrived in the harbour, including the destroyer *Bourrasque*, which sailed from Dunkirk with around 600 French soldiers. Five miles north of Nieuport, on Route Y, the destroyer came under German artillery fire. In taking evasive action, it entered a French minefield. There was an explosion. *Bourrasque* began sinking after apparently hitting a mine, although the captain, a survivor, would insist that the ship had been a casualty of the German gunfire. Two Royal Navy drifters, *Ut Prosim* and *Yorkshire Lass*, helped with the rescue effort, but there was heavy loss of life.

With Tennant at Gort's headquarters, Commander G. O. Maund had taken over his duties at the mole. Maund reported, 'Towards the close of the day a great number of ships had arrived, and I accordingly decided to accept the risk of further losses, and ordered the vessels waiting in the roads to proceed alongside and embark troops. Strong air attacks were launched by the enemy, but fortunately they were mostly concentrated against wrecks in the roads. Time and again they sent waves of bombers and directed their attack, not against our ships loading troops, but only against these wrecks in the roads. We got a great deal of amusement and satisfaction from this, for loading was proceeding apace with no casualties. At the same time, I decided that the rate of embarkation must in some way be speeded up as the capacity of the ships now alongside was more than adequate for the rate of flow of troops.'[20]

Maund rigged up a loudspeaker and told the thousands of troops, 'Remember your pals, boys. The quicker you get on board, the more of them will be saved.' The appeal worked 'like a miracle'.[21] Despite being tired and without food and water for days, soldiers responded 'splendidly' along the length of the mole for some two hours. During that time, more than 15,000 troops were embarked.

The destroyer HMS *Sabre* was no stranger to attacks, and during the afternoon, taking Route Z towards Dunkirk, shore batteries opened fire. Speed was increased and it began to zig-zag, but there were several hits. A shell passed through the petty officers' mess deck and then the magnetic compass, with a splinter allowing water to penetrate one of the oil fuel tanks. As there was not enough fuel for a round trip, the destroyer returned to Dover for repairs. For a time, *Sabre* was steered using the sun.

That evening a plane attacked the destroyer HMS *Anthony* as it took troops to Dover, dropping what appeared to be five depth charges. The first four went off together but did not affect the ship. But the fifth depth charge, close to the starboard beam abreast the bridge, rocked the ship, causing some damage. The captain, Lieutenant Commander Norman Thew, commented, 'When the lights went out and the ship considerably shaken, it was quite understandable that the army officers and soldiers in mess decks and enclosed spaces below attempted to gain the upper deck as quickly as possible. A "panic" was entirely prevented by the various ratings present in the spaces who forcibly stopped and explained that the shakes were our own depth charges.'[22]

There were some bizarre sights. Two miles off Dunkirk, the minesweeper HMS *Sharpshooter* picked up a naked soldier on a laundry basket. 'He didn't have a stitch on,' said one of the sailors. Later the minesweeper was in collision with the ferry *St Helier*. They were entangled in wreckage and another vessel produced towing lines and pulled them apart. *St Helier* 'carried on with her business' but *Sharpshooter* was towed back to Dover by the colourfully named tug *Empire Henchman*. The 50-mile trip took 13 hours.

During the day, British and French troops continued to flow through the Dunkirk perimeter. Poor flying conditions hampered the Luftwaffe, but German ground forces, surprisingly, did not press home their advantage, largely because a command reorganisation had not gone smoothly. Part of the depleted Panzer force found the terrain difficult, an artillery unit ran out of ammunition and there was some stubborn defence. Montgomery's 7th Guards Brigade repulsed an infantry division near Furnes, and French and British troops thwarted assaults across the Basse Colme Canal.

Vice Admiral Somerville wrote to his wife, 'We're having a hell of a time as you may imagine and it's not at all easy for us. A tremendous task we've been given and personally I think we're doing much better than I expected. Not so the poor soldiers across the water but one must make allowances for them in view of their deplorable situation. Thank God there's some fog today and so far the bombing does not appear to have been at all bad. It was frightful yesterday.

'The chief trouble is to get any sleep but I manage odd half hours and two to three hours each night. Glad to hear you've got so much to do as it helps to keep one's mind off it. Reggie Parish [captain of *Vivacious*] is just now absolutely dead to the world. I never saw anyone so played out. I believe his officers and men are equally done in so I'm not sending him to sea though we are sorely in need of destroyers. Spoke to Bill Adam [believed to be Lieutenant General Ronald Adam, nicknamed Bill] and Lord Gort on the telephone just now. Former sounded very nervy and bad tempered, latter was quite cool and pleasant. They must be having the hell of a time. Winston and I usually hold light converse on the telephone at 6.30 am. As he always has his teeth out it's not so easy.'[23]

(Churchill wore dentures made by London dental technician Derek Cudlipp. At Churchill's request they were designed to preserve his distinctive lisp. Cudlipp's son Nigel told the BBC in July 2010, 'When my father's call-up papers came, Churchill personally tore them up. Churchill said he would be more important to the war effort if he stayed in London to repair his dentures. Churchill used to flick out his dentures when he was angry and throw them across the room. My father used to say he could tell how the war was going by how far they flew.')[24]

Ramsay was so pleased to get five hours sleep the previous night, 'the best I've had for days', that he told his wife. But the challenges continued to mount 'and everyone is getting cooked to a turn. It simply can't last much longer at this pace, and what happens when we have to stop doesn't bear thinking about. It's inevitable that thousands and thousands will never be able to be got off.' He added, 'It is so restful and nice to be able to turn my thoughts to Bughtrig [the family home] away from all this turmoil.'[25]

Friday 31 May

Time was running out for Ramsay and his team in the tunnels beneath Dover Castle. As day six of the evacuation began, there were still around 92,000 British troops trapped in Dunkirk, along with 156,000 French soldiers. The Admiralty informed Ramsay that it was now government policy to give British and French personnel 'equal opportunity' in the evacuation.

During the night, every effort was made to get a continuous flow of merchant ships to Dunkirk, but Captain Tennant reported at 0320 that they had failed to enter the harbour. The darkness and enemy shelling must have been factors. The destroyer *Malcolm* was badly damaged after crashing into the mole but was able to embark 1,000 soldiers and return to Dover. The previous day the destroyer had carried some 1,000 soldiers, as well as two German prisoners, who were kept in the forecastle cable locker. *Malcolm* would make a remarkable eight trips to Dunkirk.

During the night, German planes were busy laying mines. At 0605, Tennant was able to report that embarkation was satisfactory in spite of shelling but 'I would again stress the need for more ships and constant fighter protection'. Nearly four hours later he was concerned that the sun was coming through, casting light on 'a big target of ships in the harbour'. Tennant made another request for air protection over the next two hours.[1]

In the early hours, Rear Admiral Wake-Walker transferred to *Express* from *Worcester*, which headed to Dover with a full load of soldiers. He managed to snatch some sleep sitting down on the bridge and leaning against 'some instruments with very sharp corners'. Later he boarded *Keith*, which became his flagship. A suitable flag was found to denote his presence. Up until then he had been using a Red Ensign to indicate which ship he was in. The destroyer moved up and down the coast so that Wake-Walker could control the flow of ships going to Dunkirk and off the beaches, where evacuation was proving difficult. At 1035, he sent the following signal to Ramsay, 'Majority of boats broached to and have no crews. Conditions on beach are very bad due to freshening on-shore wind. Only small numbers are being embarked even in daylight. Under present conditions any large-scale embarkation from beach is quite impracticable. Motorboats cannot get close in. Consider only hope of embarking any number is at Dunkirk. Will attempt to beach [a] ship to form a lee to try and improve conditions.'[2]

Ramsay replied stressing the importance of using the beaches for as long as possible. But Wake-Walker sent another signal, 'Dunkirk our only real hope.' His great fear was that German shelling might put the mole out of action, and he asked if those guns, firing from the west, could be silenced. He signalled to the shore urging soldiers to move to the port, noting, 'From seaward, everything that happened on the beach could be clearly seen. Bodies of men marched along – some in good order, others in groups and knots. At one time a battalion in perfect order marched down through a winding road from the dunes to the shore and I was told later that it was the Welsh Guards.'[3]

That morning's final edition of the *Daily Express* splashed on the evacuation with the banner headline 'TENS OF THOUSANDS SAFELY HOME ALREADY'. There were subheadings saying, 'Many more coming by day and night' and 'SHIPS OF ALL SIZES DARE THE GERMAN GUNS'. The main front-page story began, 'Under the guns of the British fleet, under the wings of the Royal Air Force, a large proportion of the BEF who for three days had been fighting their way back to the Flanders coast, have now been brought safely to England from Dunkirk. First to return were the wounded. An armada of ships – all sizes, all shapes – were used for crossing the Channel. The weather which helped Hitler's tanks to advance has since helped the British evacuation. Cost to the Navy of carrying out, in an inferno of bombs and shells, one of the most magnificent operations in history, has been three destroyers, some auxiliary craft and a small steamer.' A separate story on the front page quoted an Admiralty communiqué, which stated, 'The German High Command has claimed to have inflicted very large losses upon naval units and the transports which they protect. As usual these bear no relation to the facts.' The communiqué confirmed that the destroyers *Grafton*, *Grenade* and *Wakeful* and certain small auxiliary craft had been lost.[4]

Ships of all sizes and shapes. Over the years, the legend of the Little Ships of Dunkirk would grow, and 31 May would be a turning point. On 14 May, the BBC had broadcast an Admiralty request that all owners of self-propelled pleasure craft between 30ft and 100ft in length should report within 14 days if they had not already done so. Less than two weeks later, the small craft section of the Ministry of Shipping was telephoning boat builders and agents asking them to collect craft suitable for taking troops off the beaches near Dunkirk. The emphasis was on boats with a shallow draft, particularly yachts and launches. Such was the urgency of the operation that many owners could not be contacted. The boats were taken regardless. And at least one owner reported to police that his boat had been stolen. Tough Brothers, of Teddington, Middlesex, collected some 100 of them from the upper reaches of the River Thames. They were checked and taken by tugs to Sheerness and after fuelling went on to Ramsgate, where Royal Navy officers, ratings and experienced volunteers took over. Only a few owners, including some fishermen, remained with their boats.[5] Early in the afternoon of 31 May, towing began of a large number of small boats from Ramsgate, with a destination of the French beaches. MTBs provided an escort but at five knots it was slow going.

Charles de Groot, a lieutenant in the Royal Navy Volunteer Reserve, who was helping to organise boats at Tilbury, said, 'We got a most enthusiastic response, not only volunteering their boats but also their personal help. The other thing that happened was the problem of crewing them, and in lots of cases navy personnel went in to clubs and pubs and we had far more volunteers than we really needed.' Some of the boats needed repairs so that they could make it beyond the Thames estuary. Fuel, food, water and first-aid kits were provided. Later the lieutenant went to Ramsgate and Dover and saw troops returning. Some of them were in 'a shocking state'.[6]

Charles Muggleton was 15 when the call went out for volunteers. He had some experience because his school had a sailing boat moored at Lee-on-Sea, Essex, and he and a friend, Tony, saw the appeal as 'a great adventure'. Muggleton recalled, 'Tony and myself said, "We'll go", and we almost did go. At the last minute Tony's mother came flying down to the beach and took us, saying, "Your mother will go mad". So we never went. Opposite us were twin boys who were 16 and they went over and they never came back. That was the first thing that struck you, that war was war.' Muggleton went on to join the Royal Navy and served as a landing craft coxswain on D-Day.[7]

Albert Barnes was only 14, a galley boy in the Thames tug *Sun XII*, based at Wapping, East London, when he went to France. The tug had been docking a ship when a police boat came alongside and they were told to go to Gravesend. *Sun XII* towed two barges full of ammunition to a beach near La Panne. 'We had to go at top speed towards the beach and then cut the tow so the barges could drift in,' Barnes explained. 'Soon as they got ashore Jerry came over and they went up. Loudest bang I'd heard before that was firework night, November 5th.' Two days were spent towing boats with soldiers to the bigger ships. The crew saw Stukas attacking a hospital ship, which had 'red crosses everywhere'. When the tug returned to London the owner's son told the crew to paint the funnel because it was dirty. 'You can imagine the answer he got,' said Barnes. 'When I eventually got home I knocked at the door and my mother said, "Where have you been?" and I said over to France. She said, "You don't mean Dunkirk?" So I said that's the name.' Like Muggleton, he later joined the Royal Navy and took part in the Normandy landings, helping to tow part of the Mulberry harbour.[8]

On the morning of 31 May, six cockleboats, *Renown*, *Reliance*, *Resolute*, *Defender*, *Endeavour* and *Letitia*, set off from Leigh-on-Sea. Off Gravelines, some 40 German bombers attacked them, but they managed to zig-zag out of harm's way. That night, *Renown* had engine trouble and signalled *Letitia* for help. *Letitia*'s skipper, Arthur Dench, recounted, 'They made fast to our stern and we towed them, about three and a half fathoms of rope being the distance behind us. That was at 1.15 am, and tired out, the engineer and seaman and signaller went to turn in, as our work seemed nearly done. We were congratulating ourselves when, at about 1.50, a terrible explosion took place, and a hail of wood splinters came down on our deck. In the pitch dark you could see nothing and after the explosion we heard nothing. And we could do nothing except pull in the tow rope which was just as we had passed to *Renown* about three quarters of an hour before, but not a sign of *Renown*.'[9] *Reliance* was close to *Renown* when the fishing boat was 'blown to smithereens', killing all four crew. *Reliance*'s skipper, Alfred Leggatt, said they carried on with the evacuation, spending about 36 hours taking soldiers to ships. 'The only cup of tea I got was on the way back to Ramsgate and that went down very well,' Leggatt recalled. 'I smoked about 3,000 cigarettes in the time. Nobody would dare go down below to make a cup of tea because they were frightened the boat would blow up. I remember saying that if I ever get home I would go in a monastery and spend the rest of my life there. We had the fright of our lives. I was absolutely scared stiff and I've been scared stiff ever since. I was very pleased to get home again.' The cockleboats rescued about 1,000 soldiers in total. Leggatt's fear did not stop him joining the Royal Navy. He became a coastal forces officer and took part in the St Nazaire raid in March 1942.[10]

Ramsay, still under immense pressure, would no doubt have approved of these examples resilience, of which there were many. The crew of *Windsor* witnessed a remarkable episode. The destroyer picked up a 17-year-old lad who had set off from Hastings in a fishing boat. He was sunk twice in one morning. *Windsor* took him to Dunkirk. 'Alongside the mole there was a megaphone appeal for someone to help crew a fishing boat,' said Ordinary Seaman Stanley Allen. 'Some of the crew had been machine-gunned and they were desperately short. And this boy of 17 who had been sunk twice volunteered immediately and he got cheered off the ship by the sailors. One old three-badge able seaman – which meant he'd had 13 years of undetected crime – said to me, "With youngsters like that, how can we effing well lose." It did us the world of good, it was a real tonic.'[11]

Four fast War Department launches, *Swallow*, *Marlborough*, *Haig* and *Wolfe*, joined the armada after leaving Ramsgate in the early hours. Major Robin Hutchins of the Grenadier Guards was in command of *Swallow*, and he described the scene that greeted him at 0600: 'Dunkirk was under a pall of smoke from fires which appeared to be mainly to the south and west of the port. There were numerous wrecks outside the harbour and along the beaches. There were large numbers of troops on the shore as far as it was possible to see to the eastward, and the beach was strewn with all forms of motor transport. Along the foreshore were a very large number of pulling boats, aground, capsized or damaged, and abandoned. There were also a considerable number of motorboats, motor launches and yachts aground and, in most cases, abandoned, and several wrecks close inshore. About one mile out in the Dunkirk Roads were numerous destroyers and other vessels waiting to embark troops, but scarcely any boats were running between the shore and these ships.'[12]

Hutchins spent most of the morning towing boats with soldiers to the destroyer *Impulsive*. Most of the men were 'very weak and very helpless'. He asked the destroyer to send a signal to Ramsay requesting more cutters and powerboats to speed up embarkation. In the afternoon, he boarded *Keith* and suggested to Wake-Walker that remaining troops should go to Dunkirk. That evening, *Swallow* headed back to Ramsgate, with the hard-worked engines failing just outside the harbour. The launch, with towed boats, had taken between 700 and 800 troops from the beaches to warships.[13]

Enemy attacks, of course, were not the only danger. Sandbars, the tide, wrecks, submerged debris and fast-moving destroyers were constant hazards for the little ships. *Golden Spray*, a beach boat from Deal, had carried six loads of troops when it was caught by the wash of a destroyer trying to avoid a bombing attack. Water flooded in and *Golden Spray* soon sank.

Frederick Hannaford, skipper of the trawler *Provider*, recalled, 'One incident which stands out vividly in my mind was the action of part of my crew on the morning of May 31st. The naval officer in charge of my ship had asked a few motorboats which were laying about if they were going to get some troops off the beach, and the reply he received was that there was not sufficient water to get close enough. On hearing this four of my crew, the mate, boatswain and two deck hands all volunteered immediately to take a chance and go themselves. Of the two deck hands one was aged 58 and the other 20 years. It was only possible for three to go, so the younger man insisted that the other deck hand should keep aboard the *Provider*. The young deck hand's name was Penn. The three pushed off, arrived at the beach and picked up a load of soldiers. A motorboat went alongside to tow them back. Unfortunately, the motorboat, in starting off with its load, pulled too hard and swamped the small boat. All were thrown into the water. Only two of my men were found and brought back to *Provider*. The young deck hand Penn had lost his life.'[14]

It was a bad day for the French navy. A torpedo from an E-boat blew the bow off the destroyer *Cyclone* as it headed to Dunkirk from Dover. The ship remained afloat and managed to limp back to the English port. On 3 June, it arrived in Brest for repairs but was scuttled later that month to prevent it being seized by the Germans. Some 20 minutes after the attack on *Cyclone*, two other E-boats torpedoed the destroyer *Siroco*, which capsized with the loss of 59 crewmen and more than 600 troops. The sloop HMS *Widgeon* picked up 166 of the 252 survivors. The destroyer HMS *Leopard* suffered bomb damage off Dunkirk. At the port, the steamers *Ain el Turk* and *Cote d'Azur* and three trawlers were bombed and sunk.

During the afternoon, *Keith* took Wake-Walker to a spot off La Panne after reports of heavy shelling. The destroyer became a target and moved out of range. An observation balloon over Nieuport was directing the fire, and the admiral asked for it to be shot down. Planes were sent but the Germans hauled down the balloon, only for it to reappear. The shelling continued. Because of the danger, Wake-Walker urged General Gort to embark as soon as possible but he refused to leave before the arranged time – 1800. The rear admiral headed back to Dunkirk, witnessing a 'terrific' air battle. 'I saw three Spitfires shot down, one went inland over the dunes, still under control, one came down towards the sea at a fairly gentle angle and when only 100 feet or so up the pilot seemed to be pulled out by his parachute and came down in the sea with his parachute open – the plane went on for quite a way and then flew into the water. The third pilot baled out a good way up and came down a couple of miles away. An MTB and a motorboat in sight went off to try and pick them up and the captain of the MTB told me later that the pilot they got to was shot to pieces and they salved his parachute for identification purposes. I am afraid the other was not found.'[15]

Wake-Walker found he needed to be in several places at once. The overall picture remained unclear. He did not know when vessels would appear, and Ramsay and his team could not help much because communications were still a problem. Even the arrangements for getting Gort became confused. Wake-Walker arranged for *Hebe* to be off La Panne but, unknown to him, Dover sent over four MTBs and MASBs (Motor Anti-Submarine Boat) for that purpose. Shortly before 1800, the rear admiral approached La Panne again in *Keith* and *Hebe* signalled 'General on beach abreast of you'. A group were at the water's edge and *Keith's* boats were sent. When the first boat returned, Wake-Walker was surprised to discover that it had not carried Gort. Then it emerged that the general was already on board *Hebe*. There was a heavy air attack as his staff officers were being taken off the beach. The admiral was able to get some revenge on Brigadier Leese, who had been disparaging about the navy. Leese was kept on *Keith's* bridge 'to see something of what the naval problem was'.[16]

One hour before Gort was due to embark, four dive-bombers attacked *Hebe*, dropping 12 bombs, three of which fell very close to the minesweeper, which was also machine-gunned and 'badly shaken'. *Hebe* shot down one of the planes. Once the general was on board, *Hebe* went off at high speed, altering course frequently and staying as far away from *Keith* as possible. With air attacks continuing, *Hebe's* captain, Lieutenant Commander John Temple, believed that the Germans had information that Gort and his staff officers were on board the destroyer.

Wake-Walker returned to Dunkirk where 'I saw for the first time that strange procession of craft of all kinds that has become famous – tugs towing dinghies, lifeboats and all manner of pulling boats – small motor yachts, motor launches, drifters, Dutch skoots, Thames barges, fishing boats, pleasure steamers.' He was particularly anxious that some of the tows should go to La Panne. Later, *Keith* went to Bray-Dunes and the admiral discovered that the La Panne boats were stopping there. An order was given that they should continue along the coast. Leese was still on *Keith's* bridge and 'I remember pointing out to him how easy it was to talk about distributing boats and craft at certain places along a ten-mile stretch of coast, but that it was a very different thing to get it done in practice, in the dark, by craft which had not been there before and with no lights to help them. The inevitable tendency was to stop at the first place they came to where other craft were assembled.' Hopefully, the brigadier took on board this lesson.[17]

Once it was dark, *Keith* remained off La Panne. The rearguard was falling back and it was hoped that it would take time before the Germans realised.

Shelling was continuous. *Malcolm* reported that parachute mines were being dropped to westward. At 2300, Wake-Walker received an urgent message from the Admiralty. Where was General Gort? And why were the MTBs sent to collect him given other tasks? The admiral sent an MASB to *Hebe* to collect the general. 'To my horror it came back almost at once to say that Lord Gort had just left *Hebe* in a motor launch … I waited anxiously for the boat to arrive. Presently out of the dark a boat appeared and came alongside, still not the right one and I had a bad moment thinking of the possibilities of the boat getting lost.' After about half an hour, the right boat appeared, and Gort and Leese were transferred to the MASB, which headed for Dover, much to Wake-Walker's relief.[18]

Major General Harold Alexander was now the most senior British Army officer at Dunkirk. And there was more confusion. Captain Tennant discovered that Gort had given 'totally different instructions' to Alexander and General Bertrand Fagalde, the French commander responsible for holding part of the perimeter. Gort told Fagalde that Alexander would place his divisions under the French general's orders to help the evacuation of his men. Tennant recalled, 'General Alexander, however, was told by Lord Gort in my hearing that he was to do nothing to imperil his army and was ultimately responsible for their safety and evacuation.' The captain advised Alexander to go to La Panne, where there was still a telephone link, and speak to the Secretary of State for War, Anthony Eden. This he did. Eden advised him to use his discretion and carry on with the evacuation. Admiral Jean-Marie Abrial, in command of Dunkirk port, asked Tennant to take charge of the British and French embarkation. Tennant agreed and asked for French officers to help, and they were provided.[19]

That day, 31 May, Churchill flew to Paris for a meeting of the Supreme War Council, accompanied by Lord Privy Seal Clement Attlee, General Dill, Major General Hastings Ismay and Major General Spears. They went to Prime Minister Reynaud's room at the War Office, where Marshal Philippe Petain was among the French representatives. The first issue raised was the Norwegian crisis and there was agreement on evacuating their joint forces. Then they turned to Dunkirk. Churchill revealed that 165,000 men, of whom 15,000 were French, had been taken off.

One of the main reasons Churchill went to Paris was to ensure that the same orders were given to British and French troops. The three British divisions holding the centre would cover the evacuation of all the Allied forces. He hoped that a total of 200,000 troops would escape, which would be 'almost a miracle'. Churchill admitted that four days earlier he would not have bet on a total of more than 50,000.[20]

CHAPTER 13

Saturday 1 June

The Royal Navy had not suffered any major losses the previous day. Nor had the merchant fleet. The evacuation always seemed to be producing challenges, but Ramsay was no doubt praying that Saturday, 1 June, would be another disaster-free 24 hours. Hermann Goering had other ideas. Despite his boasts, the Luftwaffe was failing to deliver the decisive blow – the annihilation of the BEF and the French forces trapped in and around Dunkirk. Goering ordered an all-out air assault. Daylight would see the evacuation fleet paying a high price.

Two hospital carriers that had sailed the previous night returned to Dover shortly before dawn, but only one succeeded in entering Dunkirk harbour. Four personnel ships also failed to use the cover of darkness to join the evacuation, berthing in daylight. One of the vessels, the steamer *Prague*, which had made two successful trips, was bombed and badly damaged on its return journey. The destroyer HMS *Shikari* and two other vessels took off most of the troops it was carrying and *Prague*, with the help of a tug, continued to England, the captain reporting, 'Having arrived at a spot slightly north of the ruins of Sandown Castle, about a mile north of Deal, the ship was gently beached, port anchor laid out, and all active participation in the evacuation of Dunkirk ceased.'[1]

On the beaches, it became clear that La Panne was no longer an option for evacuation. The area was coming under heavy machine-gun fire, the enemy were that close, and troops were moving westward. Bray-Dunes was also becoming too dangerous. In a message to Ramsay, Wake-Walker again emphasised that rescue work should be focused on Dunkirk harbour. The vice admiral replied, 'While leaving this to your discretion it is essential that beaches should be used until found impossible.'[2]

At Bray-Dunes, a minesweeper was aground, and Wake-Walker asked the captain of a tug carrying some soldiers to go in and try to tow it off. 'The captain paid no attention and obviously was only concerned to get away,' the rear admiral recalled. 'I finally trained a gun on him and told an RNVR sub-lieutenant who was on board to take charge, put the soldiers on board the *Sabre* [destroyer] who was nearby and go off to help the minesweeper. It was not nice to have to threaten these men who were really volunteers, but it had to be done. I could not risk ships and men for the sake of some volunteer's feelings and nothing else seemed to have any effect. The real trouble on this and another occasion later was that the tugs were told to go over with pulling boats in tow and load up and they regarded themselves as transports only. I was never informed of this or their orders and regarded them as tugs and for the use as tugs.'[3]

At 0400, it was misty with low cloud, which brought some relief. Unfortunately for the rescuers, the weather improved. There were still many men on the beaches, but most of the small craft had returned to England. Wake-Walker sent another message to Ramsay saying he was directing all available vessels to Dunkirk. As the mist and cloud dispersed, so more planes appeared but not all of them were the enemy, and there were cases of ships firing at the RAF. Even *Keith*, with Wake-Walker on board, opened up with the aft machine gun despite a ceasefire order, which the gunners could not hear. With *Keith*'s high-angle ammunition running low, the rear admiral decided to send it to Dunkirk to pick up soldiers and return to Dover. He planned to transfer his flag to the destroyer HMS *Basilisk*. Before he had time to do that a heavy bombing attack developed.[4]

Ivanhoe, abreast of Dunkirk and carrying some 1,000 soldiers, was one of the targets. Three bombs were dropped from about 1,000ft. Two were near misses but the third caused extensive damage, leaving 26 dead and 30 wounded. Because of fire, the foremost magazine was flooded. *Havant* and the minesweeper HMS *Speedwell* went alongside and took off the soldiers and the wounded. *Ivanhoe* remained afloat and was able to make seven knots, despite damage to the boiler rooms. The vessel was attacked twice more and smoke floats were set off in the bow to simulate that the ship had been struck 'and this ruse had the desired effect and undoubtedly saved the ship from further damage'. *Ivanhoe* eventually reached Sheerness and entered a dry dock to stop it sinking.[5]

Before Wake-Walker had time to transfer to *Basilisk*, a wave of between 30 and 40 Stukas appeared off Bray-Dunes, and *Keith* took evasive action. In the wheelhouse, everyone was lying down and the quartermaster was steering by using the lower spokes of the wheel. Then came three loud explosions and the ship heaved. One bomb dropped astern, jamming the helm. More planes dived, releasing bombs.

'Everyone on the bridge was lying or crouching down but there was not much room and I could only find room to bend a bit,' said Wake-Walker. 'It was an odd sensation waiting for the explosions and knowing that you could do nothing. When they came it was obvious that the ship had been hit. She shook badly and there was a rush of smoke and steam from somewhere aft.'[6]

A bomb had gone down one of the funnels and burst below. Because of the danger of fire, torpedoes were jettisoned and depth charges were made safe. The ship had no steam. MTB *102*, under the command of 21-year-old Lieutenant Christopher Dreyer, came alongside and took off the rear admiral and his staff. 'In the MTB I first went to two tugs which were not far away and sent them to the *Keith*, and then made for Dunkirk,' said Wake-Walker. 'As we left I saw another attack develop on her and once more watched the bombs dropping. One bomb hit her under the bridge on the port side. First there was a white splash and then the black smoke of the explosion. When I last saw her she had a heavy list to port and her HA [high angle] gun was still firing.' *Keith* was hit twice more and most of the crew were taken off by the tugs *St Abbs* and *Vincia*.[7]

As *St Abbs* continued rescue work, a bomb hit amidships and it disappeared within 30 seconds. Thirty men from *Keith*, which sank, were lost. Sailors in the water were bombed and machine-gunned. Telegraphist Reginald Heron managed to swim to *Vincia*, grabbing one of the tyres hanging over the side. After being dragged 'at a rate of knots' he was hauled on board. 'We were all in our underwear or various dress,' Heron said. 'We were crowded on the deck of this thing and I always remember this officer who was in his pyjamas for some reason and he was in the foc'sle waving his arms over his head and saying "Survivor, survivor" to these Germans who completely ignored all this survivor business. There was the odd person killed in the tug but they didn't do much damage. I think there were so many targets they were at a loss to get some organisation into their strafing. Whatever they fired at they were hitting something or other.' It was Heron's second lucky escape. He was in the destroyer HMS *Blanche* when it hit a mine and sank in the Thames estuary in November 1939. Heron was a keen ballroom dancer and, during spells of leave, he would go Streatham Locarno in London, where he met a girl called Violette. She disappeared from his life after a brief affair. Later he learned that she was Violette Szabo, the Special Operations Executive agent who was awarded a posthumous George Cross.[8]

After taking 500 troops from the stricken *Ivanhoe*, the destroyer *Havant* headed for Dover at full speed. In the channel to the west of Dunkirk, it became a target for dive-bombers and shore batteries but escaped by zig-zagging. *Havant* had just turned to the north-west at the end of the channel when two bombs penetrated the engine room. A large bomb fell in the water 50 yards ahead, exploding as the ship passed over it. Ammunition lockers blew up and there were many casualties in the engine room and among the soldiers on deck. The destroyer was out of control and heading towards sandbanks but was eventually stopped. The minesweeper HMS *Saltash* and a large yacht came alongside and took off the soldiers. *Saltash* began towing *Havant* but bombers inflicted further punishment, and the captain, Lieutenant Commander Anthony Burnell-Nugent, gave the order to abandon ship. Later *Havant* rolled over and sank. Praising his crew, the captain commented, 'All went about their duties in a quiet and orderly manner despite grim scenes of carnage on the upper deck. During the various stages of disembarkation from *Havant* there was never any haste to leave, the soldiers and the wounded were always thought of first. About half of my seamen were ordinary seamen under 20.'[9]

Basilisk was another destroyer that succumbed to air attacks, and the captain, Commander Maxwell Richmond, a future vice admiral, had some telling observations. 'I would like to emphasise that the older destroyers with pom poms using belted ammunition and 4.7in guns with only 30 degrees elevation are no match for a determined air attack. Our Lewis guns had also been recently surrendered. When ships of this type are operating within range of enemy air attack losses must be expected unless adequate fighter protection is afforded. In all, the enemy launched four big air attacks at about hourly intervals during the forenoon of 1 June. The first, second and fourth were apparently unopposed by any British aircraft. On the third occasion an intense air battle could be heard in progress above the clouds and no effective bombing took place. I would also like to state that from my observation the enemy aircraft even when opposed were always more numerous than our own, and in the subsequent air battles our fighters although outnumbered fought most courageously and effectively but generally lost more planes than the enemy. From our point of view the BBC bulletins describing the air actions off Dunkirk entirely misrepresent the true situation.'[10]

Among the Royal Navy's other losses was the minesweeper *Skipjack*, which was carrying some 275 troops, nearly all of them below decks. In the space of two minutes, five bombs hit the ship and it turned turtle, trapping the soldiers. *Skipjack* sank after 20 minutes, with the loss of 19 of the crew. Few soldiers survived. The gunboat HMS *Mosquito* was abandoned after it was bombed and set on fire after embarking troops. Other vessels were attacked but survived.

The French destroyer *Le Foudroyant* sank in less than three minutes after being bombed off Dunkirk. That afternoon, the French minesweepers *Denis*

Papin, Venus and *La Mousaillon* were all lost within seven minutes of bombing as they sailed in convoy.

The transport ship *Scotia* embarked about 2,000 French troops, before sailing for Sheerness, avoiding wrecks and small craft heading for Dunkirk. Then 12 enemy bombers, in three formations, were spotted coming from astern. 'The shots from their machine guns dropped like hail all round the bridge and funnels and in the water ahead,' said Captain William Hughes. 'One bomb struck the ship abaft the engine room on the starboard side and another on the poop deck starboard side. Immediately the third four [planes] swooped over us and one of their bombs dropped down the after funnel while the others dropped on the stern. During all this time our guns kept firing but with no effect on the enemy. Up to then we were going on full speed and manoeuvring with the helm. An SOS had been sent out. I ordered another to be sent, but I was informed that the wireless cabin had been shattered and the wireless operator blown out of his room, but he had escaped injury.

'All these bombs had caused extensive damage and the ship was gradually sinking by the stern and heeling over to starboard. I therefore gave orders to abandon ship. The engines had been put out of action.

'We carried ten boats, but three of them had been smashed by the bombs. The troops, being French, could not understand orders and they were rushing the boats, which made it very difficult to man the falls – the port boats being most difficult as the vessel was heeling over to starboard. The chief officer had been given a revolver to use by a French officer, threatening to use this helped matters a little. However, they obeyed my mouth whistle and hand signs and so stood aside while the boats were being lowered.'[11]

The destroyer *Esk* left Dunkirk at full speed in answer to *Scotia*'s SOS. Hundreds of troops were taken off after the destroyer's bow was positioned close to the sinking ship's forecastle head. Hundreds more were plucked from the sea. Rescue work continued as the enemy returned, dropping bombs and machine-gunning men swimming and clinging to wreckage. After checking that there was no one else left alive in his ship, Captain Hughes boarded *Esk*. Other craft helped to pick up survivors and the destroyer sailed for Dover. Some 330 men lost their lives, including 28 of the crew.[12]

The steamer *Westward Ho*, serving as a minesweeper, was perhaps the luckiest vessel. It also embarked French troops – 900, including a general and his staff. Soon after leaving Dunkirk, *Westward Ho* was bombed for half an hour, an estimated 90 bombs falling, but the vessel survived, although six men were killed and 21 wounded. 'This must be considered very slight under the circumstances and I regard it as a miracle that we escaped at all,' said its captain, Lieutenant A. L. Braithwaite. The steamer opened fire at the attackers with two Lewis guns, a Bren gun and a 12-pounder, destroying three of the planes. The general was so relieved to reach Margate that he immediately decorated two of the crew with the Croix de Guerre for downing the enemy.[13]

When Wake-Walker arrived at Dunkirk in MTB *102* that morning, he intended liaising with Major General Alexander but he was away, as was Captain Tennant. A staff officer told him it was planned to continue the evacuation from the harbour and the beaches. The rear admiral decided to go to Dover and confer with Ramsay. The MTB was bombed and machine-gunned on the way over. On arriving, he was given a clean shirt and a pair of trousers but still looked 'a rather untidy figure' when he went to the castle and saw Ramsay and Somerville, who had heard of the attack on *Keith* and were 'pleasantly surprised' to see him. After sending a telegram to his wife, Wake-Walker had lunch with Ramsay at his house in the castle grounds. It was a sunny day 'and the view over the channel seemed so peaceful that, in spite of the large collection of ships, it was hard to believe that Dunkirk was so short a distance away'.[14] After the meal, he slept for a couple of hours in Somerville's bed and then went to Ramsay's headquarters to hear the plans for the night.

A tunnel in a hill led to the headquarters, of which Wake-Walker gave a good description: 'First down a steep slope with floor and walls of concrete, then into a wide passage through walls of chalk with layers of huge flints, dimly lit by an occasional lamp. This opened at the end into a large oblong chamber at right angles to the passage and divided up by boarding into a number of offices. Past these a narrow passage led to the end and the VA's office. Here the chamber finished in a large window and door out on to a narrow railed-in platform on the sheer face of the cliff. Immediately below you looked down 300 feet into the chimney pots and gardens of houses on the foreshore, and beyond the harbour was spread out in clear view. No naval officer can ever have had a better view of his command.

'One of these offices in this casemate, as the chamber was called, was known as the Dynamo Room, from the code word that had been given to the Dunkirk operation. Here the presiding genius was Captain [Michael] Denny, who was responsible for the general details. With him there were about 20 or more officers, soldiers, Board of Trade and sea transport officials, and the work they did was marvellous. They were controlling, organising, fuelling, supplying, not only men-of-war but a variety of merchant vessels. Sometimes the crew of a merchant vessel would refuse to go to Dunkirk again – within a few hours the sea transport officer had got another crew and the ship would sail. At Ramsgate, the Nore and various other places besides Dover, ships and boats were collected and organised, but the head and control of the whole was in this room, where they worked continuously and tirelessly against time day and night.'[15]

It was decided that embarkation would take place between 2100 and 0330 the next day. Ferries capable of carrying as many as 3,000 men would go to the mole and a large number of ships and small craft would cover one and a half miles of beach east of Dunkirk. The Royal Navy would provide ferries with naval officers to act as advisers and sailors to 'stiffen' the crews. French destroyers would use the west quay. The RAF was tasked with providing cover from 1900 and 0700 when ships would be on passage to and from Dunkirk.[16]

Charles Lightoller must have been the best known of the small ships' skippers, as he was the most senior officer to survive the sinking of *Titanic*. A retired commander in the Royal Naval Reserve, he was also a World War I hero, having won the Distinguished Service Cross and Bar. He set off from Ramsgate in his motor yacht *Sundowner*, accompanied by his son Roger and a Sea Scout, Gerald Ashcroft. On the way, *Sundowner* narrowly missed a floating mine and survived an attack by three fighters. It came across the motor cruiser *Westerly*, which was badly damaged and on fire, and took off the five people on board, 'giving them the additional pleasure of again facing the hell they had only just left'.[17] Lightoller was not without humour. The attacks continued but *Sundowner*, 'extremely quick on the helm', managed to dodge them by waiting until the last moment to take evasive action.

Before leaving for Dunkirk the boat had been stripped of everything moveable to create more room. It was licensed to carry 21 people. At the mole, Lightoller began embarking troops. 'My son, as previously arranged, was to pack the men in and use every available inch of space, which I'll say he carried out to some purpose. On deck I detailed a naval rating to tally the troops aboard. At 50 I called below, "How are you getting on?" getting the cheery reply, "Oh plenty of room yet". At 75 my son admitted they were getting pretty tight – all equipment and arms being left on deck.

'I now started to pack them on deck, having passed word below for every man to lie down and keep down. The same applied on deck. By the time we had 50 on deck, I could feel her getting distinctly tender, so took no more. Actually we had exactly 130 on board, including three Sundowners and five Westerlys. During the whole embarkation we had quite a lot of attention from enemy planes, but derived an amazing degree of comfort from the fact that the *Worcester*'s AA guns kept up an everlasting bark overhead.'[18]

The return to Ramsgate was 'unmitigated hell'. Some of the 'splendid' soldiers acted as lookouts and Lightoller continued to use his evasive tactics during air attacks. Another son, a bomber pilot who had been killed earlier in the war, had discussed tactics with his father 'and I attribute in a great measure our success in getting across without a single casualty to his unwitting help'. On arrival, there was disbelief that *Sundowner* had carried so many men, with one petty officer remarking, 'God's truth, mate. Where did you put them?'[19]

It was arranged that Wake-Walker would leave Dover and return to Dunkirk in MASB *10* early in the evening of 1 June, and on his way to the harbour he stopped in the town to buy 'a pair of pants and some food'. In a typically British gesture the crew of the anti-submarine boat had provided the rear admiral with his own flag, made out of a cleaning cloth with a painted red cross and dots. With the flag flying, MASB *10* left the harbour to the salutes of ships it passed.

At about this time, Ramsay received a disturbing signal from Dunkirk: 'Things are getting very hot for ships; over 100 bombers on ships here since 0530, many casualties. Have directed that no ships sail during daylight. Evacuation by transports therefore ceases at 0300. If perimeter holds will complete evacuation tomorrow, Sunday night. General concurs.'

Ramsay passed on the message to Wake-Walker as he sped towards France. A few miles off the French coast, two MTBs were spotted heading towards MASB *10*. 'They were not British and it seemed quite likely they were Germans,' the rear admiral recorded. 'We had turned towards them but as I felt it was my business to get to Dunkirk and not to get involved in a scrap with the MTBs I gave orders to go back to our course and go full speed. As we did so the others turned towards us and for a time it looked as if we would not avoid them, but we gradually drew away and they turned back to their former course. I think they must have been French as I don't fancy Germans would have left us alone.'[20]

The MASB reached Dunkirk without further incident and Wake-Walker went to Bastion 32 to confer with Alexander and Tennant. The major general's headquarters was a small bare room lit by a single lamp. The rear admiral detailed Ramsay's plans. He was relieved to learn that the French were holding a line behind the rearguard, and it was planned that the British troops would withdraw through this defence, which would remain in place. After a drink, he went to the mole and was joined by Tennant, who was wearing a tin hat with the letters SNO, 'cut out of silver paper and stuck on with sardine oil – it looked very distinguished all the same'. As they stood talking a Lysander army reconnaissance plane flew over and several Bofors guns opened up, with Tennant exclaiming, 'I'm sure that damned fellow is a Hun – he has been flying over here all day.' Wake-Walker then realised it was the plane he had requested to check if the mole was being shelled. He 'felt rather sorry for the poor chap, though he seemed none the worse. I explained the situation and hoped I had calmed their fears. After this excitement we returned to the MASB and had some food. The party ashore had not had much to eat and the beer, fruit, some raisins and chocolate which I had brought over besides more ordinary food was much appreciated.'[21]

As they sat eating, a man in brown overalls suddenly appeared in the cabin and declared, 'I am the sole survivor of the *Keith*.' It was the destroyer's navigating officer, who told how survivors were picked up by a tug, which sank after being bombed. He had swum to shore, some distance from Dunkirk. After being given clothes, he walked to the port, believing no one else had been able to swim to safety. The rear admiral admitted, 'It gave me a great shock at the time, but fortunately it was not true as many men were picked up and only[!] three officers and 33 men were lost and 16 wounded.'[22]

That evening there was a signal from the Chief of the Imperial General Staff, General Dill, who advised Alexander, 'We do not order any fixed moment for evacuation. You are to hold on as long as possible in order that the maximum number of French and British may be evacuated. Impossible from here to judge local situation. In close cooperation with Admiral Abrial you must act in this matter on your own judgement.'

Ramsay was able to point out that in spite of the losses, 60,000 troops had been landed in Britain over 24 hours, 'thanks to the unremitting determination of naval vessels who all executed a succession of round trips, interrupted only by necessary refuelling and who accounted for 70 per cent of this total. The majority of the surviving vessels had been operating ceaselessly for at least five days, and officers and men were approaching a condition of complete exhaustion.' Having to suspend the evacuation during daylight hours was a blow, and Ramsay was concerned at the increasing number of air attacks, which 'the RAF were unable to smother with the means at their disposal'.[23]

As darkness fell in Dunkirk, a sloop arrived followed by minesweepers, destroyers and tugs. The mole was outlined against the glow of fires that were still burning to the west in the town. Shelling was continuous. At midnight, Wake-Walker spotted two masts sticking out of the water, with the masthead light on one of them still burning. A trawler had just been sunk.

CHAPTER 14

Sunday 2 June

This was a crucial day, with 2 June set to mark the evacuation of the BEF's rearguard. As planned, vessels sailed for Dunkirk in the early hours of darkness, and Ramsay dared to think that the operation was going smoothly. As the destroyer *Whitshed* arrived off Dunkirk, it found French destroyers firing at aircraft heard overhead and asked if they were sure that they were the enemy. There was no reply.

Ramsay was concerned that all three routes to and from Dunkirk (X, Y and Z) were coming under fire from German batteries. The batteries targeting Route X were between Le Clipont and Les Huttes, about a mile north-east of Gravelines, and the RAF attacked them early that day with 24 Blenheim bomber sorties. Fighter patrols over routes being used by vessels were also carried out. One patrol, consisting of five squadrons, engaged a large enemy force over Dunkirk, later claiming to have shot down 18 bombers and ten fighters for the loss of seven Spitfires.

The destroyer *Icarus* left Dunkirk at midnight and taking Route X collided with 'a trawler' in poor visibility. The destroyer was not badly damaged and the official report for that day stated it was not known 'what damage was sustained by the trawler'. But according to an engine room artificer [era], Andrew Begg, it was a tug packed with soldiers and 'there must have been a hell of a loss of life'. He added, 'The tug was cut in two. We couldn't stop.' *Icarus* later received a message from Ramsay that there were magnetic mines on the route. The destroyer changed course but then faced the hazard of British minefields. Begg recalled, 'I always remember at 2 o'clock in the morning the chief era came along to me and whispered, 'We're in the middle of a British minefield, that's why we're going at five knots. For goodness sake don't let the rumour get round in case the soldiers panic. Fortunately we didn't hit one and we came out. We speeded up but it took us all night to get back to Dover. That was the last trip we did.'[1] In total, *Icarus* brought back 4,704 soldiers.

When *Whitshed* berthed at the mole, it surprisingly found few soldiers. The captain, Commander Edward Condor, went ashore, spotted a bicycle and rode off to round up troops with the aid of a loud hailer. The bicycle 'also provided useful transport for two wounded men'. Before sailing, Condor helped to berth two other destroyers and directed troops to board them. *Whitshed* returned to Dover with 512 troops.[2] The destroyer HMS *Winchelsea* sailed with 1,100. These were the last two destroyers to leave before the morning deadline.

But soon afterwards a problem arose at the mole. A motorboat from the minesweeper *Lydd*, anchored about half a mile east of Dunkirk's harbour entrance, had picked up a brigadier who asked that a signal be sent to Ramsay on behalf of Major General Alexander. It transpired that there were too many French troops crowding the mole, which was only five feet wide, and their own west quay. British soldiers could not be embarked from the harbour. Alexander wanted the rearguard to be taken off from the town's east beach. Ramsay ordered all ships known to be outside the harbour to take part in a beach evacuation. But the deadline was looming, as the vice admiral noted, 'Owing to the time in transit and coding it was feared that this signal would reach few ships still on the coast unless they had remained on their own initiative after 0300, the previously ordered time of withdrawal.'[3] The Admiralty, in fact, wanted destroyers to continue the operation until 0700 but Rear Admiral Wake-Walker did not receive this message in time.

Off the coast in MASB *10*, Wake-Walker described the scene: 'To me there were two contrasting aspects – darkness looking out to seaward, and landward dark silhouettes showing against the steady glow of fires and the occasional flash of bombs. To seaward lay the ships visible as dark blurs only, waiting off the harbour entrance for their turn to come in to the piers, looming up large and distinct as they drew near. Looking shoreward the whole town and harbour were shut in by a pall of smoke overhead, which was lit up by the glare of fires in several places inland. Against the glare the piers, harbour and town were sharply silhouetted, and on the piers and quays an endless line of helmeted men in serried ranks sometimes moving, sometimes stationary.'[4]

Between 0200 and 0900, six personnel ships returned to Britain with about 5,500 troops. The ferry *Royal Daffodil* brought back 1,500. But there was still considerable doubt as to the numbers remaining, possibly 6,000 British troops, including the rearguard. The previous evening it was thought that there were 25,000 French troops, but that number had risen to 50,000 and then 60,000.

With the evacuation suspended at daylight, Wake-Walker returned to Dover, arriving when much of the town was still asleep. A car was waiting for him and he was taken to the castle where he spoke briefly to Somerville and then retired to the vice admiral's bed, pointing out, 'It was very convenient to have him on duty at that time of day leaving a vacant bed. I slept heavily and woke suddenly as two fellows came into my room – it was Berthon, captain of the *Keith* and his first lieutenant. They were black with oil fuel and in the clothes they had been rescued the day before but they had come to let me know they were safe. I looked at them only half conscious and dropped off to sleep again at once, with a feeling of thankfulness.'[5]

After a bath, breakfast and a few moments in the sun Wake-Walker 'felt fit for anything' and made his way to the 'dungeon office' to discuss what was meant to be the last stage of the evacuation, from 2100 to 0300 on 3 June. Ramsay sent a signal to his destroyers and minesweepers: 'The final evacuation is staged for tonight, and the nation looks to the navy to see this through. I want every ship to report as soon as possible whether she is fit to meet the call which has been made on our courage and endurance.'[6] The response was overwhelmingly positive. It was planned to use Dunkirk harbour only, with small French craft embarking from the beach east of the port. To make full use of the mole, personnel ships, destroyers, sloops and minesweepers would arrive at half-hourly intervals, so that three or four ships would be berthed at the same time. A large number of tugs, skoots and drifters would also be used. Wake-Walker asked for a couple of fast boats to act as 'runners' for him.

That morning, Ramsay received an urgent message from Dunkirk, pointing out that a large number of wounded remained at the port and requesting hospital ships during the day. The message added, 'Geneva Convention will be honourably observed it is felt and that the enemy will refrain from attacking.' Ramsay noted, 'As this appeared to be the only way of evacuating the wounded, observing that the whole facilities of the port during the night evacuation hours would be required for fighting troops, it was decided to send two hospital ships.'

Worthing and *Paris* were clearly marked as hospital ships. The sailing orders were given in plain language, not code, so that the Germans would be aware of the mercy mission. Britain would 'scrupulously' observe the convention.

Worthing was the first to sail, early in the afternoon. Visibility was good. About 90 minutes later, it was attacked off the French coast. The master, Captain C. G. G. Munton, reported, 'Twelve aircraft were sighted dead ahead and were immediately recognised as enemy aircraft. One of them detached, dived at me, and commenced machine-gunning my ship. I increased to 24 knots and put my helm hard a-starboard. The enemy aircraft then attacked with nine bombs of heavy calibre. As the ship was then swinging very fast on her helm the bombs fell on the starboard quarter and port bow and one amidships off the starboard side. Two of the bombs fell within three or four feet.

'Concussion was very violent and some pipe castings were broken in the engine room, permitting water to enter, but this was quickly remedied. Some superficial damage was sustained … I was carrying all the marks and signs of a hospital ship according to Geneva Convention and this was, without doubt a shadow of doubt, a deliberate and sustained attempt to destroy a hospital ship.'[7]

Worthing returned to harbour. It was not the first time that the enemy had flouted the convention. But this time the Germans were specifically warned that hospital ships were being sent. *Paris* had been used before to bring home wounded soldiers, who were helped by army nurses. The vessel was about to sail when the wireless operator picked up *Worthing's* call that it was being attacked. *Paris's* master, Captain E. A. Biles, signalled to shore asking if he should still go to Dunkirk. He was told to proceed. Biles weighed anchor 'at once'. It was not long before three enemy planes were spotted. *Paris* took evasive action as bombs dropped close by, the explosions bursting steam pipes in the engine room and putting machinery and lighting out of action. The ship was out of control. Biles hoped that a rescue vessel would be able to tow *Paris* back to Dover.

'Immediately after the bombing the wireless operator sent an AAA message by the emergency set as the mains set was blown to pieces,' the captain recorded. 'We also hoisted the distress signal – fired rockets and hoisted ensign upside down. About 50 minutes later a flight of about 15 enemy planes approached from the same direction, three of which broke off, circled the ship and dropped about ten bombs. One of these either went through the bows of No 2b lifeboat or the force of the explosion blew the bows right off, throwing all the occupants into the water. The ship was severely shaken and damaged. Remaining lifeboats were immediately lowered and sent to the rescue of those in the water. No 4b boat when lowered into the water was immediately swamped as part of her side was blown in. Myself, the chief officer and quartermaster were left on board.'[8]

A Royal Navy motorboat rescued the captain and his two officers and took lifeboats in tow. The crew and nurses, including casualties, were later transferred to a tug and taken to Dover. Three other tugs attempted to save

Paris, but it sank after a further air attack. Ramsay observed, 'Thus the last attempt to evacuate the wounded by hospital carrier from Dunkirk was brought to nought.'[9]

The writer A. D. Devine would be more forthright: 'Others of the hospital carriers that took part in what was perhaps the most gallant work that ships of their kind have ever done were to sink off every front under the barbarity of the Nazi air. The wilful callousness of these things is beyond description.'[10]

During the afternoon of 2 June, Captain Tennant informed Ramsay that the French frontline was still holding except for an area east of Bergues. At 1700, Ramsay's armada for the final evacuation began sailing. It included 13 personnel vessels, 11 destroyers and nine fleet sweepers, as well as drifters, tugs and skoots. The composition of the French contingent was 'unknown'.

Two fast RAF motorboats, No *243* and No *270*, under the command of Commander James Clouston, also left Dover. Clouston, a pier master at the mole, had reported to Ramsay. Six miles off Gravelines, eight Stukas attacked the boats, which were carrying RAF and naval personnel. Sub Lieutenant Roger Wake, in No *270*, spent the next ten minutes evading machine-gun bullets and bombs. The boat's only defence was a Lewis gun. 'When I next had time to look round for the other boat, only her bows were visible and the whole crew were in the water,' Wake recorded. 'I closed the position and slowed down to pick up survivors, but Commander Clouston ordered me to leave them immediately and proceed at full speed to Dunkirk. I increased speed and was shortly afterwards attacked again, and during this attack my boat was repeatedly hit by incendiary machine-gun bullets and my starboard engine was put out of action. The speed of the boat was reduced to six knots.'[11]

The boat eventually reached Dunkirk. There were only two survivors from No *243*, one of whom said he saw Commander Clouston dead in the water several hours before he was picked up. Wake was convinced that if his boat had rescued survivors, the extra load, with an engine out of action and water seeping in, would have made their arrival in Dunkirk 'most unlikely'. On landing, the young sub lieutenant took on some of Clouston's duties at the mole.[12]

Wake-Walker returned to Dunkirk in MASB *10*, accompanied by Somerville. They were attacked on the away and later picked up three Belgian soldiers who were in a small boat. 'They were not too pleased at being taken back to Dunkirk but were later decanted into a destroyer,' Wake-Walker recalled.[13] The tale of a British soldier falling asleep in an obscure part of a destroyer and waking up after going to Dover and then back to Dunkirk was probably not unique.

The first destroyers to reach the French port that evening were *Sabre* and *Shikari*, which embarked a total of 1,200 troops. A steady stream of vessels kept up the work. MASB *10* picked up Alexander and his staff, transferring them to the destroyer *Venomous*, which returned to Dover with 1,100 troops.

Henry Faure Walker, a captain in the Coldstream Guards, found himself in a minesweeper after being badly wounded in a bomb explosion on one of the beaches. The officer recalled, 'Luckily I became conscious in time to stop a charming sailor from giving me a thorough washing. He said, "I'll give your face a wash, sir, and you'll feel better." And I said, "Please don't touch my face because if you do it will come off." It was so badly burned it was black and the face would have come straight away. The same applied to my hands. I was in very great pain.' Faure Walker was taken to Folkestone.[14]

At 2330 on 2 June, Tennant sent the signal, 'BEF evacuated.' He embarked in MTB *102* with a naval demolition party that had destroyed key port facilities and an RAF flying officer dressed as a Belgian peasant.

CHAPTER 15

Monday 3 June

Ramsay's focus on 3 June was the evacuation of the French troops remaining in the Dunkirk area. It had been arranged that ships would be at the mole soon after midnight. By 0030, four vessels were alongside. But there were no soldiers to embark. For Wake-Walker, this was 'a most disheartening night'. He received a report that troops had been held up because of the need for a counter attack. When some appeared, there were problems, as the rear admiral recorded, 'Even when the French did come it was almost impossible to get them to the ships at the end of the pier – they all wanted to get into the first one they came to, and the pier was so narrow that they blocked the way to any ship beyond. At last they started to trickle down but by then it was obvious that many of the ships waiting outside could not be used and I had to send back empty two personnel ships, three destroyers and several fleet sweepers.'[1]

When darkness gave way to light, more soldiers appeared. The chaos continued. 'I was hailing them to make them run down the pier,' Wake-Walker reported. 'Even then they were quite hopeless. I can remember seeing men, who were on their way to a ship that was alongside the end of the pier, turn and run back down the pier because they saw another ship coming alongside further in.'[2] The French had failed to replace the Royal Navy sailors who had been able to organise a relatively orderly evacuation.

Only minesweepers berthed near the start of the mole picked up enough soldiers. HMS *Niger* slipped at 0120 with more than 400. As it was turning, a French craft crossed its bows and was rammed but with little if any damage. A few moments later, the craft returned and rammed *Niger*. The French skipper was taken on board the minesweeper and handed over to the military authorities in Folkestone.

At 0230, the destroyer *Vanquisher* sailed for Dover with only 37 troops, and HMS *Codrington* left shortly afterwards with 44, in company with *Express*, which did not embark any soldiers.

At 0300, Wake-Walker ordered vessels to leave. At about this time, three blockships were brought in with the aim of thwarting the enemy's use of the harbour. The leading blockship blew up after hitting a mine. MTBs took off the crews. The rear admiral once again headed back to Dover in his MASB and rested for a couple of hours before breakfast. Ramsay was left frustrated, noting that between midnight and 0300 'a lifting capacity of about 10,000 was left empty'.[3]

That morning, a conference was held in the castle's 'dungeon'. It was agreed to stick to the original plan but also to use the west pier as the French apparently had insufficient ships to berth there. Ramsay was concerned, however, about the state of his exhausted crews, particularly those in the destroyers, which had been making round trips under difficult navigation conditions and 'unparalleled' air attack. Such was his concern that he warned the Admiralty that these sailors faced being tested 'beyond the limit of human endurance' and fresh forces would be needed if the evacuation continued beyond that night.[4] As Wake-Walker noted, 'Each night had been thought to be the last and then each day the ships had been asked for one more effort.'[5]

Ramsay was right to be concerned about the mental health of his men. Oliver Anderson, a chief petty officer in the minesweeper HMS *Sutton*, recalled, 'The crew were in a terrible state when it all ended. All we seemed to live on were cups of tea and cigarettes, maybe a few biscuits, the odd bully beef stew. One of the officers lost his nerve. He had been on the beach and things were nasty. Just as he was approaching [*Sutton*] we had one or two near misses and this set him off. We managed to pacify him.'[6]

Alfred Cromwell, a leading signalman in the minesweeper HMS *Kellett*, told of the toll that the lack of sleep was taking. 'Two stokers collapsed and were burned on the fourth day,' he said. 'We had landed one telegraphist and one ordinary seaman in straitjackets because they'd just gone absolutely mad through tension and seeing action. The chief era (chief engine room artificer) was evacuated because he had gone berserk. He was trying to get five minutes rest in his mess – our engines were old and he had a job to keep them going – and we were machine-gunned and a cannon shell went through the ship's side and grazed his shoulder. I think that would have sent me mad.'[7]

On the morning of 3 June, Ramsay decided he could not order ships to go that night. Instead, he sent a signal asking which vessels would be able to sail. The response was heartening – ten transports, six destroyers, eight minesweepers, four paddle sweepers, two corvettes, two yachts, one gunboat, ten drifters, five skoots and one tug, plus a large number of small craft. That night's evacuation was set to take place between 2230 and 0230 on 4 June.

When the sun rose on 3 June, fighting between French and German ground forces resumed. The Dunkirk perimeter was under greater pressure on all sides, especially in the south. General Bertrand Fagalde launched a counter attack with four divisions, supported by tanks, in an attempt to slow the enemy's advance. To the west, the French would spend most of the day trying to prevent the Germans crossing the Bourbourg–Dunkirk Canal at Cappelle-la-Grande. The causeway at the village of Les Moëres also saw fierce fighting. During the afternoon, Admiral Abrial reported that the enemy were in the suburbs of Dunkirk. But the Luftwaffe carried out few sorties at the port, mainly because of Operation *Paula*, the planned assault on airfields and factories around Paris. And with German troops gaining ground with the end in sight, there was the danger of planes attacking their own side.

Ramsay's armada sailed in the afternoon as planned. The vice admiral had been led to believe that there were some 30,000 French to be evacuated, but it was thought that only 25,000 could be taken off in the time frame, and only then if the soldiers moved with the greatest speed at all points of embarkation. In light of that morning's difficulty in getting the French to board vessels quickly, it was decided to send a naval berthing party of four officers and 50 seamen, led by Commander Herbert Buchanan, who had survived the bombing and destruction of the destroyer *Valentine* on 15 May.

Wake-Walker returned to Dunkirk, this time in MTB *102*, which had taken him off the doomed *Keith*. A scene of chaos greeted him. 'I got over at 2200 to find the harbour swarming with French fishing craft and vessels of all sorts. They were yelling and crowding alongside the east pier [mole], which was already thick with French troops.' He was concerned that these craft would delay the transports and destroyers 'but I managed to get them to go on up the inner harbour and out of the way in time'.[8]

The destroyer *Whitshed* had set off with the naval berthing party. The captain, Commander Edward Condor, reported that the crew were in 'very good heart' with the harmonica band playing. The destroyer arrived soon after the rear admiral but had trouble berthing because of the chaos, as well as a challenging tide and a north-easterly wind. And French troops refused to help tie up the ship.

Lieutenant John Wise, in the skoot *Pascholl*, gave a telling account of the vessel's arrival in Dunkirk harbour. 'The town was blazing furiously and presented a truly memorable spectacle,' Wise recalled. 'The harbour was congested, some of the ships there being wrecked, and in cases already ablaze.

Difficult navigation was intensified by our not being able to find the nouveau avant port, our peregrinations nearly putting us on the putty [aground] twice. In desperation we went alongside the packet boat quay of the inner harbour, secured and got ladders aboard. Commander Troup, waiting on the quay, immediately asked our capacity and I foolishly but optimistically replied, "Oh, between 500 and 1,000."

'Poilus [French infantry] in reasonable order commenced to invade the ship and were embarked in an orderly fashion, each man being disarmed before being allowed to descend into the hold. One of the most memorable and inspiring sights was that gallant old gentleman Commander Hammond, complete with Mae West lifebelt, his Captain Kettle [a character who first appeared in an 1895 novel] beard sticking out from under his "battle bowler", rushing fearlessly up and down the jetty, helping here, advising there, and constantly enquiring of me, "How many more do you think we can get aboard?"

'Meanwhile some of the other schuits [skoots] had secured nearby. One ran aground and was, I believe, abandoned. A destroyer came up astern and in securing hopelessly wedged us in, and carried some of our quarterdeck gear away with her bow hawser. When the hold and deck was full of Froggies – not a Tommy was to be had – we ceased embarkation but had to wait for the departure of the destroyer astern. The congestion at the time was chaotic, ships going astern into others coming ahead, French destroyers shrieking their sirens, small craft nipping here and there, rendering the exit most dangerous.'

Pascholl arrived at Ramsgate without incident, but Wise was disappointed that they had not been able to take more soldiers, explaining, 'It was not possible to carry more than the approximate 300 that we had, which included ten officers but no sick or wounded, especially as the Frog insisted on embarking with his bed, kitchen range etc.'[9]

Perhaps the smartest ship that night was the destroyer *Malcolm*. Its officers had not expected to make another trip to Dunkirk, instead planning to hold a party in port. Once again they rose to the occasion, setting sail and wearing their dinner jackets and bow ties.

CHAPTER 16

Tuesday 4 June

In the early hours of June 4, the naval berthing party under the command of Commander Buchanan worked tirelessly to embark French troops from the mole and the west pier. It was still not clear how many men needed to be rescued. With a deadline of 0300, the armada did not want to be found by the enemy when darkness gave way to light.

One of the naval officers, Commander Hugh Troup, was fortunate in finding French officers to help him at his pier, but the men under their command proved difficult. Troup recorded, 'The French soldiers were very loath to be separated from each other, their companies or their officers, but by promising them they would only be separated for two hours and would meet again in England they moved quicker. I embarked at least 10,000 troops.' The commander had arranged for his boat, which sailed from Ramsgate, to return at 0300 for the trip back, but it failed to appear because of engine trouble. Luckily, there was another boat and Troup left with General Maurice Lucas, commander of the 32nd Division, and some of his officers. Around 1,000 French troops remaining on the pier stood to attention as the general saluted and then departed.[1]

Passenger ships had been busy collecting men. *Princess Maud*, a ferry turned troopship, was struck in quick succession by the transport *Cote d'Argent* and a French trawler soon after arriving in the harbour but managed to berth at the mole. 'Troops then clambered aboard all ways, no gangways available,' the master, Captain Henry Clarke, reported. 'Dogs of all kinds got on board somehow. There was no confusion whilst a steady line of men was directed along the jetty by several members of the crew. At 0150 we were fairly well packed, so I cast off after being told that was the last of the troops. Whilst swinging a shell fell in the berth we had just vacated.'[2]

Royal Sovereign arrived at the west pier after a collision and left 'overladen with troops'. The passenger ship had made six crossings, rescuing a remarkable 6,858 men. *Princess Maud* and *Royal Sovereign* were the last passenger ships to leave. The next day a member of *Royal Sovereign*'s crew wrote to his sister, 'We have had a very exciting time and I am glad and thankful to the bon adieu it's all over … I tell you, how we are still afloat is a miracle. It has been a hell I never want to go through again. My nerves are all to hell. We have been bombed, shelled, machine-gunned and chased by MTBs but we were in God's hands. We had 78 planes bombing us one evening off La Panne beach, and of the seven or eight transports and sloops around us we were the only whole one left when they were chased off by Spitfires.'[3]

The paddle steamer *Princess Elizabeth*, which had been a ferry between Southampton and the Isle of Wight, made its third trip to Dunkirk. After embarking about 380 troops from the mole, it was ordered to cast off and clear the harbour. The steamer's total was 1,673. The sister ships, *Brighton Belle*, *Devonia* and *Gracie Fields*, did not survive. (After the war, *Princess Elizabeth* had a chequered career, eventually returning to Dunkirk after being bought by the local authority. It became a floating restaurant and a memorial to the evacuation.)

The destroyer *Sabre* played a prominent role, making ten round trips. Early on 4 June, it left Dunkirk with nearly 600 troops. The captain, Lieutenant Commander Brian Dean, reported that the soldiers were in excellent spirits and 'keenly appreciated being addressed in their own language, however imperfectly. Jokes about the comparative comfort of *Sabre* and *Normandie* were well received.' Dean was surprised that the destroyer's engines, 22 years old and submerged in salt water for 48 hours after a collision the previous year, had held out. He noted, 'To avoid bombs and shell fire it was necessary to make most exacting demands on the engines such as might well have taxed those of a new ship. In every case the response was immediate, all that could be desired, and far greater than could be reasonably expected. It is submitted that this reflects great credit on the engine-room department, to whom is unquestionably due the fact that we are all still alive and unhurt and our ship safely in dock, and the far more important fact that upwards of 5,000 troops were safely transported.'[4]

Robert Wynn, a civilian and the future Lord Newborough, made five trips to Dunkirk as skipper of a yacht that was being used as an air force rescue boat. 'You saw all sorts of boats,' he said. 'The spirit was very good. Everybody who had a boat went. I saw a fellow going across in a canoe, so I hailed him, "What the hell are you doing?" He said, "I can take one other." I never saw him again.'[5]

Wynn's boat was badly damaged by a shell but the crew managed to return to Ramsgate. Wynne then volunteered to join a fast air-sea rescue vessel. 'It was late evening when we left Ramsgate and just before dusk we made a rendezvous with a small vessel. To my surprise I noticed that we took on board an admiral of obviously great importance. His appearance gave one a feeling of confidence. He was quiet and of few words, obviously extremely tired but showing tremendous determination. [This was probably Rear Admiral Alfred Taylor.]

'On reaching Dunkirk we stopped for a few moments on entering the main harbour while he looked around to see what ships were there, and to give him time to sum up the general position. We realised by this time that this was the last night of the evacuation and that it was important to get off all the troops possible and get away all the ships able to leave. The admiral told us to proceed right up to the end of the harbour to a point where two large ships were lying alongside the quay. We made fast to the jetty near a large crane. There was a lot of gunfire in the town and a good bit of machine-gun fire not far from where we were.

'Without any hesitation the admiral jumped up on to the quay and appointed me as his number one. He did not as much as wear a steel helmet and his only armament was his walking stick, not even a revolver, which gave us a feeling of terrific admiration for him. If it was good enough for him to proceed in such a manner it was certainly good enough for us to follow him. We had not been on the jetty very long when he turned to me and asked me to go amongst the dead and try to find the identity discs belonging to the British who had fallen.

'After a while it seemed that a whole battalion of French troops arrived on the scene. The admiral ordered them to board one of the ships, but to our amazement they refused. They seemed perfectly convinced that if they did they would be sunk or bombed and therefore preferred to remain where they were on the jetty. To our relief some British troops arrived with high spirits and eventually both ships were filled to capacity. The gunfire by this time was very close and when the admiral had walked down the full length of the jetty to the end of the harbour to make sure for himself that no one was left who could be got away, and that no ship was left that could move, he finally gave us orders to embark in our vessel and make for the entrance to the harbour.

'No sooner had we started to move away from the jetty than a shell made a direct hit on the crane which had been towering above us. We could not have been more than a few yards away when it crumpled and fell into the sea, just missing the stern of our little vessel.'[6]

On the admiral's instructions, the boat went to Dover. Wynn had been an officer in a cavalry regiment in India when he was given a medical discharge, later happily admitting that there was nothing wrong with him. He disliked the army, only joining at his father's insistence, 'as one did in those days'. Soon after his exploits at Dunkirk, he applied for a commission in the Royal Navy Volunteer Reserve, passing the medical A1. As the captain of MTB *74* he took part in the St Nazaire raid in 1942 and became a prisoner after his vessel was sunk. Awarded the Distinguished Service Cross, he ended up in Colditz Castle, later being repatriated after feigning a serious back condition.[7]

Admiral Abrial left Bastion 32 for the final time and boarded an MTB for Dover. General Falgade and two other French admirals departed at the same time. On arriving, Abrial went to see Ramsay and reported that the troops still defending Dunkirk had run out of ammunition. Because of the enemy's advance, Abrial believed it was no longer possible to continue the evacuation. Operation *Dynamo* was officially ended early that afternoon.

The destroyer *Shikari* was the last ship to leave Dunkirk, 40 minutes after the 0300 deadline. By this time, the mole was under attack, with one shell explosion causing many casualties. *Shikari* returned to England with 400 soldiers, including General Robert Barthelemy, commander of the Flanders garrison. Ramsay was informed that a total of 27,000 troops had been evacuated during that night's operation.

The night was not without tragedy. The French minesweeper *Emile Deschamps*, carrying 500 men, struck a magnetic mine as it neared England, five miles off the North Foreland. It sank quickly and there were only about 85 survivors.

During the afternoon of 4 June, Wake-Walker went to Ramsay's headquarters and found the atmosphere comparatively relaxed after the tensions of the past week. Ships were being sent back to their home ports to give 48 hours leave, and 'I made arrangements to return to their proper owners various articles of clothing I had acquired, and returned to London with my staff by train. The French admiral and a general also travelled up by this train but kept severely apart from one another. I slept in the train a good part of the way and woke up to the thought of returning to my office desk in London – it was rather like waking up from a dream. Curiously enough I slept that night for no longer than my normal hours and never felt any lack of sleep in the least. I found, however, that I had lost 7lb in weight.'[8]

Although the evacuation had ended, naval and air search teams were still sent out to scour the Channel, and French troops were picked up by patrols and taken to Dover, Margate and Ramsgate. Soldiers also arrived in French and Belgian trawlers, a total of around 1,100 men.

***

Ramsay recorded that the evacuation from 26 May until 4 June saved 338,682, although some vessels had not recorded their figures. Ramsay's destroyers brought back the highest number, 103,399, followed by the personnel ships, 74,380, and minesweepers, 31,040. The total included some 125,000 French and 16,000 Belgian and Dutch soldiers. Around 850 vessels of all shapes and sizes took part in Operation *Dynamo* and nearly 240 were lost. Ramsay's destroyer fleet paid a high price, with six sunk and 23 damaged.

Ramsay, rightly, has been seen as the saviour of Dunkirk. The evacuation could so easily have been a disaster. The success was a reflection of his character. Attention to detail always had been paramount, even if it seemed to relate to something that appeared to be minor. Here was an officer who was always immaculately dressed. Here was an officer who had wanted his ship to be the best in the fleet. He could even write pages on the art of painting a vessel. Nothing escaped his eye, as his highly critical report on the state of the destroyer *Broke* during World War I showed. Ramsay was obsessive when it came to detail. And it was this obsession that he brought to the tunnels beneath Dover Castle.

He chose his senior staff carefully. Anyone he inherited who could not live up to his high standards did not last long. Skilled at organising, he also knew the value of delegating. Although he could at times appear aloof, Ramsay's presence inspired loyalty. The many men and women working in the tunnels endured long hours, as did the crews of the rescue vessels. And Ramsay was persuasive when it came to liaising with other naval commands, especially over the provision of ships.

Despite frequent poor communications with the evacuation fleet and those organising the withdrawal of troops in Dunkirk and from the beaches, Ramsay was usually quick to respond to new challenges, changing routes and times. As ever, he remained forthright. After the First Sea Lord ordered that the newer destroyers should be withdrawn because of heavy losses, Ramsay argued strongly the case for their return – and won. He was determined to do everything possible until the official end of Operation *Dynamo*.

On 4 June, the Chief of the Imperial General Staff, General Dill, wrote to Ramsay 'at the first possible moment', acknowledging his outstanding contribution. 'I should like to convey to you personally my very sincere thanks for the magnificent effort made by you and all those who acted so nobly under your command,' the general wrote. 'In these sentiments I know the whole of the British Army will join me. The number of British and Allied troops which you have been able to carry across the sea under a rapidly improvised plan has our unbounded admiration. I wish I could personally thank all ranks under your command for yet another example of their traditional heroism and, in many cases, personal sacrifice.'

General Gort told Ramsay that the Royal Navy had been 'truly magnificent', adding, 'Never will the army forget the superb effort made by you and those under your command to achieve, in face of constant and heavy air attacks, what at first looked like being an almost impossible task.'[9]

The Admiralty sent out a general message, in which it was stated, 'Their Lordships appreciate the splendid endurance with which all ships and personnel faced the continuous attack of enemy aircraft and the physical strain imposed by long hours of arduous work in narrow waters over many days. The magnificent spirit of co-operation between the Navy, Royal Air Force and Merchant Navy alone brought the operation to a successful conclusion.' The message ended, 'Their Lordships also realise that success was only rendered possible by the great effort made by all shore establishments, and in particular by the Dover command, who were responsible for the organisation and direction of this difficult operation.'[10]

Max Horton, who would play a crucial role as Commander-in-Chief, Western Approaches, in the fight against the U-boat menace in the battle of the Atlantic, told Ramsay, 'In the last few weeks I have often thought with thankfulness that it was you in charge at Dover.'[11]

Ramsay received many letters of congratulation, but perhaps the most moving one came from a Mrs S. Woodcock, who lived in the Essex village of Hatfield Peverel. She wrote, 'As a reader of the *Daily Express* and after reading in today's paper of your wonderful feat re Dunkirk, I feel I must send you a personal message to thank you. My son Leslie was one of the lucky ones to escape from there. I had a phone message on Tuesday last from a relative to say Leslie had arrived at Southampton. I have not seen him yet but hope to before he returns to France. He is somewhere in England and that's good enough. My youngest boy, John Woodcock C/JX 161188 HMS *Curacoa*, died of wounds received in Norway on April 26th so you can guess how thankful I feel and grateful to you. John would have been 17 years old on Thursday 13th. Once again I thank you.' After signing the letter she added a PS, 'I wish you and your family all the very best in the world. From a grateful mother.'[12]

Of course, 4 June was the day that Churchill made his famous 'we shall fight on the beaches' speech in the House of Commons. The prime minister admitted that originally he thought only 20,000 or 30,000 troops might be saved. But the Royal Navy, with the help of merchant seamen, had 'strained every nerve' to bring British and Allied soldiers to England, 'out of the jaws of death and shame'. Churchill also went out of his way to praise the RAF, knowing that there had been criticism of the apparent absence of planes. He insisted that the achievements of pilots were underrated. Crucially, Churchill told members of Parliament – and the nation, 'We must be very careful not assign to this deliverance the attributes of a victory. Wars are not won by evacuations.'[13]

In his detailed assessment of the evacuation, Ramsay pointed out that Dover had received many signals from the beaches urging that the operation should be focused on Dunkirk harbour. There were frequent complaints of 'no ships' and 'no boats'. But at Dover the evacuation could be viewed in 'truer perspective'. And between 28 May and 1 June no fewer than 100,000 troops were lifted from the beaches.

Unusually good weather helped the evacuation, although any northerly wind produced surf that hampered the rescue of men from the beaches. On returning to England, the despatch of troops proceeded 'with great smoothness' under War Office organisation.

The enemy had resorted to minelaying by planes, intensive air attack, action by MTBs, gunfire from coastal artillery and submarine operations. The minelaying began on the night of 28–29 May and was maintained 'with great intensity' over the next two nights. Route X and the entrances to Dover and Folkestone harbours were among the targets.

On the evening of 29 May, ships were massed in Dunkirk harbour and the Luftwaffe attacked in great strength. Ramsay noted that it was only by 'good fortune' that the harbour channel was not blocked by sinking ships, adding, 'From then onwards the scale and vigour of the air attack increased, and during 1 June all ships in Dunkirk, off the beaches, or in the approach channels, were subjected every two hours to an unprecedented scale of air attack by aircraft in such numbers that the RAF were unable to deal with the situation.'[14]

Two destroyers and two trawlers using the northerly Route Y fell victim to German MTBs. When the middle Route X, some 26 miles to the south-west, was brought into use MTBs failed to appear, despite the fact that there were plenty of unescorted targets during the hours of darkness. Ramsay pointed out that these vessels would have been 'a tempting target to any enterprising commander'.[15]

At the start of the evacuation, the southerly Route Z came under fire from shore batteries near Calais. Route X was free of such gunfire, until batteries near Gravelines opened up on the afternoon of 1 June. These attacks, combined with the Luftwaffe's onslaught, led to the suspension of shipping in daylight. The U-boat threat did not materialise. Only one submarine was thought to have penetrated further than Route Y. This boat may have laid mines that sank two anti-submarine trawlers.

The RAF's role at Dunkirk has long been contentious. Ramsay's comments are worth noting: 'Not only did German air effort interrupt and reduce seaborne traffic, but it also prevented embarkation by suspending troop movement. To both naval and military observers on the coast, the situation at times was extremely disheartening. Rightly or wrongly, full air protection was expected, but instead, for hours on end, the ships off shore were subjected to a murderous hail of bombs and machine-gun bullets.

'Required by their duty to remain offshore waiting for the troops, who themselves were unable to move down to the water for the same reason, it required the greatest determination and sense of duty, amounting in fact to heroism, on the part of the ships' and boats' crews, to enable them to complete their mission.'[16]

In the early stages of the evacuation, the discipline of soldiers on the beaches was a problem. These men were largely from rear units with few officers present. Ramsay pointed out, 'The appearance of naval officers, in their unmistakable uniforms, helped to restore order and the troops responded to commands in a disciplined manner.'[17] Later there was no difficulty with soldiers of fighting formations.

There was special praise for the navy's officers and ratings who worked off the French coast in vessels ranging from destroyers to commandeered motorboats. Often they were operating in extremely difficult conditions, which required them to take independent action. Stokers and hostility-only seamen commanded many of the small boats that took soldiers off the beaches. If a craft was damaged or sunk, the crew invariably seized another boat to continue their work. Ramsay noted, 'On their return to the United Kingdom, when asked to report their proceedings, it was only in answer to direct enquiry that it would transpire that these young men had been subjected in many cases to an unparalleled bombardment from the air. They appeared to consider that this was part of the day's work requiring no comment.'[18]

It was distressing that many ships laden with troops were sunk or damaged on their return to England. But it was fortunate that the majority of soldiers were saved because the Channel was busy with vessels. The exceptions were *Wakeful*, *Crested Eagle*, *Skipjack* and *Waverley*, which all sank quickly with heavy loss of life. In total, about 2,000 troops were lost at sea after being rescued from Dunkirk and the beaches.

Ramsay acknowledged the work done by naval and civilian staff at Dover and Ramsgate, as well as at Chatham, Sheerness and Harwich. He paid tribute to the dedication of Rear Admiral Wake-Walker, Captain Tennant and his own chief of staff at Dover, Captain Morgan. Of Vice Admiral Somerville, he recorded, 'The attributes of this officer for initiative and resource are well known throughout the Service, but I venture to express the opinion that never in the course of his long and distinguished career have they been put to better use than during the operations for the evacuation of the allied armies from Dunkirk.'[19]

With Operation *Dynamo* officially over, Ramsay at last was able to relax. He headed to Sandwich for a game of golf. Far from being weary, and no doubt enjoying the fresh air after all that time below ground, he went round in 78, his best ever performance. On Wednesday 5 June, he was in London for 'important business' at the Admiralty. He told his wife Margaret, 'I've simply been unable to write since last Saturday as events reached a veritable crescendo on Sunday and Monday. But now all is done and the task is behind. The relief is stupendous, the results beyond belief. The success is mostly due to the first-class direction and management of the show, equally with the glorious courage, skill and endurance of the personnel of all the ships. The one without the other would have been ineffective.' His staff had worked like 'a perfect machine'. Surprisingly, in view of the immense strain everyone had been under, he commented, 'All alike, sailors, soldiers and airmen, said they had enjoyed it and felt so much better for the experience.'[20]

Two days later, Ramsay was back in Dover, telling Margaret, 'It is quite extraordinary that I should have stood the strain better than most, having had the responsibility for everything on my shoulders, plus the long hours and the continuous struggle with the Admiralty to make theory give way to what was practicable.'[21]

He had been well received at the Admiralty, having tea with the First Lord, Alexander, who was 'extraordinarily nice and most sensible and practical'. There was also the bonus of a visit to a hairdresser: 'It wanted cutting badly and was quite two weeks overdue.'[22]

CHAPTER 17

The Men Left Behind

There was not much remaining of Dunkirk when the Germans took over the town and port on the morning of 4 June. The devastation was immense. Most of the buildings were skeletal or completely flattened. Estimates of the destruction in the town have ranged from 70 per cent to 90 per cent. Allied bombing later in the war also took its toll. Ships and boats were lying wrecked in the harbour and on the nearby beaches. Tens of thousands of disabled and burnt-out vehicles had been left by the BEF, as well as huge quantities of equipment and supplies. The St Pol oil refineries were still belching black smoke. And the dead were everywhere. Air raids had killed 3,000 people and wounded 10,000. One German officer complained that he was unable to swim in the sea because of the bodies and wreckage.

Bizarrely, amidst the rubble, the statue of the swashbuckling Jean Bart in the main square was unscathed. Bart, a son of Dunkirk who became a famous naval officer in the 17th century, emerged as a symbol of hope that the town would one day rise from the ashes. His sword pointed defiantly towards the sky that had been the backdrop to so much misery. But on 4 June, after days of fierce and often heroic fighting, surrender was the only realistic option for the French army. General Maurice Beaufrere, commanding the 68th Infantry Division, went to the town hall in Place Charles Valentin for talks with the mayor. Contact was made with the senior German officer, and Beaufrere was driven to Malo-les-Bains for a meeting. Not long afterwards the Swastika flag was flying from the town hall.

In the closing days of Operation *Dynamo*, Ramsay had been given conflicting figures about the number of French soldiers left in Dunkirk. On the night of 3–4 June, 27,000 were saved, and it was no doubt thought that most of the soldiers had been evacuated. In fact, there were still some 40,000 who needed rescuing and many of them were gathered at the harbour, crowding the quays, as the sun rose on 4 June, looking out to sea for ships that would never appear. They were taken prisoner. One explanation for the high number was the later realisation that soldiers, especially those from rear units, had been in hiding, with cellars an obvious choice.

And there were a significant number of severely wounded British and French troops at the large red-brick hospital on the edge of the dunes at Zuydcoote, east of Dunkirk. Ramsay's hospital ships had been unable to carry out mercy missions because of attacks by the Luftwaffe. The hospital was also targeted, despite the presence of huge red crosses on the roofs. Known as the Sanatorium, it had been in constant use from 10 May and was taken over by the Royal Army Medical Corps as the number of British casualties increased. Tents were erected in the grounds to cope with the influx. Some 12,000 wounded, including Germans, were treated and about 1,000 died. Some of the patients were killed in air raids or by enemy artillery fire. When Dunkirk surrendered, the British and French wounded became prisoners of war and were transferred to other hospitals in France and Belgium. Those who recovered ended up in POW camps in Germany, though some managed to escape.

Captain Tennant's terse signal, 'BEF evacuated', sent at 2330 on 2 June, was accurate only as far as it related to Dunkirk and the beaches. There were still many thousands of British servicemen in areas of north-west and western France controlled by the Allies. Most of these soldiers, however, were in support roles. The Germans had slowed their attack on Dunkirk, but after the town fell, a second offensive, codenamed Fall Rot, was launched on 5 June, with Paris one of the key targets. With at most 65 divisions to call on, the French commander-in-chief, General Weygand, was outnumbered almost two to one. The Germans attacked on a 70-mile front from Amiens to the Laon–Soissons road. The main British forces were the 51st (Highland) Division and an under strength 1st Armoured Division, which were in support of the French Tenth Army, tasked with holding the line of the River Somme. The Panzers had been held back before Dunkirk fell, but the tanks' crews, refreshed and reinforced, were ready for battle again.

Relations between senior British and French commanders were still strained. Lieutenant General Sir Henry Karslake was scathing, 'During the whole of this period, it was most difficult to discover the French policy of protecting this part of France. All that they could say was "The Line of the Somme will be held at all costs". This meant nothing of course because the French never did hold the Line of the Somme! Two tank officers who had escaped from Arras crossed the Somme one morning at Etoile and met some German patrols south of the river. Then the "Line of the Bresle" was to be held at all costs and so on.'[1]

The 51st Division was stretched across 16 miles of the front and on 4 June it had gone on the offensive with a French division supported by tanks, attacking the German bridgehead at Abbeville. The attackers were beaten back, with the 51st suffering heavy casualties. But by the evening of the next day, the division was reinforced with some 3,000 men.

On 7 June, two German armoured divisions pushed towards Rouen, splitting the Tenth Army. The city fell the next night, and the 51st, along with the remains of the French IX Corps, was cut off in what Churchill described as the Rouen-Dieppe cul-de-sac. The commander of the 51st, Major General Victor Fortune, came to the conclusion that his men were in a hopeless position and evacuation from Le Havre was the only option. He was, however, under French command and could not take that decision alone. Weygand and Dill in London were slow to give their backing, failing to appreciate the swiftness of the German advance. Churchill would later insist that the 'disintegrating' French command was to blame. But Churchill also has been blamed for the fate of the 51st. He was pushing the French to fight on and the presence of British fighting troops was important. As early as 2 June, the prime minister had told his chief of staff, Major General Hastings Ismay, that the BEF in France must immediately be reconstituted.

When Lieutenant General Alan Brooke, who had been commander of the BEF's II Corps, arrived in Dover from France on the morning of 31 May, he experienced a 'wonderful feeling of peace'. He went home and slept for more than 36 hours. On 2 June, he was summoned to the War Office. He was 'still overcome by the wonderful transformation from war to peace. The awful load of responsibility had been laid aside, the nightmares of anxiety were gone, roads were free from refugees, demoralization no longer surrounded me on all sides, it was another glorious English spring day. From every point of view life had suddenly assumed a very rosy outlook, and I walked into Dill's room with a light heart.'[2]

Brooke's mood would soon change. The Chief of the Imperial General Staff got straight to the point. Dill wanted Brooke to return to France as commander of a reformed BEF. It was, Brooke would admit, 'one of my blackest moments'. He recognised a poisoned chalice when he saw one, recording, 'I knew only too well the state of affairs that would prevail in France from now onwards. I had seen my hope in the French army gradually shattered throughout those long winter months, I had witnessed the realization of my worst fears regarding its fighting value and morale, and now I had no false conceptions as to what its destiny must inevitably be. To be sent back again into that cauldron with a new force to participate in the final stages of French disintegration was indeed a dark prospect.'[3]

But Brooke was left with no choice. He asked if he could refit the 3rd Division and the 4th Division but was told that time would not allow it. His main force would consist of the mauled 51st Division and the 1st Armoured Division, plus the 52st Division and the 1st Canadian Division, which would be sent over. It was pointed out that the personnel of Brooke's corps headquarters had been dispersed all over England after returning from France and it would take time to assemble them. Brooke's choice of Lieutenant General Henry Pownall as his chief of staff was turned down because 'Gort required him for the writing of despatches!'[4]

Brooke then went to see Eden, who asked if he was satisfied with the arrangements. The minister was taken aback when the lieutenant general replied that he was far from satisfied. From a military point of view, the mission had no value and there was no possibility of accomplishing anything. The army had only just escaped a major disaster at Dunkirk 'and were now risking a second such disaster'. Brooke recorded, 'I wanted him to be quite clear that the expedition I was starting on promised no chances of military success and every probability of disaster. It was for him to judge whether these risks were justified in the hope of gaining any political advantage that might exist.' Although Brooke would be in command of all British forces in France, he was still subject to Weygand's orders. His only consolation was a knighthood for his services in France.[5]

Ramsay also was awarded the KCB (Knight Commander of the Bath). The vice admiral told his wife Margaret that he felt 'an awful fraud' because a great number of people had helped with the Dunkirk evacuation, 'so it is not to be expected that I would be blown out with self esteem or anything like that but I console myself always with the knowledge that if things had not gone well I alone would have borne the responsibility and the blame. So I remain quite unmoved.'[6]

He had received many letters and telegrams of congratulation and 'I really do dread tomorrow's post'. There were newspaper interviews and photographs and he also dreaded seeing the results.[7] Although wary of personal publicity, Ramsay was generous when it came to recommending others for recognition. In total, he submitted more than 1,200 names, though many were for Mention in Despatches. The honours and awards committee did some pruning, especially when it involved base staffs. The CB (Companion of the Order of the Bath) was awarded to Rear Admiral William Wake-Walker, Captain William Tennant and Ramsay's chief staff officer, Captain Michael Denny. For other officers, there were 27 awards of the Distinguished Service Order and 86 of the Distinguished Service Cross. The bravery of sailors below officer rank was recognised when a remarkable 208 received the Distinguished Service Medal.

Two men were given the rarely awarded Conspicuous Gallantry Medal – Acting Leading Seaman Ronald Thirwall and Seaman Cook Jesse Elton. Thirwall was manning a pom-pom antiaircraft gun in *Mosquito* as the gunboat returned to the Dunkirk beaches on 1 June. Twenty-four dive-bombers attacked in waves, inflicting casualties. Three of the four barrels of Thirwall's pom-pom were put out of action, but although wounded in four places, he kept firing until there was no more ammunition. One bomb went through the gunboat's engine room and straight through the bottom of the ship and it went down 'like a rock' as water poured in. Survivors were machine-gunned in the water. Thirwall was lucky to be picked up by a drifter.

When the armed boarding vessel *King Orry* sank off Dunkirk harbour on 30 May, the naval yacht *Bystander* was one of the vessels that went to pick up survivors. Cook Jesse Elton was manning a dinghy from *Bystander* and he dived into the water repeatedly to save exhausted swimmers. He was responsible for rescuing 25 men.

The honours committee had several difficult decisions, one of which involved Captain Lionel Lambert, who was considered for a posthumous Victoria Cross. Lambert was in command of the naval yacht *Grive*, which made three round trips between Dover and Dunkirk, rescuing 1,400 troops. On returning to Dover for the third time, he put ashore one of his officers who was over 60 and 'had earned a rest'. Lambert was 67 and would not rest, telling his crew he would cross again at once. The vessel was lost off Dunkirk with all hands. The committee decided that a Mention in Despatches for Lambert would be a 'poor award', adding, 'But after scrupulous debate they reluctantly agreed that this was not quite a case for the Victoria Cross, the only posthumous decoration that might be correct. Captain Lambert's courage, spirit and devotion to duty were exemplary; but, though he would doubtless gladly have done so, he was not knowingly incurring a risk of almost certain death.'[8] Ramsay agreed that this was not a VC action. It was decided to send a special letter of appreciation to Lambert's widow.

After the Dunkirk evacuation, Ramsay noted that there was a 'perilous calm after the storm'. He did not expect the French to survive for much longer because of the enemy's superiority in divisions and air power. And he had this observation, 'Those dirty Italians are only waiting for the French to crack to join in the rout.'[9] (On 10 June, Italian dictator Benito Mussolini declared war on Britain and France.)

Britain was seen as only a temporary sanctuary for the French troops evacuated from Dunkirk. Plans were soon under way to send back most of the 125,000 soldiers to continue the battle of France. After accommodation in camps in south-west England, British ships were assigned to ferry them to Brest, Cherbourg and other ports.

Only six days after Brooke's meeting with Dill and Eden, it became clear that another major evacuation would be necessary. Ramsay was spared this task, which fell to the Commander-in-Chief, Portsmouth, Admiral Sir William James, a colourful character who had the dubious nickname of Bubbles. As a boy, James had sat for his grandfather, the painter John Millais. A picture of him gazing at a bubble he had blown was featured in a well-known advert for Pears soap. Enthusiasm for Operation *Cycle*, as it came to be known, was certainly needed because of the limited time frame. Admiral James and his staff quickly assembled a fleet of transports and small craft. The destroyer force included the Dunkirk veteran HMS *Saladin*. Le Havre would be the main evacuation point, and Major General Fortune sent Arkforce – two infantry brigades, supported by artillery and engineers – to help defend the port and the surrounding area.

At 1320 on 9 June, the Admiralty signalled that Operation *Cycle* should commence. Ten minutes later vessels began sailing. But that evening, James was told that the French were being evacuated from Le Havre during the night and the rescue of British soldiers 'must be delayed'. Troop carriers were ordered to return to their harbours. Early on 10 June, a signal was received from the reduced 51st Division warning that if the Germans broke through French defences, evacuation from another port might be necessary. For James, the picture was confusing and he set off in an MTB for Le Havre to see for himself and to confer with the French naval officer in command of the port. Le Havre was ablaze and full of refugees. 'I found that the situation was as bad as it could be,' James recalled. 'The French were giving way everywhere. I hastened to the headquarters of the French admiral, who was the supreme authority in the area, and urged him to allow me to evacuate our soldiers before it was too late. He was in a very excited state and was under the delusion that the French army was disputing every inch. Weygand had ordered a retreat to the Somme and he could give no orders for evacuation.'[10] (James did not name the French naval commander in his official report. He was Rear Admiral Charles Platon, who openly expressed anti-British sentiments. He would become a fervent supporter of the Vichy government. In 1944, Platon was captured by French partisans and executed.)

After James's visit, all available passenger ships were told to sail for Le Havre for an evacuation on the night of 10–11 June. But it was still not clear how many needed to be saved, with estimates ranging from 60,000 to 300,000.

Returning to Portsmouth, James phoned the War Office and spoke to General Sir Robert Haining, stressing the plight of the 51st Division. Haining pointed out that the Highlanders were under French command and the War Office could not order their evacuation.

The division was still struggling to reach the coast and a message suggested that the earliest it could be evacuated was the night of 12–13 June. There was a change of destination. Fortune's men were heading for the fishing port of St Valery-en-Caux, about 50 miles north-east of Le Havre. As an evacuation point, it was a poor choice because of its narrow harbour entrance, with cliffs overlooking the port and its beach. James directed *Saladin* to take small craft from Le Havre to St Valery-en-Caux, and told his staff to send over more transports. His destroyers had been checking the coast between Le Havre and Dieppe.

There was an unpleasant surprise for the admiral. On the afternoon of 10 June, it was clear that the enemy had already reached the coast. The destroyer HMS *Ambuscade* was hit by shore batteries to the west of St Valery-en-Caux and another destroyer, HMS *Boadicea*, was heavily engaged while taking 60 soldiers from nearby Veulettes-sur-Mer. That evening, ships in Le Havre and off Fecamp and St Valery-en-Caux were heavily bombed. The destroyers HMS *Bulldog* and *Boadicea* were hit. Warships were ordered not to close evacuation areas in daylight unless there were urgent reasons.

James recorded, 'Considerable numbers of small craft were in St Valery harbour and off the coast during the early hours of 11 June and thus available for evacuation if required. No British troops were there except a few wounded who were taken off. It is now known that the 51st Division were delayed in their withdrawal on St Valery by a block of French mechanical transport. In any case evacuation had not yet been approved by the French High Command.'[11]

On the morning of 11 June, *Saladin* reported that the 51st Division was formed in a hollow square round St Valery-en-Caux and arrangements were being made for evacuation when darkness fell. Accurate firing from shore batteries continued. *Codrington* was straddled at 18,000 yards and MTB 69 was hit coursing through the water at 35 knots. The Luftwaffe also carried out dive-bombing attacks on ships. The steamer *Bruges* was badly damaged and beached at Le Havre to prevent it sinking.[12]

At 1700 that day the evacuation at Le Havre began and Rear Admiral Platon finally approved the rescue at St Valery-en-Caux. But thick fog later prevented vessels from closing on the port, and early on 12 June, *Saladin* reported that the town appeared to have been captured, with the beach under heavy fire. A naval liaison officer with the 51st described the situation as most critical. A skoot managed to take off 80 troops from a beach near the port but several boats were lost. Soldiers who made their way to the beach at Veules-les-Roses were picked up despite intense machine-gun fire. As daylight broke, James asked the RAF for maximum support and destroyers tried to silence the batteries, but they were sited 'so as to be immune from ships' attack'. He received a report that the 51st was still in St Valery-en-Caux and fighting to hold its perimeter. But with the enemy occupying the strategic cliffs overlooking the port, it became clear that further evacuation was impossible.[13]

At around 0800, a white flag was seen fluttering from a steeple near the headquarters of the 51st Division, and an order was given to cut it down and to arrest whoever was responsible. It emerged that the offender was a French officer. French troops in support of the 51st had surrendered. Two hours later, his men trapped and with little ammunition, Fortune took the same decision. He surrendered to Panzer commander General Erwin Rommel. An officer of the Seaforth Highlanders admitted, 'All the men were so utterly exhausted after twelve days of continuous marching and digging without proper food or rest and with heavily fighting on eight of those days, that the majority were almost incapable of carrying on even if they had sufficient ammunition and arms.'[14] More than 10,000 Highlanders were taken prisoner, along with thousands of French troops.

The German shore batteries had presented a major problem, but a French cruiser had a spectacular success, as one of the naval officers, Captain Archibald Lovett-Cameron, sailing off Fecamp, recounted, 'Then occurred what was the prettiest piece of naval work I have ever seen in the whole of my experience. The French cruiser headed for land and while still on our port bow opened fire at the top of the cliffs. He steamed straight in firing as he went at the German battery on the hill until he was right close in under the cliffs. He then turned to starboard and opened out again and fired with his stern guns, the Germans replying with what looked like two 6in guns from the splashes. The Frenchman was under very close and accurate fire. The cruiser went on firing and to our delight we saw the ammunition dump on the hillside beside the battery blown up into the air, cascades of projectiles and cartridge cases and boxes and all the other paraphernalia went up with it, and the easterly German ceased fire. After that the Frenchman engaged the other gun and put it out of action with three or four rounds. It was a most gallant performance. The attacking of shore batteries by a ship at any time is rather difficult. In this case the batteries were placed on the top of a cliff, and they were heavy enough to damage this cruiser and sink her.'[15]

James was certain he knew the reason for the loss of the 51st: 'French affairs were then in flabby hands.' Dill contacted him, 'I feel that I must write to you personally to let you know how immensely we in the army admire and appreciate the immense and gallant efforts made by you and all those under your command to rescue our troops from their dangerous position in and about Havre. To save the whole of the 51st Division was beyond your power but that you managed to save so many of them under the conditions prevailing is little short of miraculous.'[16]

Operation *Cycle* ended on 13 June. According to James's figures, about 11,200 men were evacuated from Le Havre. From the area of St Valery-en-Caux 1,350 British and 930 French were taken off. Some British soldiers may have been evacuated in French ships.

As with the Dunkirk evacuation, failure of communications was a major factor. There was always conflicting information about the time, place and number to be rescued. The senior naval officer at Le Havre, Captain Ion Tower, found he had to rely on a dispatch rider as his only method of communication with the 51st Division. He was also surprised that the army abandoned so many vehicles and guns, as well as other equipment, much like Dunkirk. In his view, a lot could have been saved. 'No request from the military authorities was received in this respect,' he noted. 'A certain amount was put on board by the beach party on their own initiative.'[17]

On the day that the 51st Division surrendered, Lieutenant General Brooke set off for France on the mission he never wanted. At Southampton, he discovered that the duty boat taking him to Cherbourg was a 'dirty little Dutch steamer with 100 Frenchmen on board and only capable of 12 knots'. To make matters worse there was no food. The boat finally arrived off the French port at 2130 but Brooke was unable to land until 0600 the following day, 13 June. And the War Office had been pushing him for the past week to get over as quickly as possible. It was, he decided, 'an absolute disgrace'.[18]

That morning Brooke went to Le Mans to confer with British officers, including Lieutenant General Karslake and Major General Philip de Fonblanque, who had organised logistics for the BEF. He was shocked to learn that there were still 100,000 men of the BEF remaining, a significant number of them in support roles. Instructions were given to evacuate as many of these personnel as possible, leaving only enough to cover four divisions. Brooke told Karslake there was no need for him to remain in France and the lieutenant general replied that he had a plane standing by 'and was off at once!'[19]

The next day at Orleans, Brooke met a 'wizened' Weygand, who admitted that the French army was disintegrating and he had no reserves. That morning,

German troops entered Paris, which was declared an open city to save it from destruction. The French government fled to Tours and then Bordeaux. Weygand had a 'wild' plan to defend Brittany, but there was eventual agreement that it would fail. In Brooke's view, there was only one course left, stop any more troops coming over from Britain and evacuate those in France. In London, Dill agreed but said he would consult Churchill.

In the evening, Dill was at 10 Downing Street and in a phone call told Brooke that Churchill wanted the British to continue supporting French troops. The prime minister came on the line and emphasised the point.

Brooke was in no mood to be diplomatic. 'I replied that it was impossible to make a corpse feel, and that the French army was, to all intents and purposes, dead, and certainly incapable of registering what had been done to it. Our talk lasted for close on half an hour, and on many occasions his arguments were so formed as to give the impression that he considered that I was suffering from cold feet because I did not wish to comply with his wishes. This was so infuriating that I was repeatedly on the verge of losing my temper … At last, when I was in an exhausted condition, he said, "All right, I agree with you."'[20]

On 15 June, Operation *Aerial* (also known as *Ariel*) was launched. Admiral James was responsible for evacuating troops from the ports of Cherbourg and St Malo, and Admiral Sir Martin Dunbar-Nasmith, Commander-in-Chief, Western Approaches, had responsibility for directing operations from Plymouth using Brest, St Nazaire and La Pallice. Brooke observed, 'It is a desperate job being faced with over 150,000 men and masses of material, ammunition, petrol, supplies etc to try and evacuate or dispose of, with nothing to cover this operation except the crumbling French army.' To add to the difficulty he was told by Dill to keep two brigades of the 52nd Division in France for 'political reasons'.[21] Shipping was available at Cherbourg, and Brooke saw this as more time wasting. The next morning, Dill phoned him and said the two brigades could be evacuated. Liners would be used to embark men at the larger ports.

At lunchtime on 17 June, Brooke received another call from Dill saying there were reports that the French had stopped fighting. Shortly afterwards, it was confirmed that the 84-year-old vice premier, Marshal Petain, had broadcast a ceasefire. The priority now was to speed up the evacuation in case French negotiations with the Germans led to the internment of British personnel. Later that day, Brooke headed to St Nazaire, where he and his staff were due to board a destroyer and return to England. Then came news of what would be the biggest loss in British maritime history, the sinking of the *Lancastria*.

The Cunard liner, requisitioned by the British government, had been anchored off St Nazaire as part of the evacuation fleet. The ship had many thousands of service personnel and civilians on board when it was attacked by German bombers. *Lancastria* sank within 20 minutes. There is no accurate figure for the number of people who had boarded the liner. The captain was told to take as many as possible and the crew gave up counting. There were around 2,500 survivors and the death toll may have been 4,000 or higher.

Brooke's destroyer was engaged in the rescue work, but the anti-submarine trawler *Cambridgeshire* was available to sail for Plymouth. 'When we arrived on board we found that she had just been saving 900 survivors from the *Lancastria*,' the lieutenant general recalled. 'She was in an indescribable mess, soaked in fuel oil and sea water with discarded wet clothes lying all over the place. Everything sticky with this beastly black fuel oil, all the walls, chairs, furniture etc black with it.' During the voyage one of the crew 'went more or less mad and had to be held down on the deck … he kept shouting about wanting to save people'. When Brooke arrived at Plymouth, he thanked God again 'for allowing us to come home. I also thanked God that the expedition which I hated from the start was over.'[22] For Admiral James, Operation *Aerial* ended on 18 June, and his vessels largely had escaped the attention of the enemy. RAF fighter patrols thwarted German dive-bombers, although the destroyer HMS *Fernie* and the Dunkirk veteran *Sabre* were bombed towards the end of the operation.[23] For Admiral Dunbar-Nasmith, *Aerial* ended on 25 June. According to War Office figures, the total number of personnel rescued was 186,327, including 139,812 British, 24,352 Poles and 17,062 French. Czechs and Belgians were also evacuated.[24]

Reynaud, who opposed an armistice with Germany, resigned in despair as France's prime minister, to be replaced by Petain. On 22 June, the French signed an armistice. Hitler took revenge on Germany's World War I defeat by insisting that the signing take place in the same railway carriage in Compiegne Forest that saw the 1918 armistice. From 25 June, much of France came under German occupation, with a region in the south controlled by a French administration led by Petain and based in Vichy.

Between 55,000 and 85,000 French military personnel were killed during the battle of France. Many more were wounded or reported missing. The figure for German dead has ranged from 27,000 to 45,000. Britain had fewer than 10,000 killed in action.

CHAPTER 18

Mutiny

In 2016, The National Archives in Kew, south-west London, released two files that had been kept secret for a staggering 76 years, 46 years longer than the usual rule for releasing official documents. These files focus on the behaviour of some of the captains and crews of ships belonging to the Isle of Man Steam Packet Company during the Dunkirk evacuation. They were considered highly sensitive because they contain accusations of desertion and cowardice made by such prominent island figures as the Lieutenant Governor, Earl Granville, and the editor of *The Isle of Man Times*, George Brown.

The Isle of Man Steam Packet Company has a proud history dating from its formation in 1830, with ships taking passengers and freight to and from Douglas and UK and Irish ports. In World War I, the Admiralty requisitioned 11 of the company's 15 steamers and four of them were lost. After World War II broke out, ten of its vessels were commandeered.

In 2018, the company's view of the performance of its ships at Dunkirk was completely at odds with the allegations. Its website stated: 'Dunkirk was perhaps the company's finest hour, with the *Mona's Isle* being the first vessel to leave Dover for Dunkirk and the first to complete the round trip during the evacuation. Eight company ships took part in the historic mission, rescuing a grand total of 24,699 British troops from certain death (as a matter of interest, this means that one in 14 lives saved during the Dunkirk evacuations was brought by an Isle of Man Steam Packet Company vessel).'[1]

The Manx allegations were so serious that Vice Admiral Ramsay spelled them out in a report to the Admiralty on the use of personnel vessels; the main merchant ships.[2] Five of the eight Isle of Man steamers that took part in the evacuation caused problems for Operation *Dynamo*. They were *Tynwald*, *Ben-my-Chree*, *Lady of Mann*, *Manx Man* and *Manx Maid*. *Tynwald* transported 7,534 troops in five voyages but should have made a sixth trip. Trouble broke out before the fourth voyage on the evening of 1 June 1940 when the captain, Wilfred Qualtrough, refused to sail.

Qualtrough explained, 'I had a signal from the master of the *Malines* [a London and North Eastern Railway steamer] last night to say he and the master of the *Ben-my-Chree* had considered it hopeless to proceed to Dunkirk. Our crews have been continually on their feet all the week and especially the deck officers who have had to be on their feet for so long. I myself have had four hours rest for the week and am at present physically unfit for another trip like what we have had. If it is absolutely necessary to go I will abide with the masters of the other ships decision.' He added, 'There are two more of the crew going ashore now absolutely nervous wrecks and certified by the naval doctor.'[3]

Tynwald was berthed at Folkestone on the evening of 1 June and a relief crew was sent for. Armed naval guards were posted as sentries to stop anyone from leaving the ship. The crew 'contented themselves with shouting abuse at the sentries'. The men were allowed to leave when the relief crew arrived, although the chief officer, second officer, wireless operator and carpenter elected to remain on board. With a naval officer and ten ratings 'as moral stiffeners',[4] *Tynwald* sailed on the evening of 2 June and completed a round trip without incident.

It should be pointed out that *Tynwald* was originally under the command of Captain John Whiteway during Operation *Dynamo*, and he was awarded the Distinguished Service Cross. Other crewmen were also decorated.

Ben-my-Chree transported 408 troops in two voyages but should have made four trips. Ramsay reported that the captain was 'evidently in league with the masters of the *Tynwald* and *Malines*'. *Ben-my-Chree* failed to sail on the night of 1–2 June. Asked whether he would continue to help with the evacuation, the captain, George Woods, replied, 'I beg to state that after our experience at Dunkirk yesterday, my answer is No.'

The ship was also berthed at Folkestone and naval guards were placed on the gangways. Members of the crew demonstrated that they intended to leave and were forced to remain on board at the point of fixed bayonets. A relief crew took over and *Ben-my-Chree* sailed but did not complete the trip because of a collision.

Lady of Mann did four trips carrying 2,902 troops. The last two trips were carried out with a naval officer and ten ratings on board 'as an insurance'. But there was no trouble.

Manx Man carried 233 troops in three voyages. But on the night of 2 June refused to sail again. A new crew was put on board, with the engineers remaining, but the steamer failed to make Dunkirk. On returning, the original captain and some of his crew joined the ship, but it stayed in harbour because of a shortage of engineers.

Manx Maid never completed a trip. It should have sailed three times and on the last occasion offered an engine breakdown as an excuse. Ramsay noted that the ship was 'given up as hopeless'. After an appeal most of the crew volunteered to serve in other vessels.

Ramsay's senior sea transport officer at Dover quickly made the management of the Isle of Man Steam Packet Company aware of the problems with some of its vessels, particulary *Tynwald* and *Ben-my-Chree*. The company's general manager replied, 'I need hardly assure you of the surprise with which the directors and management of this company learned a few days ago that practically the whole complement of each of the above named vessels [*Tynwald* and *Ben-my-Chree*] had refused to volunteer for further service in the momentous task which so successfully has since been accomplished at Dunkirk.

'It is understood that all members of the Merchant Navy actually were given the opportunity of deciding whether they would take part in the work of evacuation and while in all probability the officers and crews with which we are concerned were extremely tired and perhaps nerve-wracked that, presumably, would be common to all others. It may be, however, that it is not for us to judge on the question of loyalty and duty to the country in a time of great need but my directors are bound to be concerned by the fact that our officers left their vessels, without any reference to us, as we understand, in charge in each case of only a first mate.' The company's board planned to meet within days to consider 'the whole position'.[5] Rumours about the behaviour of the crews swept the Isle of Man for several months, and in September, the Lieutenant Governor, Earl Granville, a retired vice admiral, sent a damning letter to the Second Sea Lord, Admiral Sir Charles Little.

'You have probably heard of the disgraceful behaviour of a large number of the personnel, both officers and men, of the Isle of Man steamers at the evacuation of Dunkirk,' Granville wrote. 'Here, we don't want any of these men to receive any of our unemployment relief or assistance from our war distress tribunals; furthermore it appears that some officers who were loyal and took command of ships when the masters had deserted, have been placed under "deserters". It seems to be very difficult to sort out the sheep from the goats, without a proper investigation, and any tribunal doing this must not have a Manxman on it.' Granville pointed out that there was local demand for a full inquiry.[6]

The previous month it had been decided not to give the shamed captains the usual gratuity that masters receive for having their ships requisitioned for government service.

Granville's call for an inquiry left the Admiralty with a legal problem, as the Second Sea Lord explained, 'The position is that these vessels were ordinary merchant ships used as transports by the Ministry of Shipping. The crews were on ordinary mercantile orders and were not under naval discipline. This being so, it seems impossible even if desired to appoint a naval board of enquiry or tribunal to investigate failures to obey orders. Such a board of enquiry would have no powers over men not subject to naval discipline and could not even oblige them to attend.'[7]

It was also doubtful whether the Ministry of Shipping had the power to order an inquiry. Admiral Little added, 'From the reports it is clear that some of the officers and men behaved very badly and if I may say so you are the best judge, knowing local opinion, as to whether this should be made public or not.'[8]

The captains of the *Tynwald*, *Ben-my-Chree* and *Manx Man* were suspended but later reinstated. George Brown, editor of *The Isle of Man Times*, was quick to express his opinion. 'That seems to me to be wrong unless their unpardonable behaviour is being overlooked.'[9]

It appears that the Admiralty did carry out some form of inquiry because Brown requested a copy of the findings. He asked the Admiralty, 'Do you not think it would be fairer if the findings of the Admiralty court into these matters were made public, or at all events were divulged to the Isle of Man Steam Packet Company, so that they would know how to act? At the moment, the men are accused publicly of abandoning their ships and acting as cowards, and this is an exceedingly serious charge.

'I understand there is an Admiralty report. It has not been issued, and I am wondering whether you could let me see a copy of it privately, so that we shall know how to govern ourselves when referring, if ever, to this matter. If the charges made are true and are substantiated, then no punishment could be too severe for the men in question.'[10]

The Manx steamers were not alone in causing problems for Ramsay's men. The Southern Railway ferry *Canterbury* made two trips to Dunkirk, but on 28 May, the captain refused to make a third voyage. A senior navy officer went on board and explained the gravity of the situation and ordered him to sail at 2230. It was then discovered that some of the crew had been given leave. A naval officer and ratings were put on board to 'stiffen' the remaining crew and *Canterbury* sailed at 0930 on 29 May. It was bombed returning from Dunkirk and after landing troops did not take any further part in the operation.

After completing one trip, the captain of *St Seiriol*, a ferry of the Liverpool and North Wales Steamship Company, refused to sail again. A naval officer with armed ratings went on board at 1000 on 29 May and the master, R. D. Dobb, was put under open arrest. At Dunkirk, the steamer picked up survivors from *Crested Eagle* and *Grenade* and also embarked soldiers from a beach.[11]

The master's refusal to sail was completely ignored by his company, whose chairman told the Ministry of Shipping, 'No praise is too high for the gallantry of Captain Dobb in the opinion of my directors.' Of the second voyage, the chairman stated, 'On the night of 29 May he took his vessel well in shore and put the remaining lifeboat out to go to the beach, and also was successful in picking men from the water who were survivors from other ships which were sunk by enemy action and then brought his ship safely to port with a complement of BEF men despite intense air bombing.'

The chairman ended his letter, 'After the strain and anxieties of these two trips and after the strenuous work during the previous week, the whole of the crew were thoroughly shaken and the military doctor at Dover, after he had examined them, decided without hesitation that the master and all hands were unfit to carry on any longer, consequently they all returned to their homes.'[12]

Captain Dobb also gave a written account of his ship's two trips but made no mention of his refusal to sail. Nor did he reveal that he had been placed under open arrest. *St Seiriol* took no further part in the evacuation.[13]

Ramsay also drew attention to the behaviour of the master of *Malines*, a steamer of the London and North Eastern Railway. The vessel made two trips to Dunkirk and then, on 2 June, disappeared from Dover without informing the naval authorities. Later it was discovered that it had gone to Southampton. Asked to provide an explanation, the captain, G. Mallory, pointed out that his crew had been badly shaken by enemy attacks. 'When, finally, the crews of the Manx steamers refused to sail it was evident that my crew was on the edge of revolt. After consultation with reliable witnesses, both marine and military, I considered the odds against a successful prosecution of another voyage too enormous, and the outcome too unprofitable to risk the ship. My draught does not permit me to reach the beaches at Dunkirk, and the quay appears to be untenable. This ship having suffered damage while rescuing the crews of two destroyers, and having grounded and damaged the propellers in the shoals around Dunkirk, I have decided, on my own initiative, to return to Southampton, and if possible, dry dock and put the ship in condition for further service, especially as we cannot now maintain a speed of more than 14 knots.'[14]

Ramsay told the Admiralty that the outstanding merchant ships were *Royal Daffodil* (General Steam Navigation Company), which made seven trips, and *Maid of Orleans* (Southern Railway Company), which did six trips. *Royal Sovereign* (General Steam Navigation Company) also made six trips, and *King George V* (David MacBrayne Ltd) and *Cote d'Argent* (French) each did five trips. The masters of *Royal Daffodil*, *Maid of Orleans*, *Royal Sovereign* and *King George V* were all decorated.

The Royal National Lifeboat Institution has been keen to promote the part that its vessels played in the evacuation of Dunkirk. On the afternoon of 30 May 1940, the Ministry of Shipping asked the organisation to send as many of its lifeboats as possible to Dover. Lifeboat stations from Gorleston, Norfolk, to Shoreham, Sussex, were alerted, and 19 vessels went across the Channel as part of the Little Ships armada. But RNLI personnel manned only two of the lifeboats. The others were mostly crewed by the Royal Navy. What the institution is not keen to promote is the fact that three of its crews refused to take part in the evacuation and exasperated naval officers ended up commandeering all the lifeboats, apart from the Ramsgate and Margate vessels, which had already set off for Dunkirk and were later recognised for their bravery.

The coxswain of the lifeboat at Hythe, Kent, Henry 'Buller' Griggs, led a protest soon after arriving in Dover. He complained that his vessel, *The Viscountess Wakefield*, weighing 14 tons, was likely to run aground in rescue work from beaches. Apparently unaware of the extremely high tides at Dunkirk, he insisted that winches would be needed. Griggs then asked a number of questions, in particular on pension rights for families in the event of lifeboat men being killed. On this point, he was given an answer but demanded a written assurance. When this was refused, Griggs said he would not go. His crew supported him, as did the men of the Walmer and Dungeness lifeboats. With time precious, the navy simply took over the lifeboats and Griggs and the others were given railway vouchers and told to go home.

The RNLI held an inquiry and Griggs was blamed for the crews' refusal, 'and it is considered that this failure to perform a duty at a time of great national emergency reflects discredit on the lifeboat service and can in no way be excused'. A report added, 'The naval authorities, being unable to risk such behaviour by the crews of other boats which had not yet arrived, had no other course open to them but to summon ratings of the Royal Navy to man the boats.' When the other lifeboat crews arrived at Dover, they were disappointed to learn that they would not be able to take part in the evacuation, 'which will in days to come be recognised as one of the greatest epics of the sea'.[15]

Griggs, who had been a member of the Hythe lifeboat crew for 38 years, was dismissed from the service. His motor mechanic, a relative, suffered the same fate. The crews of the Walmer and Dungeness crews were reprimanded. The only lifeboat lost at Dunkirk was *The Viscountess Wakefield*. After the war, the RNLI decided it would no longer station a lifeboat at Hythe.[16]

The Ramsgate lifeboat, *The Prudential*, helped to bring off some 2,800 men from the beaches over 30 hours, much of the time under fire. The coxswain, Howard Knight, was awarded the Distinguished Service Medal. The work of the Margate lifeboat, *The Lord Southborough*, won praise from the captain of the destroyer *Icarus*, Lieutenant Commander Colin Maud. 'I had not any power boats and they did magnificent work bringing loads of about seventy at a time to the ship,' he reported on the challenges of 30 May. 'Unfortunately the weather began to deteriorate and the lifeboat could not get close to the shore so the whalers ferried troops to the lifeboat and when full she brought them to *Icarus*. This was about 0600, and shortly after both whalers were capsized ashore and the lifeboat began getting into difficulties when embarking troops ashore.'[17] Coxswain Edward Parker was also awarded the Distinguished Service Medal.

Ramsay was aware of the bravery of the Ramsgate and Margate crews but he did not forget the trouble caused by the Hythe lifeboat revolt. In a letter to his wife Margaret in March 1941, he suggested that she should drop the RNLI from her list of charities because of the crews' refusal. 'There's a gross exaggeration about saving thousands from Dunkirk,' he wrote. 'Only two lifeboat crews went over, from Margate and Ramsgate, but many lifeboats were without proper crews, being made up of volunteers and sailors detailed.'[18]

Merchant Navy seamen and lifeboat men were not the only ones causing headaches for Operation *Dynamo*. The Royal Navy also had problems with reluctant sailors. Ramsay was given a special alert about the destroyer *Verity*, whose captain, Lieutenant Commander Arthur Black, had been badly wounded.

Verity's Lieutenant Eric Jones reported, 'The morale of the ship's company had been undermined by the shelling from shore batteries and aerial bombing during the last few days. It is considered that this was exaggerated by long hours and lack of sleep. This situation came to a climax during the first dog [watch] when one rating attempted to commit suicide. This incident caused a marked increase to the men's uneasiness. Shorting afterwards a report was made by the leading seamen that the ship's company were considering breaking out of the ship.'[19]

Vice Admiral Somerville went on board the ship and addressed the crew, and the destroyer was given a break from evacuation duties, allowing the men a night's rest. On 29 May, they showed determination in repelling dive-bombing attacks off Dunkirk and 'seemed in good fettle' on the return journey. But after the destroyer berthed at Dover 12 members of the ship's company disappeared. Three were held at the dockyard gate and three returned in the early hours saying they had lost their nerve. The ship was ordered to stay in harbour.[20]

The minesweeper *Hebe* worked off La Panne, rescuing a total of 1,140. On 1 June, it returned to Dover to take on oil and ammunition and have boiler repairs. The captain, Lieutenant Commander John Temple, was about to face a dilemma, as he recorded, 'During the following 24 hours one officer and 28 members of the crew collapsed due to shock and were sent to *Sandhurst* [a repair ship with medical facilities] for treatment. I reported this fact to Vice Admiral Dover who ordered me to sail for Portsmouth at 0900 on 3 June and give leave.'[21] Even *Hebe*'s surgeon collapsed, mumbling that he could not face another trip to Dunkirk.

How genuine were these cases? According to Harold Biles, an engine room artificer at the time, he felt nothing but shame about the behaviour of some of the crew. He recalled, 'We were embarking more stores and ammunition back in Dover. An RAF plane flying low overhead was the starting point. A seaman looked up, screamed and fell into convulsions with hysteria. It was contagious and he was joined by three or four others. Later in the day an order was issued, amazing and ill judged. Anybody feeling the stress of the last week was told to leave the ship and assemble on the dockside in preparation for going to hospital. About 20 men left the ship and I can still see their grins as they trooped over the gangway. The majority were malingerers but in fairness the prospect of that final trip was frightening as the Germans were almost on the French beaches.'[22]

Biles, along with the chief engineer and coxswain, went to the captain and told him that the ship was now so short of crew that a further sailing was impossible. 'And so we remained alongside while other craft made the trip, some never to return.' *Hebe* played no further part in Operation *Dynamo*. Speaking on the eve of his 98th birthday, Biles, who won a Mention in Despatches, said, 'This was the greatest blow which sometimes I feel to this day.'[23]

One view from the Royal Naval Medical Service: 'It seems probable that, had not sleep been denied to the crews of so many ships through force of circumstances, there would have been hardly any hospital admissions for psychiatric reasons as a result of this operation. In actual fact, there were probably many more hospital admissions than were warranted by the number of genuine cases because, under the conditions existing at Dover, admission to hospital was often the only means of securing sleep, rest and meals for some men who were badly in need of relief. There came a time when some seamen had been on almost continuous watch for six days.'[24]

CHAPTER 19

Threat of Invasion

Ramsay was given ten days' leave in June 1940 and he joined his wife, Margaret, and children, David and Charles, at the family home in Berwickshire, where he 'loved every moment' and wished it had 'gone on for ever'. On his way back to Dover, he stopped off in London. There was something troubling him. With Italy at war with Britain, he headed to Gieves the military tailor and had the 'offending' ribbon of the Crown of Italy, a World War I award, removed from his uniform. Later, there was an appointment at Buckingham Palace, where he had a long conversation with King George VI. In a room with no one else present, the king, using his own naval sword, knighted Ramsay.

Back in Dover, Ramsay was under no illusions. Although much of the British Army had been saved, the country was in a desperate position. He remained on the front line. And there were other threats. Italy was seeking victory in the Mediterranean, the Soviet Union had a pact with Hitler, and Spain and Japan were emerging dangers.

After the fall of France, Hitler believed that such a weakened Britain would be ready to accept a peace agreement. He had, of course, seriously underestimated Churchill's resilience. In early June, the prime minister expressed his defiance and was even looking at going on the offensive. He had in mind amphibious warfare, telling Major General Ismay that it was important to force the enemy to keep large forces along the coasts of the countries they had conquered.[1]

When Hitler realised that Britain was not going to succumb to his demands, he too looked at amphibious warfare, not hit-and-run raids but a full invasion, which was a growing fear in Britain. His military chiefs had been looking at the possibility, and on 16 July, they were ordered to begin serious planning. This would be Operation *Sea Lion* [*Seelöwe*].

Ramsay would emerge during the war as a superb planner of invasions from the sea. He was aware that they required meticulous planning. If he had seen the plans for *Sea Lion*, he would have been greatly relieved. They were conjured up in a matter of weeks. From the outset, an invasion of Britain needed German naval and air superiority. But the Kriegsmarine was not in a position to launch a decisive supporting role. It did not have a huge fleet and it had been badly mauled during the conquest of Norway. There were only three cruisers and four destroyers available for such an operation. The head of the German navy, Grand Admiral Erich Raeder, knew that these vessels were no match for the Royal Navy's Home Fleet. Nevertheless, he was obliged to make preparations. The Luftwaffe believed it would take two to four weeks to achieve air superiority. A successful invasion would also depend on other factors – the weather, tides and a low risk of accidents. Landing craft, of course, were essential, plenty of them. But the Germans did not have any, apart from a couple of prototypes. It was decided to use river barges and more than 2,000 were collected from Germany, France, Belgium and the Netherlands. Most of them lacked engines and needed towing by tugs or trawlers. Some of the barges had the bows cut off so that ramps could be fitted for tanks, lorries and other vehicles. In addition, there was an armada of motorboats. The invasion force would set off from a number of ports, including Le Havre, Boulogne, Calais, Dunkirk and Ostend. After several revisions, the Germans planned to send a first wave of nine to 11 divisions across the Channel to land at targets along the Kent and Sussex coast, stretching from Hythe to Worthing. Dover would be attacked later, not from the sea but on land.

On the south and east coasts of Britain, defences were quickly built up and army reinforcements sent. Military leaders thought it would be a morale boost if the prime minister visited the threatened sectors, and Churchill agreed. An early trip saw him meeting Montgomery, now commanding the 3rd Infantry Division, who had his headquarters at Lancing College in Sussex. Churchill and the major general drove along the coast until they came to Brighton. They dined at the Royal Albion Hotel, opposite the Palace Pier. The hotel was empty, a consequence of evacuation, but there were still a number of people on the beach enjoying the good weather. Churchill was amused to see a platoon of Grenadier Guards making a sandbag machine-gun post in one of the pier kiosks. It brought back childhood memories of seeing performing fleas.[2]

Reminiscences aside, Churchill was left unhappy because of Montgomery's troop deployment, telling Eden, the Secretary of State for War, that the 3rd Division was spread along 30 miles of the coast when it should have been held in reserve, ready to move to any invasion flashpoint. And the soldiers lacked transport.

That July, Brooke replaced Ironside as commander of Home Forces. The newly promoted acting general had impressed Churchill, even after making the prime minister painfully aware of the futility of continuing to support the French army. On his return from France, Brooke was given Southern Command. After several inspections, he was left in despair: 'The more I see the nakedness of our defences the more appalled I am. Untrained men, no arms, no transport and no equipment. And yet there are masses of men in uniform in this country but they are mostly untrained, why I cannot think after ten months of war. The ghastly part of it is that I feel certain that we can only have a few more weeks left before the Boche attacks!'³

His headquarters as C-in-C Home Forces was St Paul's School in Hammersmith, west London, which he found dirty and not well equipped. When he arrived on 19 July, he discovered that Ironside, placed on the retired list with the rank of field marshal, had already gone, leaving only a note saying 'he arranged with the owner of the Rolls-Royce he had been using for me to take it over and the best of wishes. That was all! Not a word concerning the defences or his policy of defence etc, absolutely nothing!'⁴

On coastal defence, Brooke held similar views to Churchill. He preferred light defences along the beaches to delay landings, with highly mobile forces in the rear to deliver aggressive action before the enemy could get established. 'I was also relying on heavy air attacks on the points of landing and had every intention of using sprayed mustard gas on the beaches.'⁵

Ramsay also was focused on defence. His ships were busy carrying out reconnaissance patrols, and naval and air forces were on alert to strike if the enemy attempted to cross the Dover Strait. Beaches were mined, and fortifications improved in Dover and at the harbour.

The vice admiral told his wife, 'The dark period of danger for invasion has passed without anything occurring, and so we have gained this much time for increasing our preparations, which are coming along well. There is much remaining to be done, of course! I daresay the Hun was not ready, as the preparations for such an expedition are enormous. He may select a good moonlight period or wait for the next one, but in the meantime every day helps us. The PM came yesterday. I met him at the station, and brought him up to my office where I had all the military talent from the region to meet him. He was in excellent form, and after a while we went for a tour of the district lasting some hours, and I got back at nine o'clock.'⁶

Bertram Ramsay as a 20-year-old sub lieutenant in the Royal Navy.

Ramsay's father William, an officer in the 4th (Queen's Own) Hussars.

Ramsay with his young wife, Margaret, who became his confidante.

The battleship HMS *Dreadnought*, which Ramsay joined as a lieutenant in 1906.

The battleship HMS *Royal Sovereign* – Ramsay's last sea command in 1935.

Sir Roger Backhouse. Ramsay clashed with the Commander-in-Chief, Home Fleet, likening him to Mussolini. (National Portrait Gallery)

Admiral of the Fleet Sir Andrew Cunningham who was the First Sea Lord at the time of the D-Day landings. (IWM A 9760)

Admiral of the Fleet Lord Keyes, who criticised Ramsay during World War I but praised him in 1944. (Alamy)

Dover Castle, where Operation *Dynamo* was based in tunnels originally dug out in the 13th century.

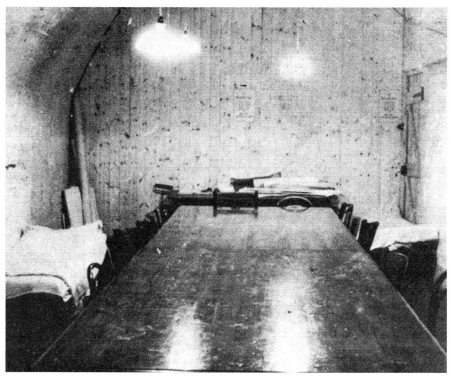

A rare picture of the main Operation *Dynamo* room. (W. J. Matthews)

Retreat. British soldiers on a Dunkirk street as they head to the evacuation ships in May 1940. (Alamy)

Debris of war. Abandoned anti-aircraft guns on one of Dunkirk's main streets. (IWM HU 2286)

Ramsay was forced to stop sending hospital ships to Dunkirk because of Luftwaffe attacks. (IWM HU 73187)

British soldiers using ladders to board the destroyer HMS *Vanquisher* at the Dunkirk mole, showing the difficulty at low tide. (IWM HU 1153)

How the *Daily Express* reported the evacuation on 31 May 1940.

British troops wading out to a destroyer off Dunkirk. (IWM HU 41240)

The stricken French destroyer *Bourrasque*, which sank with heavy loss of life after striking a mine. (IWM HU 2280)

We're home. British soldiers arriving in Dover after a destroyer dash across the Channel. (Royal Navy Museum)

Winston Churchill and Ramsay at Dover Castle in September 1940 discussing plans to counter a German invasion. (IWM H 3508)

Churchill looking across the Channel during a tour of defences on the south coast on 20 June 1941. Ramsay and General Sir John Dill are with him. (IWM H 10872)

A confident Churchill leaving Ramsay's underground headquarters at Dover Castle. (IWM H 3509)

Planning Operation *Husky* – the 1943 invasion of Sicily. Left to right, Major General Sir Francis de Guingand, Air Commodore Claude Pelly, Air Vice Marshal Harry Broadhurst, General Sir Bernard Montgomery and Admiral Ramsay. (IWM NA 4088)

Planning D-Day. A meeting of commanders in London in February 1944 with, from left to right, Lieutenant General Omar Bradley, Admiral Ramsay, Air Chief Marshal Sir Arthur Tedder, General Dwight Eisenhower, General Montgomery, Air Chief Marshal Sir Trafford Leigh-Mallory and Lieutenant General Walter Bedell Smith. (IWM TR 1541)

British commandos storming ashore on Sword beach on D-Day, 6 June 1944. (IWM BU 1184)

Witnessing the Normandy invasion. Ramsay, Eisenhower and Montgomery on board the minelayer HMS *Apollo* on 7 June. (IWM A 23929)

Flying the flag. Royal Navy commandos set up a post on one of the Normandy beaches. (IWM A 24092)

The battleship HMS *Ramillies* bombarding enemy positions. (IWM A 24459)

Killing ground. US troops met fierce resistance at Omaha beach and suffered heavy casualties. (IWM EA 25644)

Royal Marine commandos heading for the raid on the fortified island of Walcheren to open up the port of Antwerp. (Royal Navy Museum)

TAC HEADQUARTERS:
21 ARMY GROUP,
B.L.A.

22 December, 1944.

My Dear Bertie

Thank you so much for your letter and your cheque in payment of your bet. I will see that it is duly recorded in my betting book that the bet has been paid.

I hope we shall get this war won well before next Christmas.

With all good wishes to you for 1945.

~ I won't give you my views on the present situation. I might say things I should not!

As ever

B. L. Montgomery.

Admiral Sir Bertram H Ramsay, KCB, MVO,
Headquarters,
Allied Naval Expeditionary Force.

Ramsay had bet Montgomery £5 that the war would be over by 1 January 1945. The admiral paid up. (Churchill Archives Centre, Cambridge)

Minutes from death. Ramsay wearing a flying jacket before boarding a Hudson plane at an airfield near Versailles on 2 January 1945 for a flight to Brussels to see Montgomery. (*After the Battle* magazine)

Wreckage. The Hudson crashed soon after take-off, killing all on board. This was one of the pictures shown to a board of inquiry, which blamed pilot error. (The National Archives)

Clearly Ramsay was under pressure, adding, 'Last night I had the first night in pyjamas and in my own bed for quite nine days and enjoyed it immensely. How I would love to be able to sleep in my own bed at home instead.'[7]

On 26 July, Brooke was at the War Office for talks with Dill and afterwards he went to a Chiefs of Staff meeting. 'I came away feeling less confident as to our powers of meeting an invasion,' he recorded. 'The attitude of representatives of the naval command brought [out] very clearly the fact that the navy now realises fully that its position has been seriously undermined by the advent of aircraft. Sea supremacy is no longer what it was, and in the face of strong bomber forces can no longer ensure the safety of this island against invasion. This throws a much heavier task on the army.'[8]

Perhaps Brooke was being a little pessimistic. A few days later there were intensive air raids on Dover. The destroyer *Codrington*, a Dunkirk veteran, was sunk but in one of the attacks the Germans lost some 20 planes. The war would show that capital ships were vulnerable to air attack, but in July 1940, the Luftwaffe had few pilots skilled in destroying fast-moving targets such as destroyers and MTBs. Static targets such as *Codrington*, which had been undergoing boiler cleaning, were a concern for Ramsay and six of his eight destroyers for anti-invasion duties were sent to the relative safety of Portsmouth. *Codrington*'s bows were later towed to a nearby beach, much to the delight of children who used the wreck as a diving board.

Air raids were also taking a toll on Dover's remaining civilian population. Dogfights were a familiar occurrence. As one local recalled, 'By 1940, when things were really bad, we would go to the Winchelsea area caves for shelter. These caves ran from Winchelsea chalk pit through to the top of Priory Hill while there was an offshoot tunnel that ran to the back of Westmount College in Folkestone Road. These caves, dug out of solid chalk, proved very much a lifesaver over the coming years. Inside the caves there were bunk beds on one side and bench seats on the other, lighted with dull electric lights. But there was no heating.'[9]

The battle of Britain was under way, with the Luftwaffe intent on destroying RAF Fighter Command in southern England. The battle would rage until the end of October. As Hermann Goering's pilots fought for air supremacy, Grand Admiral Raeder was becoming increasingly concerned about his navy's ability to get an invasion fleet across the channel. He told Hitler that more time was needed, ruling out July, then September and eventually suggesting spring 1941. The task was made more difficult after Churchill urged the RAF to carry out heavy bombing raids on the ports where ships and barges were assembling for a crossing. Hitler, in fact, had not underestimated the difficulty of launching a successful invasion of Britain, conceding that Sea Lion would be 'an exceptionally bold and daring undertaking'. He no doubt hoped that the Luftwaffe campaign would force Churchill to come to an agreement without the need to land a huge force. His air force commander, Goering, was confident that a bombing campaign targeting English cities, especially London, would force the issue. But Hitler also had another target in sight, his ally Joseph Stalin and the Soviet Union. The oilfields of the Caucasus were one of the prizes.

In Britain, the fear of invasion remained. The Germans were increasing the number of heavy batteries along the Channel coast and these were a threat to Royal Navy patrols and convoys. Churchill gave orders for improved artillery positions in the Dover area, with guns capable of firing across the Channel. During these anxious summer months, he visited Ramsay at the castle several times. The prime minister regarded the vice admiral as a friend and remembered seeing him often as a boy at barracks in Aldershot during his service as a young officer in the 4th Hussars. At that time, Ramsay's father was colonel of the regiment.[10]

Dover, of course, was not the only focus. From July to September there was a remarkable build-up of the country's defences, helped by arms shipments from the United States and high output from armaments factories at home. In August, five infantry divisions were available for the defence of the south coast, with a possible reserve of three divisions. By the following month, there were 13 divisions, plus three armoured divisions. They were capable of acting at 'great speed', as Churchill and Brooke had advocated, and were in addition to local defence forces.

Britain may have been in peril, but there were still everyday practicalities, such as eating, as Ramsay pointed out to his wife, 'Alas, the tomatoes never reached us as the GPO [General Post Office] have written to say that the parcel was leaking juices so badly that it was damaging other parcels and on opening they found all the tomatoes were squashed. So the valiant attempt to feed me has failed and isn't worth repeating, so far as tomatoes are concerned.' He added, 'I hope you were pleased with the chocolates. I had a good day in London and saw a lot of people … did a lot of satisfactory business at the Admiralty.' Ramsay had lunch with Brooke and got 'most interesting' insights on what happened in France after the German breakthrough in the wake of Dunkirk. 'If it hadn't been for him it's highly improbable that the Lowland Division, which includes the Territorial KOSB [King's Own Scottish Borderers] would have got out at all. The whole thing was political and the French generals were callously proposing to carry out a project which they knew to be absolutely hopelessly unsound. Brooke refused to cooperate under those conditions and it was only after a heated conversation of the terms with Winston that he persuaded the latter to agree to the withdrawal of our divisions.'[11]

Later in August Ramsay told his wife about the air war, which was 'too wonderful for words and should have seriously interfered with Hitler's programme. I've been trying to think out some logical reading of his plans and it's not easy. Either he started his air blitzkrieg to bring about the destruction of our main fighter force by the date set down for invasion, and to put out of action all the aerodromes in the area chosen for the landings to take place. Or he started it just as an air war to devastate the country and demoralise the people. I incline to the former view. If I am right, then he has failed to achieve destruction of our fighters, and on the other hand has incurred considerable damage, material and morale, to his own air force. So if he intends still to proceed with his invasion plan he must conserve his air force for the chosen date. But obviously this will be a very difficult proposition. Likely periods are early next week and about 7th–10th September. So it will be interesting to see what his air action will be in the next few days, i.e. whether he continues his attacks or stops except for small raids.'[12]

On 1 September, the Observer Corps reported that the wave of German bombers and fighters passing over Dover was five miles long. The planes were on their way to attack RAF bases and the London docks. Dover was not spared and Ramsay noted that 23 barrage balloons were shot down. By the afternoon, 15 had been replaced but in the evening a further 12 were destroyed.

A week later Ramsay wrote to his wife Margaret, 'Things have advanced rapidly since my last letter and there is every indication now that invasion is intended and that it will come in the next few days, possibly even before you get this. So we must brace ourselves for the avalanche and all that will accompany it, and trust that everywhere the attack will be defeated and the Huns driven out or captured.

'It will be a frightful struggle, with the whole German air force operating in support, near or far. By this day next week we shall know the result and will, we hope, be able to celebrate a great victory. This is going to be an anxious time for you, darling, and I wish I could be with you to hold your hand, but everybody is in a like position and each has got to bear his or her burden bravely. I shall make myself think of the peace and quiet of

Bughtrig and the happiness we all have had there together, and look forward to resuming life there with you and the children.

'I had the Duke of Kent here on Friday for an hour, on his round of visits to air force stations. He was very pleasant. He said that the King had wanted to come to Dover but he was not allowed, quite rightly.'[13]

On reflection, Ramsay was relieved that he had been forced to retire after falling out with Admiral Backhouse because he ended up spending four happy years at Bughtrig, which left him mentally and physically refreshed when the call came to return to service. As Rear Admiral W. S. Chalmers observed, 'The four years of happy home life had mellowed and strengthened him, increasing his sense of proportion, clarity of mind and physical stamina. Had he remained on the active list it is possible that he might have driven himself too hard, and might well have found himself burnt out in a high ranking but less important shore command.'[14]

Several days after telling Margaret of his invasion fears, he had lunch at the castle with Churchill, who had been inspecting coastal defences with a party of senior officers, including the First Sea Lord, Admiral of the Fleet Pound, and Brooke. 'The PM was in very good form but realises the frailty of the situation,' Ramsay noted. 'Ismay, who goes everywhere with him, told me that he went and saw the poor people's battered houses in the East End [of London] and the people went wild with enthusiasm. Stopped his car, pulled him out, patted him on the back and gave him a marvellous reception. They said, "Good old Winnie, we knew you'd come. Go on, give them hell and we'll stick it. Don't worry about us." The PM was so overcome that he shed copious tears. It was most inspiring. I should have shed them just to see it happening. Everywhere the people collected and cheered him.'[15]

Ramsay was impressed with the behaviour of his large contingent of Wrens during air attacks. 'They drive their cars about in the most exposed places during raids and bombardments and take it all as a matter of course.' But he gave orders that Wren cypher officers were not to relieve one another if there were attacks. On one occasion, two of them were spotted running to the cypher office covered in chalk. One explained that they were hurrying to relieve colleagues who had not had any tea or supper. And why were they covered in chalk? 'Well, a salvo has just struck the cliff below us – but don't tell the admiral!' On another occasion Ramsay went to the cypher office and found the Wrens knitting. He was told there was 'nothing to do at the moment' so it was either knitting or telling naughty stories. He told them to carry on knitting.[16]

According to Churchill, 15 September was the crux of the battle of Britain, with the Luftwaffe carrying out its heaviest daylight raid on London. That evening, the prime minister, who had been at the headquarters of No 11 Fighter Group in Uxbridge, Middlesex, was informed that 183 enemy planes were shot down for the loss of fewer than 40 aircraft (post-war information would put the enemy's losses that day at 56). Bomber Command was busy pounding shipping in ports from Boulogne to Antwerp. Two days later, Hitler decided to delay *Sea Lion*, which was postponed until July 1941 and then the spring of 1942. Before that spring Raeder persuaded Hitler to drop the operation completely.

On the day that Hitler delayed the invasion, Ramsay was passing on his view to his wife: 'Well here we are, the 17th, and yet no invasion. Not that it implies it is not coming but only that preparations were not completed when the bad weather set in two days ago. It would seem that merchant vessels and barges sufficient to convey an enormous force are now distributed where they are required and now it is just a question of waiting until the weather is suitable. They will want several days fine weather and not just one or two, or they will have their initial landing force cut off without supplies, which would be grand from our point of view.'

The battle of Britain was effectively over by the end of October 1940. Although Fighter Command suffered heavy losses, the Luftwaffe lost more planes, a ratio of around two to one. A high level of aircraft production and intensive pilot training helped to boost the RAF. Luftwaffe tactics switched to the Blitz, the largely night-time bombing of London and other cities such as Bristol, Portsmouth, Coventry, Glasgow and Cardiff. These raids caused widespread destruction and heavy civilian casualties, with some 43,000 killed and 139,000 wounded.

In Berwickshire, with her two children, Ramsay's wife was a world away from the horrors of war. In one of his letters, Ramsay wrote, 'I hope that you are able to manage that great horse box – it must be a beast to drive and I hope that you've got someone to accompany you.' Towards the end of the letter, he added, 'I hope you've enjoyed your mornings out with the hounds on Starlight and that you've got over your stiffness. How have the hounds been doing and who else has been out?'[17] Perhaps the vice admiral was feeling homesick.

After Dunkirk, the threat of invasion was not the only immediate concern of Churchill and his military leaders. A major worry was the French navy, a significant force that could not be allowed to fall into German hands. In

June, before France agreed to an armistice, the commander-in-chief of the navy, Admiral of the Fleet Francois Darlan, had given an assurance that this would not happen. There was the option of sailing all his ships to British, American or French colonial harbours. But when Petain formed a government, Darlan agreed to serve as minister of marine and he changed his mind about cooperating.

The ships were in different locations. Two battleships, four cruisers, eight destroyers, several submarines and other vessels were already at Portsmouth and Plymouth after leaving northern French ports before they fell. At Portsmouth, Admiral James, who had masterminded the Le Havre evacuation, arranged for 1,000 leaflets to be printed explaining that the ships would not be allowed to return to France but the crews could choose whether to fight with Britain or go home. Boarding parties, made up of 1,000 sailors, 500 marines and an infantry battalion, distributed the leaflets. The plan went 'without a hitch'. James recorded, 'There was no trouble; most of the officers and sailors looked very cheerful as they marched to the assembly point in the dockyard; for them a period of tension was ended and they knew where they were.' Many of the men elected to fight on in the Free French Navy.[18]

A battleship, four cruisers and other ships were at Alexandria in Egypt, under the watchful eyes of the British. There were also vessels at Algiers, Casablanca, Toulon and Martinique. The battleship *Richelieu* was at Dakar, Senegal. But as far as the British were concerned, the most important ships were at the Algerian port of Oran, Mers-el-Kébir. They included the modern battlecruisers *Dunkerque* and *Strasbourg*, which Churchill regarded as 'much superior' to the German *Scharnhorst* and *Gneisenau*. There were also two battleships, several light cruisers and a number of destroyers and submarines. If the Germans or Italians seized these vessels, it would have seriously compromised the balance of naval power in the Mediterranean.

On 1 July, the Admiralty instructed Vice Admiral Somerville, in command of Force H at Gibraltar, to prepare for Operation *Catapult* on 3 July. Somerville's fleet, comprising the battlecruiser HMS *Hood*, battleships HMS *Valiant* and HMS *Resolution*, aircraft carrier HMS *Ark Royal*, two cruisers and 11 destroyers, sailed for Mers-el-Kébir. Somerville was keen to avoid force, but the Admiralty told him, 'Firm intention of HMG that if French will not accept any of your alternatives they are to be destroyed.'[19]

The French commander, Admiral Marcel-Bruno Gensoul, was given four options: put to sea and join British forces; sail with reduced crews to any British port; sail with reduced crews to a French West Indies port; or scuttle his ships. Gensoul, who objected to dealing with a French-speaking Royal

Navy officer who was only a captain, allowed negotiations to drag on, and Somerville reluctantly gave the order to attack. The battleship *Bretagne* was blown up in the action, and *Dunkerque*, the battleship *Provence* and the destroyer *Mogador* were all damaged and then run aground by their crews. The bombardment killed 1,297 Frenchmen for the loss of five aircraft and two crewmen. *Strasbourg* managed to escape to Toulon. On 8 July, Swordfish torpedo bombers from *Ark Royal* mounted another raid on Mers-el-Kébir and *Dunkerque* was badly damaged.

Richelieu was damaged at Dakar during Operation *Menace* in September. British and Free French forces had attempted to seize the strategic port but met stiffer Vichy resistance than expected. The failure was a bitter blow for de Gaulle, who led the Free French. Britain had agreed to support the operation because it wanted to protect trade routes off west Africa and to show its backing for de Gaulle. One of the Royal Navy's casualties was *Resolution*, badly damaged after a torpedo attack.

Not surprisingly, the attack on Mers-el-Kébir was widely criticised in France. Churchill had his own view, 'The elimination of the French navy as an important factor almost at a single stroke by violent action produced a profound impression in every country. Here was this Britain which so many had counted down and out, which strangers had supposed to be quivering on the brink of surrender to the mighty power arrayed against her, striking ruthlessly at her dearest friends of yesterday and securing for a while to herself the undisputed command of the sea. It was made plain that the British War Cabinet feared nothing and would stop at nothing.'[20]

Ramsay's view: 'The Dakar business was really most unfortunate and has set back the Free France movement, which up to then had not been going too badly.'[21] (On 27 November 1942, the Germans tried to seize the French fleet at Toulon but most of it was scuttled. A total of 75 vessels were destroyed, including *Strasbourg*.)

One of Ramsay's concerns in August 1940 was the morale of crews manning anti-submarine and minesweeping trawlers at Dover. Most of the men were civilians, including milkmen, tailors and farmhands, who had received only basic training. Crews were on constant alert during patrols, facing the danger of attack from the air, E-boats and enemy coastal bases with long-range weapons. Even in harbour, men were unable to get enough rest because of air raids and warnings.

Ramsay told the Admiralty, 'There is no doubt that the ship's companies of vessels which have been at Dover for any length of time are showing signs of strain, and the number of skippers, mates and ratings who report sick on the grounds of nervous trouble gives rise to anxiety. The senior medical officer informs me that in the majority of cases there is nothing wrong with these men beyond the fact that their morale is not very high and that they are experiencing a kind of fear complex.

'It has to be remembered that the officers and ratings of the patrol service are not a highly disciplined service like the Royal Navy and have not the advantages of trained and long service officers and petty officers to encourage and hold them together, and set an example.'[22]

Ramsay acknowledged that vessels at Dover had suffered considerable casualties in the past three months. Surgeon Lieutenant Gerald Garmany reported that 35 cases had been treated since 1 June, though it was not clear if this covered vessels other than trawlers. Two men were found to be hysterical, one weeping and gnashing his teeth. Three others were psychotic. But when it came to anxiety, Garmany concluded that many cases were 'obvious malingerers'. Of 30 such cases, only eight were over 35 years of age.

The surgeon lieutenant pointed out that civilians with training as little as two weeks had been sent to trawlers to work under very exacting conditions, 'Their team spirit is but ill developed and their sense of discipline is very poor in many cases.' Garmany added, 'This lack of preliminary training seems in these men to leave them in their own hands, some option, between say, firing a gun and scurrying below which they later explain, without any sense of dishonour, by some such phrase as "my nerves went to pieces".' Too much sympathy tended to increase a man's belief that he was being asked to do something beyond endurance. (After the war, Garmany became a prominent psychiatrist at Westminster Hospital and pioneered the removal of patients from long-term incarceration in vast mental asylums.)

Ramsay suggested that vessels should be based at Dover for only three months. He noted, 'The effect of changing station is very largely a psychological one in that men are inclined always to think that they are in the most exposed station and that others are having a better time. The knowledge that change of station is part of a general Admiralty policy, for the benefit of skippers and ships' companies should therefore have a good effect.'[23]

The vice admiral did not hesitate if he thought an officer was not up to the task. The captain in command of the minesweeping trawlers was replaced.[24]

CHAPTER 20

1941

Undoubtedly the year 1940 was intense for Ramsay, but he knew that he had coped well with the demands. He must have wondered what the next 12 months would bring. Britain remained in a perilous position. On a personal note, the New Year began in a promising way, with another spell of leave at Bughtrig. Returning to a foggy and damp Dover was the hard part. Ramsay told his wife, 'Being at home again has made me want to be there more than ever, and it is so difficult to come away and leave all that I love best in life behind.'

It was not long before Churchill took Ramsay's mind off Berwickshire and they faced the task ahead. The prime minister paid another visit to the castle, and after brandy and coffee they went on a two-hour tour of the local defences. This trip came shortly after a key meeting of military chiefs, when Brooke had complained that there were still shortages of rifles, ammunition, armoured cars and tanks. Brooke recorded, 'This did not please Winston at all, and after the meeting he complained to Dill that he considered it most ungrateful of me to complain of lack of equipment after all that had been done for me. Considering the period we had been at war, I consider that I had every right, and indeed it was my duty, to draw attention to the shortages that prevailed.'[1] There was no room for complacency.

Another visitor to Dover Castle was Wendell Willkie, a lawyer who had challenged Franklin D. Roosevelt unsuccessfully in the previous year's US presidential election. Ramsay found Willkie, a former Democrat who became the Republican nomination, talkative and 'quite exhausting'. But he remained a patient listener because his visitor favoured American military support for Britain and would, with yet more political somersaulting, emerge as an ally of Roosevelt. Willkie also had a meeting with Churchill. Ramsay was convinced that the US would enter the war at some stage 'if only they would take the courage and look far enough ahead'.[2]

Visitors aside, Ramsay was kept busy watching over the Dover Strait, orchestrating sea and air patrols, protecting convoys and attacking enemy shipping.

In Dover, there was a constant reminder of war. January 1941 saw the Germans using incendiary bombs for the first time, some 100 falling over a wide area of the town in a single raid, but there was little damage because of swift action by firewatchers. The sound of explosions across the Channel was almost a daily occurrence as the RAF continued to attack ports. The Luftwaffe kept up its attacks on Dover, and in one small area, 118 houses were destroyed and 172 badly damaged. Despite these attacks, morale among civilians and military personnel remained high, with the town's three local cinemas usually packed. A petition for a roller skating venue, signed by hundreds, was sent to the local council, which decided there were higher priorities.[3]

One priority for Ramsay in April was money – the family finances. With his usual attention to detail, he listed for his wife their likely expenditure for the next 12 months (£s):

David's schooling	30
Fuel	100
Telephone	36
Stamps	6
Doctor	25
Chemist	15
Children's clothes	40
Subscriptions	20
Hunt	40
Car petrol and repairs	20
Drink	30
Cigs	25
Your clothes	30
Travelling	15
House repairs	15
Forage	40
Garden	15
Petty cash	20
Presents	10

The total came to £532 and Ramsay added a further £100 for insurance. Against this was income of £670. But once again he was concerned that they would be liable for 'super tax' because Margaret had a private income, and he suggested she put £175 out of every £450 received in a special account and then 'your balance would always be a true statement of how you stand'. There was further advice: 'I wouldn't get rid of an indoor servant.' It seemed that their finances were healthy enough to exclude that possibility, and Ramsay conceded that the aim was to have 'a well balanced household' and 'let's be comfortable'.[4]

On 24 May, the Royal Navy suffered a major blow, when the battleship *Bismarck* sank the battlecruiser *Hood* in the Denmark Strait. The 'Mighty Hood' exploded and disappeared in less than three minutes, and only three of the crew of 1,418 survived. Three days later *Bismarck* was destroyed.

Britain was fighting on several fronts. The battle of the Atlantic was raging as convoys struggled to bring in supplies while U-boats took a heavy toll. Campaigns in the Mediterranean and in North Africa were at crucial stages.

On 17 June, Ramsay was in London and he had lunch with Brooke, who came from a meeting with Churchill and military chiefs. Brooke complained that most of the men at the meeting were 'moth-eaten old admirals'.[5] The general did not include Ramsay in that category. (The outspoken Brooke, in fact, was an admirer and years later he would write, 'Personally I look back on the many contacts I was privileged to have with Ramsay as some of my most cherished memories. His great charm, inspiring personality and the breadth of his outlook placed him in that category of men whom one meets only rarely in a lifetime and whose loss deprives one of an irreplaceable friend.')[6]

That month, in the early hours of 22 June, Hitler abandoned his non-aggression pact with the Soviet Union and gave the order for Operation *Barbarossa* – the invasion of his ally. It had been delayed for about a month because of campaigns in Yugoslavia and in Greece, and that would prove to be costly when the Russian winter intervened. The Germans committed almost 150 divisions, some three million men, and 3,000 tanks and 2,500 aircraft. In addition, there were 30 divisions of Finnish and Romanian troops. But even that vast number would be more than matched by the Soviets. Nevertheless, Stalin and his generals were taken by surprise when the Germans launched their offensive along a 1,800-mile front. With Hitler looking east, it seemed in Britain that Operation *Sea Lion* was a fading possibility, though Ramsay and the other defenders could not afford to relax. Churchill thought that if Germany succeeded in the Soviet Union, then *Sea Lion* would become a priority again.

Brooke's view was that: 'As long as the Germans were engaged in the invasion of Russia there was no possibility of an invasion of these islands. It would now depend on how long Russia could last and what resistance she would be able to put up. My own opinion, and an opinion that was shared by most people, was that Russia would not last long, possibly three or four months, possibly slightly longer. Putting it at four months, it certainly looked as if Germany would be unable to launch an invasion of England until October, and by then the weather and winter would be against any such enterprise.

'It therefore looked as if we should be safe from invasion during 1941. This would put me in the position of devoting the whole of my energies towards converting the defence forces of this island into a thoroughly efficient army capable of undertaking overseas operations if and when such operations became possible.'[7]

Churchill was staggered that the Soviets had allowed the Balkans to be overrun by Germany, failing to realise that Hitler was about to launch the biggest land invasion in history. The leaders in Moscow had been seen as calculating, but they were now being shown up as 'simpletons'. The pact conjured up by Vyacheslav Molotov and Joachim von Ribbentrop in 1939 had allowed Stalin to embark on a campaign of aggression, much like Hitler. The Soviets quickly occupied eastern Poland, Estonia, Lithuania, part of eastern Finland and eastern Romania. It is perhaps surprising how quickly Churchill offered help to the duplicitous Stalin. But the priority was to fight Nazi Germany.[8] Britain, alone in the first half of 1941, now had a new ally, Hitler's former conspirator, Stalin. In August, Britain sent its first Arctic convoy of military aid, which arrived at Archangel.

As Ramsay had forecast, the United States entered the war, provoked by the Japanese air attack on Pearl Harbor on 7 December, which took a heavy toll on the US Navy. There were also coordinated strikes on the US-held Philippines and Guam, and Britain faced a new and unwanted front after the Japanese also targeted Malaya, Singapore and Hong Kong. As Ramsay pointed out, 'Our position in the Far East, and elsewhere, has been made very difficult.'[9]

Ramsay was scathing about the lack of defence at Pearl Harbor: 'The more I hear about the disaster the less I can understand this complete unpreparedness. It was quite criminal in the circumstances. I should say that sooner or later Japan will gain the Philippines and northern Malaya, cutting our route to Singapore except from the south. Hong Kong will last out a long time but the question of its relief will be a most difficult one. It is unfortunate that the Japs should have set us back in this way in view of the fact that elsewhere things are going so much more in our favour. In Russia the Germans do actually seem to be on the run.'[10]

Hong Kong, in fact, did not hold out for long, with British forces surrendering on Christmas Day. Malaya fell to the Japanese on 31 January

1942 and Singapore on 14 February. The Philippines were eventually seized in May.

The loss of *Hood* in May 1941 had shocked the Royal Navy. There would be an even greater shock in the December. For some time, Britain had been aware of the threat from Japan. After much discussion at the Admiralty, and at Churchill's urging, the battleship HMS *Prince of Wales*, which had been involved in the action that saw *Hood* sunk, and the battlecruiser HMS *Repulse* were sent to the Far East to act as a deterrent. The ships were at Singapore and designated Force Z when Pearl Harbor was attacked. Tom Phillips, a newly promoted acting admiral and in command of Force Z, received reports that a Japanese invasion force was heading for the coast of north-east Malaya and he set sail with his two capital ships and four destroyers as an escort. There should have been an aircraft carrier but none was available.

Force Z failed to find the Japanese invaders and Admiral Phillips decided to return to Singapore. Early on 10 December, he received a report of an enemy landing at Kuantan, about halfway between Singapore and Kota Bharu in the north, and went off course to investigate, only to find that the information was false. It was a fateful decision. By this time, the Japanese had located the ships and waves of planes, including torpedo bombers, attacked *Prince of Wales* and *Repulse*, which were both sunk with heavy loss of life.

Captain W. S. Roskill, the official naval historian, would comment, 'Any previous doubts regarding the efficiency of the Japanese air force had been dispelled in no uncertain manner, for the attacks had been most skilfully carried out. At trifling cost to themselves they had, by sinking two capital ships at sea, accomplished what no other air force had yet achieved – and they had accomplished the feat at a distance of some 400 miles from their bases.'[11]

The role of Admiral Phillips has long been controversial. He badly under-estimated the potential of the Japanese air force, even reportedly remarking as the first attackers came within sight that he doubted the enemy had torpedo aircraft.[12] RAF cover would have been available when the ships were off Kuantan but Phillips made no such request. *Repulse*, which sank first, did ask for cover but it was made nearly an hour after the first enemy planes appeared. Ten Buffalo fighters of the Royal Australian Air Force arrived on the scene as *Prince of Wales* disappeared. Phillips went down with the ship.

Ramsay was at the Admiralty when he heard 'the staggering news of the loss of *P of W* and *Repulse*, which constitutes quite one of the worst disasters we have had to face. I'm not quite happy about the way in which they were lost as I don't think Tom Phillips has ever appreciated the fact that ships are as vulnerable as they are to aircraft attack when in waters in which the enemy have air superiority. Had James Somerville been in his place I can't see him doing what Tom Phillips did, neither would I. But the initial mistake was the *P o W* out there at all and anyway without an aircraft carrier. Tom Phillips has always been a protégé of Winston who gave him the job. He has no sea experience in this or the last war and is a fine theorist, or was poor chap, and I think it was an undesirable appointment as do many others.'[13]

Somerville was a fierce critic of Phillips and in October had warned that sending *Prince of Wales* to the Far East was 'a great mistake'. After learning of the disaster he told his wife, 'As you know I always express my doubts about the advisability of sending out someone who had no personal experience of the war at sea. Tom P has always been an advocate of pushing on regardless of the consequences and I imagine that on this occasion he hoped to catch the Japanese party landing in N Malaya. But it was obvious they would be covered with shore-based air from Thailand and I should think it very doubtful indeed if we could provide shore-based fighter support to those two ships. I personally would not have dreamt of taking two battleships like that without adequate air and sea support. In any case *Repulse* was a most unsuitable ship – I refused to have her in the Western Med because she had not been modernised and lacked proper A/A equipment. Altogether a deplorable and tragic business.'[14]

Later, Somerville told Admiral Sir Andrew Cunningham, Commander-in-Chief, Mediterranean, 'The *Prince of Wales* and *Repulse* affair seems to have been a thoroughly bad show. No air support, but in any case fancy relying on quite untried shore-based air for cover! Why the hell didn't they send someone out there who has been through the mill and knew his stuff.'[15]

Churchill had a rather different view of events, recording, 'In judging the actions of Admiral Phillips during these calamitous days it should be emphasised that there were sound reasons for his belief that his intended attack on Kuantan would be outside the effective range of enemy shore-based torpedo bombers, *which were his chief anxiety* [author's italics], and that he would only have to deal with hastily organised strikes by ordinary long-range bombers during his retirement.'

The prime minister admitted that the loss of *Prince of Wales* and *Repulse* was his greatest shock in the war.[16]

CHAPTER 21

The Great Escape

For nearly a year, the Royal Navy and the RAF had been keeping a close watch on the German battlecruisers *Scharnhorst* and *Gneisenau*, which had taken refuge at Brest in north-west France after attacks on shipping in the Atlantic. The cruiser *Prinz Eugen* also went to Brest following the loss of *Bismarck* in May 1941.

The RAF made a total of 47 bombing raids on the port. Reconnaissance showed that in 1941, from the end of July until mid-December, all the ships entered dry dock at some stage. It was reported that each vessel had received direct hits – *Gneisenau* eight, *Scharnhorst* six and *Prinz Eugen* three. But by 1 February 1942, all the ships were out of dry dock and apparently seaworthy, and it was thought that they would attempt to leave Brest. Hitler, in fact, had given orders that he did not want the ships to remain there as targets. Two destroyers, five torpedo boats and eight minesweepers arrived at the port, an indication that an escort force was being built up. This would become Operation *Cerberus* – the Channel Dash.

The Admiralty believed there were several options for the ships – head out to the Atlantic, sail to the Mediterranean or return to German waters going north around Britain or simply using Ramsay's Dover Strait. The last course was thought the most likely because Force H would be at Gibraltar, covering the Mediterranean, and the Home Fleet was in northern waters.

The Admiralty and the Air Ministry produced a plan, Operation *Fuller*, to deal with an escape using the Channel. Ramsay thought that the Germans would try to sail through the Dover Strait in darkness. On 3 February 1942, six destroyers armed with torpedoes were placed at four hours' notice in the Thames estuary to intercept the enemy. These ships were under Ramsay's orders, as were eight MTBs and six Swordfish torpedo bombers of the Fleet Air Arm's 825 Squadron. The submarine HMS *Sealion* joined two other boats patrolling off Brest. Between 3 and 9 February, minelayers sowed about 1,000 contact and magnetic mines in six fields between Ushant and Boulogne.

On the RAF's part, Coastal Command, Bomber Command and Fighter Command's No 11 Group were alerted. Coastal Command organised night patrols to cover the entrance to Brest, the line between Ushant and Île de Bréhat, and the area from Le Havre to Boulogne. No 11 Group and Ramsay arranged that after dawn fighter aircraft would carry out reconnaissance of the Channel between Ostend and the mouth of the Somme. These were known as 'Jim Crow' patrols.

Early on 12 February, two Spitfires spotted E-boats heading south from Boulogne. Radar plots also picked up enemy aircraft circling over specific areas. The enemy made a concerted effort to jam the radar chain. Later that morning, a Spitfire spotted 20 to 30 vessels west of Le Touquet. The pilot was forbidden from using radio contact during reconnaissance and reported the sighting after returning to base at Hawkinge, north of Folkestone. His report was passed to Ramsay. But confirmation that the German capital ships were at sea came from another pilot, Group Captain George Beamish, who was not involved in the reconnaissance operation. Beamish and another pilot were attacking two Messerschmitts – 'a Hun straffing expedition' – when *Scharnhorst* and *Gneisenau* were spotted by chance. Beamish returned to his base at 1109 and made his report, which was passed on.[1]

Because of the suspicious radar plots, the air staff officer at Ramsay's headquarters had already decided to warn Lieutenant Commander Eugene Esmonde, in command of the six Swordfish at Manston, Kent, that there might be possible targets. The previous day Esmonde had been at Buckingham Palace to receive the Distinguished Service Order for his part in the sinking of *Bismarck*. On 24 May 1941, despite bad weather, he led nine Swordfish in a night attack on the battleship, scoring one direct torpedo hit on the starboard side.

Ramsay reported, 'Immediately it was established that the battlecruisers were present I ordered the MTB striking force to proceed from Dover and Ramsgate and the destroyers to come to immediate notice. The latter were found to be at sea exercising – a fortunate circumstance in view of the short warning – and they were at once ordered to proceed in execution of previous orders. The commander, corps coast artillery, was informed of the situation and given permission to open fire unhampered by consideration of the movement of our coastal craft.'[2]

Fighter Command's No 11 Group and Coastal Command's No 16 Group were contacted and it was arranged that an escort for the Swordfish would be provided so that a coordinated attack could take place at the earliest moment.

There would be five fighter squadrons from No 11 Group and Beaufort torpedo bombers from No 16 Group. The rendezvous was fixed for 1225 over Manston. But this gave the fighter squadrons little time for briefing, take-off and flight to the Kent base. In the event, only one squadron of 10 fighters made the rendezvous – at 1228. Lieutenant Commander Esmonde decided he could not delay his departure and the Swordfish set off.

'This was not known in my operations room,' Ramsay recorded. 'That the plan to escort the Swordfish miscarried must be counted as a major tragedy, as it gave practically no hope of success or of survival to the Swordfish who had to face a sky full of enemy fighters, as well as very heavy flak from the destroyer screen and the capital ships themselves.'[3]

The target was thought to be about 10 miles north of Calais, and the Swordfish flew in two flights of three, with Esmonde leading. One problem was the slow speed of the Swordfish, 80mph against the 250mph of their escorting Spitfires. Enemy planes soon appeared and the Spitfires engaged them. Esmonde pressed on but all the Swordfish faced 'incessant fighter attacks', most of them receiving damage. The capital ships were spotted and the Swordfish flew through flak from a screen of destroyers and E-boats. Esmonde's plane was badly damaged and he almost lost control but recovered and kept closing on the ships. When about 3,000 yards away he was hit again and crashed into the sea.

The air gunner in the second Swordfish was killed by machine-gun fire and the observer, Sub Lieutenant Edgar Lee, tried to take over the gun but could not move the body. The third plane was badly hit and the pilot, Sub Lieutenant Pat Kingsmill, and the observer, Sub Lieutenant Reginald Samples, were wounded. The engine and the upper-port wing caught fire as the air gunner continued to engage enemy fighters. Kingsmill managed to keep control of the plane long enough to aim his torpedo at one of the large ships from under 3,000 yards. He kept flying until the engine cut out and the plane crashed into the sea. All three crew were rescued by an MTB.

The second Swordfish was attacked again and the pilot, Sub Lieutenant Brian Rose, severely wounded in the back. He held his course but a further attack burst the petrol tank, and fumes affected the pilot and the observer. With the engine faltering, Rose decided to drop his torpedo, aiming for one of the large ships at a range of about 2,000 yards. After turning past the destroyer screen, the plane crashed into the sea. Lee helped Rose out of the aircraft and, after a struggle in the water, managed to get him into their dinghy. The observer also tried to release the body of the gunner but the plane sank. They were found by MTBs about 90 minutes later.[4]

The three Swordfish of the second flight were last seen heading towards the capital ships. They never returned and there were no survivors. Ramsay stated, 'In my opinion the gallant sortie of these six Swordfish constitutes one of the finest exhibitions of self sacrifice and devotion to duty that this war has yet witnessed.'[5] Esmonde was awarded a posthumous Victoria Cross and the 12 others who died were all Mentioned in Despatches. The five survivors were also decorated. All the Swordfish were lost and none of their torpedoes found a target.

The five MTBs at Dover, under the command of Lieutenant Commander Edward Pumphrey, had cleared the harbour at 1155 and the enemy were sighted at 1223. One boat broke down and the others were 'all over the shop' because of air attacks. And the E-boat screen proved formidable. The battlecruisers were at a distance of about 5,000 yards and Pumphrey's torpedoes had a range of 5,500 yards.

Pumphrey stated, 'The problem then was to have a crack at the E-boat screen, there were twelve, with all the four boats, or whether to fire from outside the screen and I consider I made the wrong decision. I altered course to do so. I immediately had a breakdown of my centre engine and starboard engine and the speed came down to about fifteen knots. In the circumstances I thought to try to go through the screen was absolutely daft. I should only lose my tubes and probably my boat before I got the range down appreciably so I closed to about 400 yards from the E-boats. I fired the first fish about 800 yards and the second one about 400 yards from the E-boats under fairly heavy fire and then withdrew. The other boats did the same thing and I think they were quite right not to go through the screen. To have gone through with our slow boats and poorer gunfire and outnumbered three to one we should merely be blasted out of the water.'[6]

The MTBs had a maximum speed of 27 knots against the E-boats 40 knots. The fifth MTB overcame its engine problems and manoeuvring to the rear of the E-boats fired its torpedoes at *Prinz Eugen* at a distance of about 3,000 yards. None of the torpedoes from the five MTBs resulted in hits. The Ramsgate MTBs encountered engine trouble and returned to harbour after losing sight of the enemy in deteriorating weather.

Torpedo and bombing attacks by the RAF met with failure. Coastal Command had 36 Beaufort torpedo bombers at three bases, Thorney Island, near Portsmouth, St Eval, Cornwall, and Leuchars, Fife. The seven bombers at Thorney Island were nearest to the German ships but only four were in an advanced state of readiness and they set off for Manston to pick up a fighter escort. Confusion reigned and the four Beauforts, without fighters, failed to make coordinated attacks. The remaining three bombers attacked later in poor visibility and one was shot down. Torpedoes were launched but none found targets.

There were 14 Beauforts at Leuchars, but only nine carried out the mission because three of the planes did not have torpedoes and two bombers suffered engine failure. The nine rendezvoused with Hudson bombers, two of which were shot down. The 12 Beauforts from St Eval failed to find the enemy as darkness fell and two of the planes did not return.

Bomber Command launched some 240 bombers in successive waves during the afternoon, but poor visibility prevented the use of high-level attacks with armour-piercing bombs; the only effective way of seriously damaging the capital ships. General-purpose bombs were of limited value but it was hoped that using them would draw the enemy's attention away from the torpedo attacks. Little if any damage was inflicted on the ships and 15 bombers were lost.

Fighter Command also was heavily involved that day, deploying nearly 400 planes. Many dogfights took place as the RAF tried to protect the attacking force. Seventeen planes were lost. A similar number of enemy fighters were reportedly downed.[7]

The six destroyers under Ramsay's orders were HMS *Campbell* and HMS *Vivacious* of the 21st Flotilla, and HMS *Mackay*, HMS *Whitshed*, HMS *Worcester* and HMS *Walpole* of the 16th Flotilla. All were ageing ships and normally used for convoy work on the east coast. Ramsay's original plan was based on a night attack in the strait, and a daylight attack by destroyers on such a formidable force was a huge risk. Nevertheless, Ramsay had no choice that day. His destroyers were based at Harwich, not Dover, so that they could quickly reach what he thought was the best area for an attack. Ramsay reasoned, 'There was the hope that one or more of the enemy ships might have been damaged by mines or torpedoes before reaching it. Further westward in the strait or its approaches they would have been hindered by our own minefields and the numerous and powerful enemy shore batteries.'[8] At 1156 on 12 February, after getting Admiralty approval, Ramsay gave Captain Charles Pizey in *Campbell* the order to intercept the enemy.

The battlecruisers' speed had been estimated at 20 knots, but at 1300, Ramsay informed Pizey that it was much greater. Pizey decided his only hope of catching up with the enemy was to go across minefields and head to a position off the mouth of the River Scheldt, which the destroyers safely did, but *Walpole* was forced to return to harbour with engine trouble. The ships avoided several bombing attacks, including one by an RAF Hampden.

At 1517, *Campbell's* radar picked up two large ships at a range of nine and a half miles. Visibility had dropped from seven miles to four miles, which favoured the destroyers. At 1543, *Scharnhorst* and *Gneisenau* were sighted off the Dutch coast and the Germans opened fire. At 3,500 yards, Pizey decided his luck would not hold for much longer and *Campbell* and *Vivacious* fired their torpedoes. *Worcester* got closer at 2,400 yards but was badly damaged by enemy salvoes and set on fire. All five destroyers fired their torpedoes. There were no hits. *Worcester* managed to limp home.

Pizey reported, 'Gunnery conditions throughout were extremely difficult owing to the high speed and frequent alterations of course in the heavy swell. Seas were breaking green fore and aft and there was continuous spray over the bridge. Conditions for training the torpedo tubes were equally difficult. In *Campbell* the crew of Y gun were at times knee deep in water and the gunlayer at A gun was removed from his seat and thrown across the forecastle, while the engineer officer was washed through the guardrails and only saved himself by clutching a passing stanchion. These were only a few of the many similar incidents which occurred in all ships, and give some indication of the difficulties experienced.'[9]

Captain John Wright in *Mackay* told of the 'extraordinary' mixture of aircraft during the operation. 'Many of the enemy aircraft obviously thought we were friendly while a few of our own aircraft made it evident that they considered us hostile,' Wright reported. 'We on our part opened fire on several occasions on aircraft later recognised as friendly. The aircraft of both sides must have found the situation very confusing. We were fortunate in being attacked by Dorniers and Heinkels only and not by Junkers dive-bombers.'[10]

The escape of the capital ships, commanded by Vice Admiral Otto Ciliax, was a blow for Ramsay, as he admitted, 'The failure to inflict loss or serious damage on the enemy during his passage of the strait is very much felt in my command.' He noted, 'The main factor which influenced all operations was the failure to detect the enemy at daylight. Had the enemy ships been sighted then there would have been ample time to set the main air striking forces in motion so that they could make their attacks in the narrow waters of the Dover Strait, where the maximum advantage could have been derived from our numerical and tactical air superiority, combined with an accurate knowledge of the enemy's position from the RDF [radar] plot.'[11]

Remarkably, the Germans had been at sea for 12 hours before they were spotted. Churchill conceded that the escape of the capital ships through the English Channel in daylight 'astonished' the British public. Even *The Times* was scathing: 'Vice Admiral Ciliax has succeeded where the Duke of Medina

Sidonia failed: with trifling losses he has sailed a hostile fleet from an Atlantic harbour up the English Channel, and through the Strait of Dover to safe anchorage in a North Sea port. Nothing more mortifying to the pride of sea power has happened in home waters since the 17th century.'[12]

Such was the concern that the First Lord of the Admiralty, A. V. Alexander, wrote to the Secretary of State for Air, Sir Archibald Sinclair, on 13 February saying he was 'very much disturbed' by the escape and suggesting that a joint inquiry be set up immediately. That day the Vice Chief of the Air Staff, Air Vice Marshal Norman Bottomley, received a memo about the whereabouts of two key commanders on the previous day. The head of Fighter Command, Air Chief Marshal Sir William Sholto Douglas, had been at Northolt air base in Middlesex attending 'some special Belgian squadron function'. The head of Coastal Command, Air Chief Marshal Sir Philip Joubert de la Ferté, was at the Admiralty. He then went to the Air Ministry and did not leave for his headquarters until about 1330. The memo pointed out: 'The SASOs [Senior Air Staff Officers] at Fighter and Coastal Commands were therefore in charge of operations during the critical morning period.'[13]

Mr Justice Bucknill was soon appointed to lead a board of inquiry, whose other members were Vice Admiral Sir Thomas Binney, Air Chief Marshal Sir Edgar Ludlow-Hewitt and two officials from the Admiralty and the Air Ministry.

Evidence to the board revealed that air patrols on the night of 11–12 February had encountered problems with their detection equipment and there were gaps in reconnaissance. The first flight returned to base after an equipment fault, which was later shown to be only a blown fuse. One patrol was described as 'useless', and an aircraft that returned to base was not replaced. The first daylight patrol missed the big ships because it was too far to the west of the area covered. The board came to the conclusion that the detection equipment was only 50 per cent reliable 'in the best circumstances'. Night patrols were difficult, especially when it came to visual contact, but the enemy ships should have been spotted in daylight earlier than they were. No. 11 (Fighter) Group, responsible for the 'Jim Crow' patrols, was criticised for not investigating radar plots indicating that enemy aircraft were circling over specific areas and that 'something unusual was afoot'.[14]

The failure to detect the enemy earlier resulted in attacks lacking coordination. The board reported, 'It seems to us that the weak forces available needed a carefully coordinated plan for concerted action if they were to have any reasonable prospect of crippling one or more of the battlecruisers.' The board found there was no evidence of a lack of cooperation between the various commands. 'In the event it is not surprising that those in command of the various striking forces were more concerned to delay the enemy in any way possible by immediate attacks with any forces available than to risk losing the opportunity in the effort to arrange coordinated attacks.'[15]

Although Bomber Command sent a large force, it played 'a comparatively ineffective, if gallant, part in the battle'. This was largely due to the weather conditions. But the inquiry pointed out that Bomber Command crews had received little training in attacking fast-moving warships. The enemy had shown how effective dive-bombers could be against armoured ships at sea and in harbour. As Captain Wright of the destroyer *Mackay* had noted, the enemy plane most feared was the Junkers dive-bomber.

The inquiry also suggested that MTBs needed improvements to match the speed and armament of E-boats. One of the main conclusions: 'Apart from the weakness of our forces the main reason for our failure to do more damage to the enemy was the fact that his presence was not detected earlier, and this again was due to the breakdown of the night patrols and omission to send out a strong morning reconnaissance.' Tribute was paid to the 'countless acts of gallantry' later in the day.[16]

The inquiry's witnesses included Vice Admiral Ramsay, the heads of Coastal Command and Fighter Command, and Air Vice Marshal Trafford Leigh-Mallory of No 11 (Fighter) Group.

On 17 February, Air Chief Marshal de la Ferté made a serious allegation to the Secretary of State for Air. He accused Ramsay of sacrificing the Swordfish crews. He telephoned the minister that evening and the following message was recorded in a 'most secret' memo: 'Vice Admiral Dover did not fully cooperate with us in this action in that he dispatched his six Swordfish on his own initiative and was unwilling to fit their action into the general plan. Had he done so, they would probably not have suffered so severe casualties.

'When, some ten days or so ago, Rear Admiral, Naval Air Services, placed these Swordfish at the disposal of Vice Admiral Dover, C-in-C wrote to the Admiralty and telephoned the Director of Home Operations there stressing how important it was that any operations by these aircraft should be coordinated with the operations of Coastal Command. He was given an assurance that this would be done.

'C-in-C Coastal Command does not particularly wish to raise this point, but he feels that you and VCAS [Vice Chief of the Air Staff] would like to have this knowledge available in case any charges of non-cooperation be levelled against us.'[17]

In view of this allegation, it seems odd that the board of inquiry found there was no evidence of a lack of cooperation between the various commands.

In his report of the enemy's escape, Ramsay stated that the departure of the Swordfish from Manston 'was not known in my operations room'. At the inquiry the vice admiral was asked whether it had been possible to stage a combined attack with the Swordfish and the MTBs and he replied, 'I was so anxious not to hold anything back that I would put no restrictions on anything. My idea was to get everything off as quickly as possible because we had not got the warning we had hoped to get.' The First Sea Lord had told Ramsay, 'The navy will attack the enemy whenever and wherever he is to be found.'[18]

Ramsay was also questioned why the Swordfish did not have the arranged escort of five fighter squadrons. He replied, 'I was promised those but in actual fact they took off with one squadron because the others did not arrive in time. I understand that it is the custom of the RAF that if a squadron, an escort does not arrive at the time it is arranged to be over its rendezvous the bombers do not proceed, but it is fair to say on this occasion being Fleet Air Arm aircraft they were not accustomed to work with the RAF and it is quite possible that Lieutenant Commander Esmonde was not aware he had not got all his escort.' He added, 'I think he must have been impatient to get away. One cannot say any more than that because there was no survivor on his plane but knowing him and everyone who knows him feels sure that must be the case.'[19]

Ramsay pointed out to the inquiry that his operations room had been busy reporting to a large number of air authorities, as well as the Admiralty. It would have been much easier dealing with one air authority. 'One's whole idea is to keep noise and telephoning down to a minimum on these occasions with all the plots coming in and orders going out, signals coming in, it very easily gets into a babel.'[20]

He was also asked why the MTBs were so inferior to E-boats and gave the rather surprising answer: 'These boats were built to carry Italian engines and when Italy came into the war there were no Italian engines so we had to get the best engines we could from America and that is all the speed they will give them.'[21]

A few days after the escape, Churchill addressed the House of Commons and he tackled a question that had been in the thoughts of many. Why were Britain's naval forces to intercept major warships so light? The prime minister pointed out that keeping big ships at ports close to the Channel would have left them as easy targets for air attack, as happened with the German vessels at Brest. 'Further, any such disposition would have dangerously weakened the preventive measures which we have to take to safeguard our convoys and guard the northern passage, and to deal with other German ships, *Tirpitz*, the *Lutzow* and the *Scheer*.' Although the British public saw the escape as a humiliation, there was a positive side. While *Scharnhorst*, *Gneisenau* and *Prinz Eugen* remained at Brest, they were a major threat to Atlantic shipping and to the Mediterranean. It was preferable to have them at German ports.[22]

What the British public did not know at the time was that *Scharnhorst* and *Gneisenau* had not got clean away. *Scharnhorst* struck a magnetic mine dropped by the RAF in the mouth of the Scheldt. The explosion caused serious damage, bringing the ship to a halt. A long gash in the side of the hull allowed hundreds of tons of water to pour in. Power to the ship's turbines was cut off but these were restarted, and *Scharnhorst* got under way after about half an hour. Later, it hit another mine and more water flooded in. The ship eventually limped to Wilhelmshaven, continuing to Kiel for permanent repairs.

Gneisenau also hit a mine, causing flooding, but the damage was minor. After calling at Brunsbüttel, at the mouth of the Elbe, it hit a submerged wreck and more water flooded in. The battlecruiser eventually arrived at Kiel, where it entered dry dock. Only *Prinz Eugen* reached home waters undamaged.[23]

A British force, led by Admiral Sir Bruce Fraser in the battleship HMS *Duke of York*, destroyed *Scharnhorst* in the battle of the North Cape on 26 December 1943. Only 36 of the crew of 1,968 were rescued.

Gneisenau never saw action again. It was ready to leave dry dock on 26 February 1942 after repairs, but that night was extensively damaged in an RAF raid. It was later taken to Gotenhafen in German-occupied Poland. Plans to improve the ship's armament were dropped and it ended the war as a blockship. *Gneisenau* was scrapped in 1951.

Prinz Eugen had a bizarre end. In February 1942, the cruiser was sent to Norway but within days was torpedoed by the submarine HMS *Trident* and returned to Germany for repairs. It survived the war and was handed over to the US Navy as a prize. The ship was taken to the Pacific and joined a ghost fleet to see the effects of nuclear tests at Bikini Atoll in the Marshall Islands in 1946. *Prinz Eugen* was largely undamaged by the blasts but later sank because of a lack of maintenance. The pride of the Kriegsmarine remains a visible wreck off one of the islands.

CHAPTER 22

Go to It!

The escape of *Scharnhorst, Gneisenau* and *Prinz Eugen* had been an embarrassing blow for Ramsay, but the Bucknill inquiry acknowledged the limitations of the forces available to him. And Churchill, initially exasperated, soon came round to describing the escape as a retreat, a victory of sorts. Indeed, the ships never again posed a serious threat. Ramsay was still held in good standing.

No doubt, the Channel dash was overshadowed by other events in February 1942. In particular, the fall of Singapore, which Churchill described as the worst disaster and biggest capitulation in British history. It took only a week for the Japanese to seize the island fortress. If ever there was a case for a full inquiry, that was it, but Churchill decided it would be impossible to hold a royal commission while war was raging. Another setback was the retreat of the Eighth Army in Libya.

In April 1942, the Americans had been in the war for only a few months, but already they were thinking of a major offensive against Germany, although public opinion at home was in favour of focusing on the defeat of Japan. But Stalin had been pleading for a second front and Roosevelt was keen to relieve the pressure on the Soviet Union, telling Churchill that 'the Russians are together killing more Germans and destroying more equipment than you and I put together. Even if full success is not attained, the big objective will be. Go to it! Syria and Egypt will be made more secure, even if the Germans find out about our plans.'[1]

Roosevelt sent one of his closest advisers, Harry Hopkins, and chief of staff, General George Marshall, to London to discuss the way ahead. They brought a memorandum approved by US military chiefs and the president urging a quick decision on mounting a major offensive against the Germans. Immense preparations would be needed and during that time 'the enemy in the west must be pinned down and kept in uncertainty by ruses and raids'. Churchill needed no convincing when it came to mounting commando raids.

The Americans envisaged an invasion force of 48 divisions, supported by 5,800 combat aircraft. It was recognised that shortages of landing craft and shipping to transport troops from the US to Britain were immediate problems. April 1943 was seen as the earliest time to mount the invasion but late summer of that year might be more realistic. Selected beaches between Le Havre and Boulogne would be chosen for landings.

Churchill discussed the proposals with his military chiefs, and they were heartened by the American response. But the idea of mounting an invasion in Europe in April 1943 was thought unrealistic.

On 14 April 1942, Hopkins and Marshall went to 10 Downing Street for a conference with Churchill and his defence committee. The prime minister had one important reservation. It was essential to carry on with the defence of India and the Middle East. Lieutenant General Ismay took notes and he recorded that General Brooke, appointed Chief of the Imperial General Staff, stated that the Chiefs of Staff were in 'entire agreement with General Marshall on the project for 1943'.[2]

In his diary, Brooke had a rather different interpretation of the No 10 discussions: 'With the situation prevailing at that time it was not possible to take Marshall's "castles in the air" too seriously. It must be remembered that we were at that time literally hanging on by our eyelids. Australia and India were threatened by the Japanese, we had temporarily lost control of the Indian Ocean, the Germans were threatening Persia and our oil, Auchinleck was in precarious straits in the desert, and the submarine sinkings were heavy. Under such circumstances we were temporarily on the defensive, and when we returned to the offensive certain definite steps were necessary.' He added, 'We might certainly start preparing plans for the European offensive, but such plans must not be allowed to interfere with the successive stages of operations essential to the ultimate execution of this plan.'[3]

Of Marshall, Brooke formed this view: 'He is, I should think, a good general at raising armies and providing the necessary links between the military and political worlds. But his strategical ability does not impress me at all. In fact in many respects he is a very dangerous man whilst being a very charming one!'[4]

Soon after these discussions, Ramsay was given a new task. The vice admiral left Dover Castle for an underground office in Whitehall, where he would work with General Sir Bernard Paget and Air Chief Marshal Sholto Douglas on invasion planning known as Operation *Round-up*. Ramsay clearly missed having his own command and found the work a little tedious, as he told his wife, 'I attend meetings and have long visits from people who fill my head with rather dull but valuable facts; the result of each talk is to drive out most of what I took in at the previous one … Working in potted air and light makes me extraordinarily wooden-headed after an hour or two, and I shall be glad to have done with it all. But I have a fear that I may be drawn into further commitments.' He continued to miss his family. 'I wish I could have a nice long spell at home with you, even if I do have to wash up, clean my boots etc.'[5] At Bughtrig, there was a clear chain of command.

Ramsay thought his spell in Whitehall was temporary, but after a couple of weeks, he was appointed Flag Officer Expeditionary Force and the work became more interesting. On 28 April, he was invited to dinner at Brooke's flat and they had a long talk. No doubt the general made known his views on Marshall and the need for careful invasion planning. Brooke discovered that Marshall had not studied any of the strategic implications of a cross-Channel operation.

The following month saw Ramsay attending meetings with the Chiefs of Staff and at 10 Downing Street, when the prime minister was in 'excellent form'. It was in June that he said farewell to Dover. In a special message to those under his command, he stated, 'It having been decided that my absence on special duty is to be permanent instead of temporary, it is with very real regret that I hand over the Dover command, which it has been my pride and privilege to hold since the outbreak of this war. I would, therefore, take this opportunity to express my high appreciation of the splendid manner in which officers, men and women have performed their duties at all times and under all conditions, and of the wonderful spirit which has always been so strikingly in evidence.' He added, 'We shall still have to fight for many months and we must expect hard knocks before we force the enemy to abandon the struggle, but I have every confidence that the steady continuance of your work will hasten our inevitable and decisive victory.'[6]

In July, there was further promotion, Naval Commander-in-Chief, Expeditionary Force, with the rank of acting admiral. Remarkably, he was still on the retired list. Defining his duties, a letter from the Admiralty stated, 'He will be responsible for the general direction of all naval forces engaged in large-scale landing operations on the coast of France and the Low Countries, and for the transport of the expeditionary force across the sea and its landing and establishment on the enemy coast.' The admiral would be working in cooperation with the army, the RAF and the Chief of Combined Operations.[7]

Ramsay was ultimately responsible for the training of troops and sailors in the amphibious operations of *Round-up*, and he realised that some tact would be needed. Lord Mountbatten had been appointed

Chief of Combined Operations, with the rank of commodore, though he quickly rose to acting vice admiral. Mountbatten would admit that there was some early friction. Ramsay and other senior officers went to Scotland to see some of the training and the admiral was not impressed, telling Mountbatten, 'I freely admit that I am not happy about the state of training and discipline among personnel of special surface ships and landing craft and beach parties. It is not anything like up to standard, and with the great expansion upon us, it is likely to deteriorate rather than improve unless it is taken in hand now and given close personal attention and supervision. I do not think you can do this with your other commitments, and if you are to retain the latter I think you should co-opt the services of a flag officer on the active list, and turn the whole task over to him under your general direction. The state of training and discipline naturally affects me very closely, as the whole success of Round-up depends upon it.'[8]

Ramsay and the other commanders-in-chief involved in *Round-up* made Norfolk House in Westminster their headquarters. Their American counterparts also based themselves in London, led by Dwight D. Eisenhower, another officer who had enjoyed a rapid rise up the ranks. When war broke out, he was a lieutenant colonel based in the Philippines but by July 1942 had become Commander of the European Theatre of Operations, with the temporary rank of lieutenant general. He had an important backer in Marshall. Yet he had never experienced combat. He was, however, noted for his organisational ability. Ramsay's view: 'Eisenhower is a sensible chap, I think, and anxious to get on with things.'[9]

Marshall, on the other hand, was not regarded as a sensible chap. The general, Hopkins and Admiral Ernest King, US Chief of Naval Operations, arrived in London on 18 July keen to push for an early invasion of France, even considering one later that year. Brooke perhaps summed up the view of the British planners: 'He [Marshall] never fully appreciated what operations in France would mean – the different standard of training of German divisions as opposed to the raw American divisions and to most of our new divisions. He could not appreciate the fact that the Germans could reinforce the point of attack some three to four times faster than we could, nor would he understand that until the Mediterranean was open again we should always suffer from the crippling shortage of sea transport.'[10]

The British and the Americans were still under pressure from the Soviet Union to open up a second front in western Europe. But Brooke believed that the first priority was to liberate North Africa. Then the aim would be to open up the Mediterranean. Once that had been achieved, southern Europe could be threatened by eliminating Italy.[11]

Churchill also had his doubts about Marshall, believing that he was trying to assume his president's powers as commander-in-chief of American troops. There were other divisions. Brooke thought Mountbatten was 'again assuming wild powers'. And Eisenhower had a less than flattering opinion of Admiral King, believing him to be 'an arbitrary, stubborn type, with not too much brains and a tendency toward bullying his juniors'.[12] King, noted for his rudeness, was not fully on board when it came to an invasion of France, believing that his country's priority should be action in the Pacific and the defeat of Japan.

It was eventually agreed that Operation *Round-up* was too premature, and another option, *Sledgehammer*, was looked at. This would be a limited offensive in north-west France, aiming to seize the ports of Brest or Cherbourg and areas of the Cotentin Peninsula in the autumn of 1942. The next stage would be to build up troops and equipment over the following months for a breakout in the spring of 1943.

On 22 July, the Americans presented a memorandum supporting an early attack on Cherbourg. But the British thought that even Operation *Sledgehammer* had little chance of success. Brooke summed it up: 'The memorandum drew attention to all the advantages, but failed to recognise the main disadvantage that there was no hope of our being in Cherbourg by next spring!' That evening, there was a War Cabinet meeting at Downing Street and Brooke presented the case against *Sledgehammer*. It was decided unanimously not to approve the operation.[13]

Churchill noted, 'The attempt to form a bridgehead at Cherbourg seemed to me to be more difficult, less attractive, less immediately fruitful or ultimately fruitful. It would be better to lay our right claw on French North Africa, tear with our left at the North Cape, and wait a year without risking our teeth upon the German fortified front across the Channel.'[14]

The day after the War Cabinet meeting Ramsay wrote, 'Things have been in a proper mess in higher direction circles, owing to the American desire to do something quickly, yet not knowing what is possible to do. Consequently their perspective is all wrong and they have had to be shown it. However, I think that after much argument they do see now a little more clearly. No doubt after years of war we look more closely at things before we say what we will or will not do, whereas the Yanks are new to the game and have the enthusiasm of beginners.'[15]

Eisenhower had been in favour of *Sledgehammer* but he would concede, 'Later developments have convinced me that those who held the Sledgehammer operation to be unwise at the moment were correct in their evaluation of the problem.'[16]

The difficulty of mounting an assault on the French coast was soon highlighted. On 19 August, a force of nearly 5,000 Canadians, some 1,000 British commandos and 50 US Rangers was landed at the port of Dieppe in Operation *Jubilee*. The aim of *Jubilee*, masterminded by Mountbatten of combined operations, was to seize the port for a limited time, destroy installations and gather intelligence. But the Germans were on high alert and Dieppe and the surrounding cliffs were heavily defended. The raid was a disaster. Some of the planning had relied on holiday snapshots. Hidden machine-gun positions took a heavy toll. The Canadians had 3,367 men killed, wounded or taken prisoner. This casualty toll, which left so many families devastated, remains controversial in Canada. The British Army lost 247 men. The Royal Navy had 550 casualties, losing the destroyer HMS *Berkeley* and 33 landing craft. The RAF's losses were 106 aircraft. The First Sea Lord had refused to commit capital ships or cruisers, fearing their vulnerability to air attack. Understandably, the Japanese attacks on *Prince of Wales* and *Repulse* were fresh in his memory. But a fierce naval bombardment, which might have made a significant difference, had been ruled out anyway because of the risk of high civilian casualties.

Later, Mountbatten claimed that the battle of Normandy was won on the beaches of Dieppe. The raid had been postponed several times because of bad weather, and Lieutenant General Montgomery, who was involved in the early planning as C-in-C Southeastern Command, advised against continuing with *Jubilee*. Soldiers had been briefed and security breaches were feared. Churchill would admit that intelligence had suggested Dieppe was protected only by a small force of some 1,400 men. He justified the raid, however, by insisting it had been a valuable experience.[17]

Ramsay viewed Dieppe as an unnecessary and costly diversion. He was concerned that the enemy would learn too much about Allied strategy on amphibious warfare. New types of landing craft were being used. But the Germans were left unimpressed, dismissing the attack as a fiasco and seeing it as a propaganda victory. To add to the Allies' embarrassment, the Vichy leader Petain wrote to Hitler congratulating him on defending French soil.

Captain Roskill, the official naval historian, pointed out: 'The Germans decided that the Dieppe raid indicated that, when the time came for the allies to invade the European continent in earnest, their initial thrust would be aimed at capturing a large port. It is likely that this false deduction contributed greatly to the successful landing on the Normandy beaches in June 1944. On our own side the lessons learnt were many, and were promptly put into practice. We had learnt at no small cost in Norway, Greece, Crete, Malaya and indeed in all theatres of the war, that command of the air was an essential pre-requisite for success in landings from the sea.'[18]

There had been months of frustration for Ramsay, with long and sometimes acrimonious discussions about *Round-up* and then *Sledgehammer*. The Dieppe raid had shown the importance of striking at the right time. The invasion of Europe would have to wait. In August 1942, Ramsay was presented with a new challenge, Operation *Torch*.

CHAPTER 23

Operation *Torch*

With Operation *Round-up* on hold and *Sledgehammer* about to be buried, Churchill and his military chiefs continued to argue the case for an invasion of Vichy-controlled North Africa. In a message to President Roosevelt on 8 July 1942, the prime minister had pointed out that such an action would give the best chance of easing pressure on the Russian front. And it would not involve huge risk. Any resistance from Vichy would not be comparable to that which would be offered by the German army in northern France.

In American military circles, there was a growing belief that ruling out an invasion of France in 1942 should allow the US to prioritise the Pacific campaign, as Admiral King had been advocating. Roosevelt, however, was convinced that Germany, rather than Japan, remained the priority.

The memorandum that Hopkins, Marshall and King brought to London in July was from their president, and it stressed the need for definite plans for the remainder of 1942. The document listed a number of options if *Sledgehammer* was ruled out. Among them was 'a new operation in Morocco and Algeria intended to drive in against the back door of Rommel's armies'. Roosevelt stressed to his emissaries, 'Please remember three cardinal principles – speed of decision on plans, unity of plans, attack combined with defence but not defence alone. This affects the immediate objective of US ground forces fighting against Germans in 1942. I hope for total agreement within one week of your arrival.'[1]

On the British side, another reason for pushing for the invasion of French North Africa was the fear that the Germans would occupy the region, drawing in Spain and Portugal.

When it became clear that the British would not back down on *Sledgehammer*, Roosevelt told Hopkins on 25 July that plans for landings in North Africa not later than 30 October should go ahead. Marshall and King bowed to the decision of their commander-in-chief. That day in London a meeting of the Combined Chiefs of Staff formally approved the idea.

Confusingly, the proposed operation had been given the codenames Gymnast, Super-Gymnast and Semi-Gymnast. It became Operation *Torch*. The decision to go ahead with it brought Churchill 'great joy', and Roosevelt was 'very happy', noting, 'I cannot help feeling that the past week represented a turning point in the whole war and that now we are on our way shoulder to shoulder.'[2]

Churchill and his personal representative in Washington, Field Marshal Sir John Dill, thought that Marshall would be suitable as *Torch*'s supreme commander. Clearly unknown to them, Marshall had summoned Eisenhower to his London hotel, Claridge's, on 26 July and offered him the post, stating that 'while this decision was definite some little time would be necessary to accomplish all the routine of official designation'.[3] Perhaps Marshall was taking a little revenge on what he perceived as British stubbornness in the earlier talks. Or perhaps he was aware of Brooke's view of his shortcomings on strategy. Marshall and King quickly packed their bags and headed back to Washington. The following month, Eisenhower was indeed confirmed in the post. He was under no illusions of the task ahead: 'The decision to invade North Africa necessitated a complete reversal in our thinking and drastic revision in our planning and preparation. Where we had been counting on many months of orderly build-up, we now had only weeks. Instead of a massed attack across narrow waters, the proposed expedition would require movement across open ocean areas where enemy submarines would constitute a real menace. Our target was no longer a restricted front where we knew accurately terrain, facilities and people as they affected military operations, but the rim of a continent where no major military campaign had been conducted for centuries.'[4]

There were other factors – less air power, the use of 'highly vulnerable' Gibraltar as the main base and the difficulty of establishing a beachhead. It was, in Eisenhower's words, a 'violent shift' in target. But the main focus remained the invasion of mainland Europe, and the 'African venture was looked upon as diversionary in character but necessitated by the circumstances of the moment and in the hope that from it we would achieve great results'.[5]

The Americans were keen to give the impression that the attack on Vichy territory was their operation. There was still much anger in France over the British naval raids on Mers-el-Kébir and Dakar. Another US army officer, Major General Mark Clark, was appointed Eisenhower's deputy. In early August, Ramsay, as Naval Commander-in-Chief, Expeditionary Force, was told to switch his attention from *Round-up* to *Torch*. But he was heading for a major disappointment. On 3 September, Churchill told Roosevelt that 'in view of the importance of the operation' it was proposed to give the naval command to Admiral Cunningham, with Ramsay as his deputy. Clearly, behind the scenes, there had been murmurings about Ramsay. US warships would come under this command, and it seems that an officer with a higher profile, a 'fighting admiral', was more acceptable to the Americans. Cunningham, known as ABC, was certainly that. During World War I, he emerged as a daring destroyer captain, winning the Distinguished Service Order and two Bars. As Commander-in-Chief, Mediterranean, he was the victor of the battle of Cape Matapan in March 1941, when three Italian cruisers and two destroyers were sunk. Cunningham may have been a warrior, but Ramsay was the master when it came to detailed planning, as ABC would acknowledge, once joking that an officer who had worked for him for three years 'knew my methods, or perhaps should I say lack of method'.[6] Ramsay took his demotion well, comparing himself to Moses, who died within sight of the Promised Land. He would, however, live to fight another day.

Eisenhower and Cunningham were opposites when it came to their careers, the soldier who had never experienced combat and the sailor who had seen plenty of action. But the Texas-born soldier, known as Ike, soon warmed to the 'real sea dog', recording, 'He was the Nelsonian type of admiral. He believed that ships were sent to sea in order to find and destroy the enemy. He thought always in terms of attack, never of defense. He was vigorous, hardy, intelligent and straightforward.'[7] And Cunningham thought Ike sincere, straightforward and very modest.

Cunningham was already known in American military circles because in March he had been appointed head of the Admiralty delegation in Washington and the First Sea Lord's representative on the Combined Chiefs of Staff committee. He had been reluctant to leave the Mediterranean for what amounted to a desk job, and his departure was kept secret to avoid alerting the enemy. His new adversary would be Admiral King.

In his memoirs, Cunningham described King as someone of immense ability but not easy to get on with: 'He was tough and liked to be considered tough, and at times became rude and overbearing. It was not many weeks before we had some straight speaking over the trifling matter of lending four or five American submarines for work on our side of the Atlantic. He was offensive, and I told him what I thought of his method of advancing allied unity and amity. We parted friends.' Cunningham added, 'Not content with fighting the enemy, he was usually fighting someone on his own side as well.'[8]

He reported King's behaviour to the First Sea Lord, telling Pound that he had been 'abominably rude and I had to be quite firm with him'. Cunningham also became aware of 'bitter rivalry' between America's navy and army.[9]

He was still in Washington when he learned that *Torch* had been approved, and he was enthusiastic, believing it would help shipping movements in the Mediterranean, put pressure on Rommel's forces in North Africa and relieve besieged Malta. At that stage, Ramsay had not been confirmed as *Torch*'s naval commander, but Cunningham clearly knew of his involvement with *Round-up*. On 31 July, ABC wrote to Pound, 'You probably have somebody already in your mind, but if it was considered that I could be of use I should be more than willing. At the same time I don't want to push myself forward.'[10] In reality, he was keen to get the post and escape from Washington's infighting. Ramsay was sacrificed.

Even King supported Cunningham's appointment, although he was averse to US ships being under British command, suggesting that they should be independent of the main expedition. But he had no problem with Royal Navy ships being under US command. King was no doubt taken aback when the American task force leader Rear Admiral Henry Hewitt said it would be 'a privilege' to serve under Cunningham. A compromise saw the task force coming under *Torch* command after nearing the point of invasion.

That year saw another operation, *Bolero*, under way; the build-up of US forces in the UK. The aim was to send more than one million service personnel and thousands of bombers and fighters. Troopships began crossing the Atlantic in May, and the movement of aircraft started the following month. It was intended that these forces would be used for the second front in north-west Europe, originally *Round-up* and then *Sledgehammer*. A significant number were 'borrowed' for *Torch* and would later form the nucleus for the invasion of Normandy in 1944. Meanwhile, plans for the attack on French North Africa went ahead, but not always smoothly.

The plans involved three landings, Casablanca in Morocco, and Oran and Algiers in Algeria. For the Casablanca invasion, American troops would leave in convoys from Portland, Maine, and Hampton Roads, Virginia. The two other landings would involve British and US troops sailing from the Clyde. The British saw Casablanca, on the Atlantic coast, as largely irrelevant because it was too far to the west.

Preparations had started to unravel within days of the 25 July agreement, prompting Field Marshal Dill in Washington to express his concern to General Marshall. 'I am just a little disturbed about Torch,' he wrote. 'For good or ill it has been accepted and therefore I feel that we should go at it with all possible enthusiasm and give it absolute priority. If we don't, it won't succeed.

'From what our planners tell me, there are some of your people who feel that Torch is not a good operation. That, of course, must be a matter of opinion but those who are playing a part in mounting the operation must be entirely whole-hearted about it, or they cannot give it all the help it should have and overcome all the difficulties that will arise.'[11]

Marshall replied that he agreed that those involved in planning *Torch* must give their full support. 'Absolute candour among the planners is essential,' he wrote. 'The US planners are deeply concerned with the planning and implementation of several operations at this time and therefore must consider the implications of each on the others. They must foresee and make provision to meet all difficulties involved in the execution of these plans.' It would seem that there was still preference for an early invasion of north-west Europe and greater action against Japan. Marshall ended his letter, 'You may feel sure that US planners will enthusiastically and effectively support decisions made by the commander in chief.'[12]

On 22 August, the First Sea Lord asked Ramsay to prepare a progress report for the prime minister. 'It should be comprehensive in the matters it deals with but each part should be as short as possible,' Pound instructed.[13]

Two days later Ramsay sent his report. The naval outline plan had been completed. Interestingly, there was also detailed planning for an assault on the Tunisian port of Bône, further to the east. If *Torch* were successful, Tunisia would be an obvious next step. Ramsay's report covered a number of issues including the provision of destroyers as convoy escorts, the number of landing craft, air support and communications. It was planned to use 28 destroyers as convoy escorts and an additional 10 destroyers for the assault. It was not known if the Americans had enough destroyers, with Ramsay noting, 'The ability of the US to provide the requisite naval forces is therefore the crux of the western assault problem.' Arrangements were being made for aircraft carriers to have the maximum number of modern fighters. Eleven ammunition ships would be needed to support ground forces. Gibraltar was likely to be the main naval base. 'It should be noted, however, that owing to the limited capacity of the harbour many valuable ships, such as tankers and ammunition ships, must of necessity be berthed in the bay, where they will be exposed to all forms of underwater attacks.'[14] (From 1940 until 1943, Italian frogmen based at Algeciras, across the Spanish frontier, carried out a number of attacks on ships at Gibraltar.)

There was still concern about America's commitment to *Torch*. Churchill told Roosevelt that after consulting his military chiefs, and Eisenhower and Clark, it was important to fix a date for the operation. There had been too much dithering. Roosevelt was urged to give Eisenhower a date even if all forces were not in place.[15]

Then came what Churchill described as 'a bombshell'. Despite Marshall's assurance to Dill that there would be full cooperation, serious differences emerged between the two sides. The US chiefs of staff disliked the idea of committing large forces beyond the Strait of Gibraltar. One fear was Spain closing the strait with German help. Even Eisenhower was in favour of heading east into the Mediterranean to have greater impact on the campaign in North Africa. But he failed to influence his superiors.[16]

Churchill was again in contact with Roosevelt, stressing the importance of taking Algiers as well as Oran on the first day of *Torch*. In Algiers, the Allies would have the best chance of a friendly reception. It would be a 'most strategic success'. Failure to go east of Oran would give the enemy a present of Algiers and another prize, Tunis. Roosevelt was urged to fully support Eisenhower and the plans that had been made.[17]

Roosevelt replied that it was his 'earnest desire' to launch *Torch* at the earliest possible moment. The initial attacks must be made 'by an exclusively American ground force, supported by your naval, transport and air units', to lessen the risk of Vichy resistance. US troops would move on only two targets, Casablanca and Oran, consolidate them and then a week later 'your force can come in to the eastward'. In the president's view there were not enough ships and planes for three simultaneous landings.[18]

Churchill would reflect, 'I did not wholly share the American view that either they were so beloved by Vichy or we so hated as to make the difference between fighting and submission, but I was very willing that, provided the necessary forces were set in motion and the operation was not fatally restricted in its scope, we should keep as much in the background as was physically possible. I would even have agreed to such British troops as had to be used in the first assaults wearing American uniform.'[19]

The prime minister told the president he was sure that 'if we both strip ourselves to the bone' the three landings could still take place simultaneously. Roosevelt took this on board and proposed new troop arrangements for all three targets. The number of soldiers and landing craft for Casablanca would be reduced, boosting the numbers for Algiers.

Ramsay summed up the frustration by pointing out that 'all Winston's ideas have to be transmitted to Washington and they send back their own ideas which differ from ours. We are like marionettes dancing to everyone's tune.'[20]

On 5 September, Churchill told the president he was sending Ramsay, with Eisenhower's agreement, to Washington to brief Cunningham on the latest naval plans for *Torch*.

Ramsay flew to Washington with one of his aides, Commander Thomas Brownrigg, who had served in the Mediterranean. Cunningham and his wife took the visitors – used to rationing – to a well-known restaurant outside the capital. 'From the menu one ordered a chump chop and the other steak,' ABC recalled. 'Their faces when they were served with gargantuan helpings were worth seeing.'[21]

The admirals were soon busy working on plans and attending conferences. One evening, they went to the White House and spent nearly three hours talking with Roosevelt and Hopkins, mostly about *Torch*.[22]

On 8 September, Eisenhower and Clark dined with Churchill and they discussed the date for *Torch*, which had been postponed several times. The latest date was 4 November but Eisenhower said it might have to be 8 November because of troop equipment issues.

That month saw a major security scare. An RAF Catalina flying boat heading to Gibraltar from Britain crashed into the sea off Cadiz in bad weather on the afternoon of 26 September. Ten people were on board, seven crew and three passengers. The bodies of a Royal Navy officer, Paymaster Lieutenant J. H. Turner, and a member of the crew were washed ashore. It emerged that Turner was carrying a letter that revealed when Eisenhower and his deputy, Clark, would arrive in Gibraltar and it gave the 'target date of 4 November', although there was no mention of *Torch* being the target. A second letter came from the HQ, Naval Commander-in-Chief, Expeditionary Force, but it did not refer to a target or a date. A Spanish naval officer handed over the bodies to an RAF intelligence officer. It was feared that the Spain might have passed the information to the Germans, but an investigation concluded that *Torch* had not been compromised. The date of the operation, however, was changed to 8 November.[23] (The following year, Britain's Operation *Mincemeat* deceived the Germans over the invasion of Sicily by planting false secret papers on the body of a tramp, dressed as a Royal Marines officer, that washed up in southern Spain.)

Cunningham finally left America on 11 October 'delighted to be getting away from the hothouse atmosphere of Washington and actively back into the war.'[24] His role in *Torch* was still known only to a few.

During October, contact was made with French generals who were thought likely to support the Allied invasion. The American insistence on the French being convinced that *Torch* was a US operation may have been overplayed, as Cunningham would note, 'In actual fact this difference in feeling towards the Americans and ourselves was much exaggerated. Those Frenchmen who were anti-Vichy cared not at all whether it was the British or Americans who came to help them, and vice versa.'[25]

On 19 October, the submarine HMS *Seraph* (P219) sailed from Gibraltar carrying Major General Clark and other senior American officers. The party landed in Folbots west of Algiers at night for talks with General Rene Mast, who indicated that the French army and air force were unlikely to offer much resistance. (The French navy, which manned coastal guns, was a different matter.) The submarine picked up the Americans and returned to Gibraltar.

Later *Seraph* sailed close to Toulon to collect General Henri Giraud, who had been a prisoner of the Germans. He supported Allied landings in North Africa, but he refused to deal with the British. To keep him on side, the submarine masqueraded as an American boat, calling itself USS *Seraph*. Eisenhower hoped that Giraud would rally French forces in North Africa, but it soon emerged that he had greater ambitions. In talks with Ike in Gibraltar, it became clear that he was 'under the grave misapprehension' he would be in command of the entire Allied expedition. 'General Giraud was adamant,' Eisenhower recorded. 'He believed that the honor of himself and his country was involved and that he could not possibly accept any position in the venture lower than that of complete command.' This was an impossible demand. After lengthy talks, Geraud refused to have anything to do with *Torch* and at midnight went to bed, declaring, 'Giraud will be a spectator in the affair.' The next day, he agreed to participate.[26]

Cunningham's participation in *Torch* was still being kept secret. On 28 October, wearing civilian clothes, the admiral took a train from London to Plymouth, where he boarded the cruiser HMS *Scylla*, which was bound for Gibraltar. Some of his staff had flown to the Rock. Ramsay remained in London – 'our rear link'. Cunningham recorded, 'His services in that respect were inestimable. If in the strenuous weeks ahead we wanted anything we signalled direct to Ramsay and he personally arranged it at the Admiralty. This procedure was entirely new. It was found so useful that it was adopted in all subsequent operations of a similar nature.'[27] Eisenhower flew to Gibraltar on 5 November in a flight of five Flying Fortresses.

Although Eisenhower and Cunningham were given comfortable living quarters, their headquarters was in a damp and airless tunnel that had been cut deep inside the Rock. Cunningham was luckier. He also had an office in the dockyard, where he could watch the ships assembling and receive calls from commanding officers. 'It was thrilling to be amongst the seagoing navy again. I felt as though I had been away from it for years instead of only seven months.'[28]

Cunningham soon received a personal letter from his deputy. 'It wasn't easy to see you go without giving a thought to what might have been, but any such thought is swamped in no time by the knowledge that what is, is for the best, and had I been the authority in power I would have ordered things to be as they now are. There is no one I would rather have done my work for than you, and I have done it with real pleasure. I'm confident that success awaits you.'[29]

The launch of Operation *Torch* coincided with a timely morale boost for the Allies. On the night of 23–24 October, Lieutenant General Montgomery's Eighth Army launched a major offensive against the Germans and the Italians at El Alamein in Egypt. By 4 November, it was clear that Field Marshal Rommel's army was beaten, retreating west towards Tunisia. It was a turning point in the North African campaign. And Eisenhower's forces were about to push eastwards.

CHAPTER 24

The Burning *Torch*

In the days before the invasion, Cunningham and Ramsay had good fortune on their side. Despite the huge movement of shipping, German intelligence, the *Abwehr*, failed to realise in time what was taking place, even though there were agents operating freely in Spain and in Spanish Morocco, and it had observation posts along both sides of the Strait of Gibraltar.

There were some 340 ships in the British force and the merchant ships were arranged in convoys, each having to approach Gibraltar and head into the Mediterranean at specific times between the evening of 5 November and the early hours of 7 November. To help deceive the enemy, a number of ships sailed past Oran and Algiers, giving the impression that they were heading for Malta, but at nightfall they turned back. The Germans also thought that the target might be Dakar, and around 60 submarines were massed around the Azores and Madeira. An Allied convoy unconnected to *Torch* was badly mauled.

As Cunningham pointed out, 'The early stages of the operation prior to D-Day were remarkable for lack of incident. This was indeed fortunate since, in the course of this vast and complex movement, delays caused by casualties or stress of weather would have rendered the timely delivery of the assaults improbable.'[1] On the night of 7 November, the admiral went to the Rock's Europa Point and watched some of the darkened ships passing.

There was, in fact, one casualty, the American transport USS *Thomas Stone*, which was torpedoed in the early hours. The ship did not sink and was taken in tow by the destroyer HMS *Wishart*. The troops on board set off on the long trip to Algiers in their landing craft but these had to be in abandoned in rough seas. The frigate HMS *Spey* picked up the men.

From British submarines off Algiers and Oran, reconnaissance teams in Folbots were sent in. These exercises were largely successful, though there was always the danger that they might compromise security. Indeed, two officers were captured but 'they kept their heads and the pre-arranged cover plan was adequate'. The assault forces arrived off the beaches and 'contacts were made with beacon submarines as planned'.[2]

Off Algiers, there were 93 warships and merchant vessels under the command of the Royal Navy's Vice Admiral Harold Burrough. The attack on the city was launched in three main areas, the harbour and points to the east and west.

The destroyers *Broke* and *Malcolm* were given the task of reaching the harbour and disembarking troops before the French could scuttle ships and destroy installations. In the darkness, the destroyers failed to find the harbour entrance. They were soon under fire. *Malcolm* was badly hit and forced to withdraw. Only at the fourth attempt did *Broke* succeed, crashing through the boom. 'At the moment of impact we were going about 25 knots and went through it just like a knife through butter,' the captain, Lieutenant Commander Arthur Layard, reported. 'I had no difficulty in checking and turning the ship but in the darkness mistook the layout of the harbour and berthed alongside the mole Louis Billiard instead of the Quai de Dieppe as planned. My jumping party were soon ashore and the ship was secured and the brows run out, and the soldiers started to disembark at about 0515.' The ship changed berth twice but came under renewed fire and made for the harbour entrance. There were a number of hits and that night a rising sea and wind led to a heavy list. The destroyer HMS *Zetland* took *Broke* in tow, but later Layard's crew were forced to abandon the ship, which sank.[3] (This was not Ramsay's *Broke* but a destroyer commissioned in 1925 and the third vessel to bear the name.)

To the west of Algiers, 33 transports landed nearly 33,000 troops, along with vehicles and supplies, at three zones. Another force stormed beaches to the east of the port. A bombardment silenced forts guarding the harbour. Early in the day, French resistance fighters had seized the city's telephone exchange, radio station and other targets. Algiers surrendered that evening, and at dawn the next day Vice Admiral Burrough's flagship, HMS *Bulolo*, entered the harbour.

Cunningham commented, 'The actual landings when the troops reached their beaches appear to have gone according to plan and the work of the beach parties was excellent, but unnecessarily large numbers of landing craft were crippled as the disembarkations proceeded. These losses were mostly avoidable and due to lack of training and bad seamanship. In this connection it is recommended that the use of new entries, not properly disciplined, in this type of operation be avoided.'[4]

Algiers had been taken with relatively few casualties but that would not be the case with Oran. There was a similar plan to seize the port before the

French could destroy its facilities. In Operation *Reservist*, HMS *Walney* and HMS *Hartland*, two former US Coast Guard cutters, charged the harbour boom but met withering fire. *Walney* was put out of action and sank. *Hartland* caught fire and later blew up. There were few survivors among the crews. Of nearly 400 US troops on boards the ships, only 47 survived unhurt.

'The choice of the ships for this operation had rested on their American appearance, and their chance of a friendly reception lay largely in this appearance and the use of the American ensign,' Cunningham reported. 'In the face of serious opposition it could not be expected that they would succeed in their task. In the event, the moment chosen could hardly have been less fortunate, since the French alarm to arms was in its first full flush of Gallic fervour and they had not yet been intimidated by bombing or bombardment, whilst darkness prevented any American complexion to the operation being apparent. The expedition was a failure, redeemed by the gallantry displayed by officers and men of both nations as they strove to achieve their object in the face of hopeless odds.'[5]

Several senior US Navy officers had complained to Eisenhower that Operation *Reservist* was 'suicidal', but the general replied, 'I can't take your advice on this thing, I have to get my advice from Ramsay.' In fact, *Reservist*'s commander, Captain Frederic Peters of the Royal Navy, was the main planner.[6] The Canadian-born Peters survived the attack, only to die days later in an air crash as he returned to England. He was awarded a posthumous Victoria Cross. The Americans gave him the army's Distinguished Service Cross.

During *Reservist*, three French destroyers left the harbour to attack troop transports and the British cruiser *Aurora* and several Allied destroyers engaged them. One French destroyer was sunk, one was driven ashore and the third headed back to harbour. *Aurora* and the cruiser *Jamaica* later put two other destroyers out of action. But Cunningham would admit, 'It was highly distasteful for our ships to have to destroy French vessels which should have been fighting with us.'[7] Ramsay, no doubt, shared that view.

On the morning of 8 November, troops and tanks landed on beaches east and west of Oran, and aircraft from three carriers put the nearest airfield out of action. The battleship HMS *Rodney* bombarded coastal guns. Fighting went on throughout the day and continued on the next. Early on 9 November, a final assault was launched on the city of Oran and French forces surrendered at noon.

Cunningham paid tribute to Ramsay's 'sound planning and forethought' for the attacks on Algiers and Oran. And 'despite the difficulties inherent in welding together the systems of command and organisation of two nations, there reigned a spirit of comradeship and understanding which provided that vital force which brought success to our undertaking'. It had, he added, been a privilege to serve under Eisenhower.[8]

The attack on Casablanca remained an all-American operation. There were three key invasion targets, Mehdia-Port Lyautey and Fedala to the north-east of the city, and Safi to the south. A fleet of nearly 100 ships, under the command of Rear Admiral Hewitt, arrived off the coast with 31,000 troops and 250 tanks, led by the fiery Major General George Patton. The weather was a major factor, and on 6 November, Hewitt received forecasts warning that surf was 15 feet high, making landings impossible. A meteorologist with the fleet predicted there would be an improvement on 8 November, and Hewitt decided to press on with the original plan, so that the Casablanca invasion coincided with the attacks on Algiers and Oran.

The French had significant forces in and around Casablanca, and the appearance of the Stars and Stripes on 8 November did not pacify them as the Americans had hoped. Mehdia-Port Lyautey proved to be the most difficult target. The day began badly when two American officers drove under a flag of truce to speak to the local French commander. One of the officers was shot dead and the other detained. Coastal batteries opened fire soon afterwards. It was not until early on 11 November that the French stopped fighting.

At Fedala, many landing craft were wrecked and soldiers drowned. But fighting was comparatively light and by the afternoon it had ended. Safi also surrendered that afternoon. French cruisers, destroyers and submarines based at Casablanca sailed to oppose the landings, but they paid a high price. US warships and planes destroyed one of the cruisers and a number of the destroyers and submarines. A bizarre action involved the incomplete battleship *Jean Bart*. Unable to move from its berth, the ship fought a one-sided duel with the battleship USS *Massachusetts* and suffered extensive damage.

With Casablanca surrounded, Patton planned a massive bombardment on 11 November, but shortly before it was due to begin, a ceasefire was agreed. All three main targets had been taken, and Churchill described *Torch* as a brilliant success.

Ramsay wrote to his wife, 'The news is now out, thank goodness, and the necessity for secrecy no longer exists. Very few people seem to have guessed what was in train, and considering the enormous number of ships that had to be altered and fitted out, armed and loaded it is wonderful how little it was spoken about or even known.

'The operation so far has been an outstanding success and from the naval point of view has gone absolutely according to plan. What that plan entailed in the making will never be known except to those who worked on it. The weather was very bad all the way out but was favourable for the day of the landing. Everything depended on this. Our hope that the French would not put up an organised resistance has been realised to a moderate extent. At Algiers there was very little resistance because the French army had been got at beforehand and there was very little of their navy there. At Oran and Casablanca, which are naval ports, the resistance was stiff, but that of the army wasn't too great. The air force put up little resistance and we soon got the airfields, enabling us to fly in Spitfires etc from Gibraltar for the local protection of the port and shipping.'

Ramsay added, 'I suppose if I were an advertising, aggressive type of chap I would push myself to the front, but I'm not.' He wished he could have 'a nice long spell at home'.[9]

A few days later, Cunningham wrote to Ramsay saying 'nobody has contributed more to the success of this show than you have and I hope everyone knows it. Things go well on the whole and we have got further in the last five days than expected. But we are not moving fast enough. Tunis is anyone's who cares to walk in but the Huns are beating us in the race. We have started having heavy losses from the U-boats and air attacks but not out of the way for what has been achieved.

'Clark has gone to Algiers to try to sort out the rival claims of Giraud, Darlan, Juin, Nogues etc [General Alphonse Juin, General Charles Nogues]. It is indeed a tangled skein. I begin to wonder are there any really patriotic Frenchmen, de Laborde [Admiral Jean de Laborde] whom I would have sworn by appears to have let his fleet just remain in Toulon without making any effort to escape the Huns.

'Eisenhower is good but terribly mercurial. He was in the depths of despair because Oran did not fall at once. But his ideas are good. He does not to me seem to take enough part in directing the operation, but perhaps I am an interfering person.'[10]

Ramsay also received a letter of congratulations from Lord Mountbatten, who wrote, 'I have just seen Troubridge [Commodore Thomas Troubridge, in command of the Oran naval force] who has given me a first-hand account of how well everything in the naval plan worked, and knowing how much the success of all the naval arrangements was personally due to you I should like, if I may, to offer you my most sincere congratulations on such a wonderful and successful show.

'When I first heard that there had been a change of command my impulse was to sit down and write and say how very deeply I felt for you; but then I thought that perhaps it was rather out of place my doing so. Now that it is all over perhaps you will allow me to express my very real sympathy that you should have been robbed of the fruits of all the work you have put into this operation, through no fault of your own.'[11]

It soon became apparent to Eisenhower that faith in General Giraud had been misplaced. Giraud expected the Allies to switch their attention away from North Africa and invade the south of France, unaware that Britain and the US had stretched their resources 'to the limit'. On 9 November, Clark and Giraud flew to Algiers to win over the French leadership there. A broadcast called on French forces to cease fighting. As Eisenhower recounted, 'General Giraud's cold reception by the French in Africa was a terrible blow to our expectations. He was completely ignored.'[12]

It just happened that Admiral Darlan, commander-in-chief of French forces and notorious collaborator, was in Algiers visiting his son in hospital. One problem for the Allies was the fact that senior French officers felt bound to Petain's regime because they had sworn an oath of loyalty. But Darlan, as their legal commander, could release them from that commitment.

In response to *Torch*, Hitler ordered German and Italian forces to invade unoccupied southern France. The breaking of the armistice changed Darlan's position and he told Vichy forces to cease fighting. On 13 November, Eisenhower and Cunningham flew to Algiers to confer with Clark and Robert Murphy, an American diplomat who had been busy working behind the scenes. The French admiral then agreed to cooperate with the Allies. Eisenhower recorded, 'Darlan's orders to the French army were obeyed, in contrast to the disdain with which the earlier Giraud pronouncement had been received.'[13]

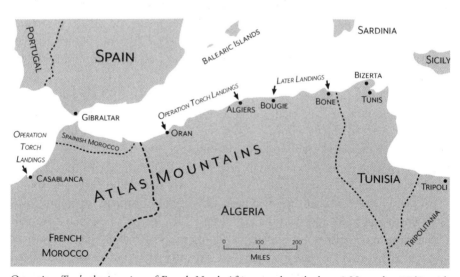

Operation *Torch*, the invasion of French North Africa, was launched on 8 November 1942, with Oran, Algiers and Casablanca as the key targets.

Darlan appointed himself French North Africa's high commissioner and, with some irony, gave Giraud command of their military forces.

The Allies had sidelined the Free French leader Charles de Gaulle. He was not even told of the planning for *Torch*. Churchill pointed out to Roosevelt, 'It is surely of the highest importance to unify in every possible way all Frenchmen who regard Germany as the foe. The invasion of unoccupied France by Hitler should give the opportunity for this. You will, I am sure, realise that His Majesty's Government are under quite definite and solemn obligations to de Gaulle and his movement. We must see they have a fair deal.'[14]

Roosevelt had shown 'vehement hostility' to de Gaulle. He replied to Churchill, 'In regard to de Gaulle, I have hitherto enjoyed a quiet satisfaction in leaving him in your hands. Apparently I have acquired a similar problem in brother Giraud. I wholly agree that we must prevent rivalry between the French émigré factions.'[15]

In Britain and the United States, there was much criticism of Darlan's involvement. Ramsay commented, 'Eisenhower has handled the difficult political situation extremely ably, far better I consider than a British general in his place would have done. The Americans are very politically minded, which on such an occasion has its advantages. From the purely military point of view our generals are much superior.'[16]

Darlan had declared that Cunningham was the only British admiral he would shake hands with. Ramsay told Cunningham, 'But you might remind him of what I did for the French at Dunkirk, 129,000 of them.'[17]

Cunningham wrote to Ramsay, 'We have been heavily shot at from home over allowing Darlan to be head of government out here. They always want to have it both ways. The fact is that our intelligence was much at fault. They gambled on Giraud's influence and thought Darlan was hated and had no influence. The exact contrary was the case. Giraud cut no ice at all and consented at once to work under Darlan, who is the only man who can deliver at least some of the goods. I would like to ask the Foreign Office just exactly what they would have done if in Eisenhower's position.'[18]

The political battles were certainly unwanted in such a crucial military campaign. Darlan, however, would not be in his new role for long. He was assassinated in Algiers on Christmas Eve. Conspiracy theories have swirled ever since. The young killer was one Fernand Bonnier de la Chapelle, who belonged to a resistance group supported by Britain's Special Operations Executive and America's Office of Strategic Services. Bonnier shot Darlan at his offices in the Palais d'Été and he was executed after facing a secret court. De Gaulle later exonerated Bonnier. It emerged that on the day of the assassination the head of Britain's Secret Intelligence Service, Sir Stewart Menzies, who rarely left London, was in Algiers.[19]

Churchill would later record that Darlan's murder had relieved the Allies of their embarrassment at having to work with him.[20]

The military success of *Torch* made Tunis the next important target. This would be the task of the British First Army, led by Lieutenant General Kenneth Anderson. But the force needed building up with men and supplies, and the more suitable harbours of Bougie and Bône, east of Algiers, were seized with little difficulty. And the Germans, realising the strategic importance of Tunisia, began sending reinforcements to Rommel.

CHAPTER 25

The Tide Turns

The success of Operation *Torch* created a problem. What next? In the early part of 1942, the Americans had been keen to launch an invasion of north-west Europe. British planners considered an offensive too risky, 'castles in the air', as Brooke put it.

But towards the end of 1942, US military leaders were being much more cautious, deciding that *Torch* had ruled out a major crossing of the English Channel for the whole of 1943. This did not go down well with Churchill, who thought that an invasion might be feasible in the July or August, confident that the North African campaign would be over relatively quickly. Even his own Chiefs of Staff were erring on the side of caution, and he thought their reports 'unduly negative', considering only Sicily or Sardinia as the next target. The ambitious prime minister told his military chiefs, 'The effort for the campaign of 1943 should clearly be a strong pinning down of the enemy in northern France and the Low Countries by continuous preparations to invade, and a decisive attack on Italy or, better still, southern France, together with operations not involving serious shipping expense, and other forms of pressure to bring in Turkey and operate overland with the Russians into the Balkans. If French North Africa is going to be made an excuse for locking up great forces on the defensive and calling it commitment, it would be better not to have gone there at all.'[1]

Churchill was still concerned that Britain and the US needed to be playing a major role in helping the Soviet Union, whose fate remained in the balance. In another message to his Chiefs of Staff, he stressed, 'I must repeat that Torch is no substitute for Round-up ... I never meant the Anglo-American army to be stuck in North Africa. It is a springboard and not a sofa.' The Americans were looking at 1944 for 'their great design'. As the prime minister saw it, 'the sum of all American fears is to be multiplied by the sum of all British fears'.[2]

To some extent, Roosevelt supported Churchill's view, suggesting that if the opportunity arose to strike across the Channel in 1943 'we must obviously grasp it'. But it was important to continue building up forces in Britain. In the meantime, North Africa would have to take precedence. And the US was more heavily engaged in the Pacific 'than I anticipated a few months ago'.[3]

The campaign in North Africa, moving east towards Montgomery's successful forces, did not go according to plan. The build-up of supplies was slow, hampered by air attacks on Algiers and Bône. Road and rail networks were poor. The Germans sent troops in large numbers to Tunis, 'and violent resistance began'. Anderson's First Army, backed by American troops, reached Djedeida, 12 miles from Tunis, but got no further and was soon forced back. A new enemy appeared, the rainy season.

Churchill suggested to Roosevelt that they should meet with Stalin to discuss the way ahead. The president agreed that it was 'the only satisfactory way of coming to the vital strategic conclusions the military situation requires'.[4]

Stalin said he was unable to leave the Soviet Union, and Roosevelt decided that the absence of 'Uncle Joe' should not prevent him from meeting Churchill. Several countries were considered for the talks, including Iceland, Bermuda and England, along with Khartoum in Sudan, Algiers and Casablanca, which was the agreed choice. Mindful of security, Roosevelt decided he would be known as Admiral Q. Churchill settled for Mr P, suggesting that they needed to 'mind our Ps and Qs'.

Churchill left Britain for Casablanca on 12 January 1943 in a converted bomber. It was a fraught flight because a petrol heater almost set the plane on fire and the prime minister decided that it was 'better to freeze than burn'. After arriving in Casablanca, there was the consolation of a comfortable villa. Before the president's arrival, Churchill went for coastal walks with the First Sea Lord and other military chiefs, noting that waves 15 feet high were crashing down on the rocks. It was no wonder that so many landing craft had been lost.

During the leaders' talks, General Sir Harold Alexander, Commander-in-Chief, Middle East, reported on the progress of Montgomery's Eighth Army, which was set to hasten Rommel's retreat. Alexander's 'unspoken confidence was contagious' and he impressed Roosevelt.

The Combined Chiefs of Staff spent ten days working on the main issues. On the North African campaign, it was agreed that Tunis should be the priority, using the Desert Army, as well as other British and American forces. Alexander would be Eisenhower's deputy and effectively in charge of all operations. Cunningham and Air Chief Marshal Sir Arthur Tedder would oversee naval and air policy.

It was acknowledged that U-boats in the Atlantic remained a major threat to Allied shipping. There was a commitment to continue to get as much aid as possible to the Soviet Union. The defeat of the Germans in Europe in 1943 was still the aim, though the military planners must have wondered if this was realistic, but they were well aware of Churchill's thoughts. In the Mediterranean, Sicily would be the next target with Operation *Husky*.

The conference had an amusing side, the 'shotgun marriage' of de Gaulle and Giraud. The haughty de Gaulle had reluctantly gone to Casablanca, and at a press conference on 24 January, the pair were forced to shake hands, Churchill recording, 'The pictures of this event cannot be viewed even in the setting of these tragic times without a laugh.'[5]

Ramsay was set to play a major role in *Husky* as the naval commander of the British assault forces, with Montgomery in command of the troops for the land battle. On the American side, Hewitt and Patton were given the corresponding roles. Ramsay had returned to the planning for *Round-up* when he learned of his new role, leading the Eastern Task Force, with Hewitt responsible for the Western Task Force. Cunningham was in overall naval command of both task forces. On 18 February, Ramsay attended a Chiefs of Staff meeting in London. Eisenhower was under pressure to launch *Husky* in the June but July was looking more realistic. The admiral pointed out that some of the landing craft from the US were set to arrive only a week or two before the assault. Crews would need a great deal of training.

Ramsay stressed the importance of close liaison between all the military leaders. It was recorded, 'In support of this he quoted an occasion where a telegram from Middle East to the US had been repeated to General Eisenhower, but a subsequent telegram substantially modifying the views expressed in the former had not been repeated. In the same way, the planning staff had lately changed part of the plan in such a way as to necessitate the provision of extra shipping. Although urgent steps would have to be taken in London to meet this new requirement, the authorities here had not been notified of the alteration of the plan.'[6]

On 2 March, Ramsay set up his *Husky* headquarters in Cairo, taking staff from London. A few days later, he complained to his wife that he was staying in a freezing flat. 'There is not a fireplace or a heater and the evenings are Arctic. I seem to be cursed with cold rooms. Our offices, which have no heating, are also Arctic, and we have to wear greatcoats in them. The flies are being an absolute curse.'[7]

A warmer climate was on offer and Ramsay went to visit Montgomery at Medenine in south-east Tunisia, shortly after an attack by Rommel's forces had been repulsed. It is surprising that two men with such contrasting personalities got on so well. 'Monty was in great form,' Ramsay wrote. 'He told me he gets thousands of letters and has had three proposals of marriage. He tries to answer or at least acknowledge every letter (except the proposals). The Eighth Army are magnificent. No other word for it. Monty the creator of it may be likened unto a popular film star, the way the soldiers rush to see him when he passes by. Monty was most optimistic about his future operations and I think you can look forward to good news shortly. There will be no stopping his army, I'm sure.'[8]

Ramsay also spent a week with Cunningham in Algiers, but there was tension. On 19 March, he wrote again to his wife, 'We've had a quiet time here, nothing much going and it is never very satisfactory living in someone else's sphere of action, especially with someone as dominating as Andrew Cunningham, charming though he may be. So I'm anxious to be off as soon as I can where I am my own boss and can get on with my own job.

'Tell me of domestic events etc that would interest me when you write. I've finished *Northanger Abbey* and *Persuasion* and loved them both. And my other literature is also exhausted so I don't know what I shall do on my long air journey back. Besides I always like to have a book by me to read in the evening and in bed. I think I shall have to read Jane Austen all over again. This is the time I could make good use of the library at Bughtrig.'[9] Once again he said how much he missed his family.

Ramsay was working closely with Lieutenant General Miles Dempsey, whom he liked 'and we see eye to eye, which makes it easier. But we don't see eye to eye in all things with those above us! ABC has his own very definite views. His judgement is excellent but his facts are sometimes wrong. There may be trouble later on, owing to his way of centralising command, in the same way as when he and I play together in ping-pong. He takes four-fifths of the balls. He's very good too.'[10] Not only had Cunningham taken Ramsay's *Torch* post but he was bossing the ping-pong table as well. Both admirals liked to win.

There were encouraging developments for the Allies in the early months of 1943. Perhaps the most significant was the defeat of the German Sixth Army at Stalingrad after months of bitter fighting. The Soviets reported on 2 February that all resistance had ended, and Churchill told Stalin it was 'a wonderful achievement'. The victory helped to take some of the pressure off Britain and the US over Stalin's demands for a major second front.

On 8 February, the Russians took back the city of Kursk. One day later, in the Pacific campaign, American forces captured the island of Guadalcanal after a land, sea and air campaign that had started the previous August. It signalled the end of Japanese expansion plans.

Three months would pass before the Allies secured victory in North Africa. The Eighth Army continued to push west towards the First Army, and American and French troops, trapping the Germans in a pincer movement. The First Army took the great prize, Tunis, on 7 May, the same day that the Americans entered Bizerta.

Alexander reported to Churchill, 'The Axis front has completely collapsed and disintegrated. We shall have to mop up pockets of Germans, but up to date probably 20,000 prisoners have been taken, besides many guns, lorries and dumps. Our casualties both in men and tanks are light.'[11]

On the day that Tunis was taken, Cunningham ordered his naval forces to patrol the Strait of Gibraltar to prevent the Germans staging a Dunkirk-style evacuation. The admiral signalled, 'Sink, burn and destroy. Let nothing pass.'[12] In the event, few Germans or Italians got away. The RAF was also keen to attack enemy shipping. Such was the enthusiasm of pilots that the bridge structures of Cunningham's destroyers were painted red to aid recognition. The Luftwaffe had already lost the battle of the air. Despite the paint precaution, Spitfires with American pilots attacked two destroyers – *Bicester* and *Zetland*. The pilots found themselves on the receiving end of some colourful language from *Bicester*'s captain, who was known as Baron Bicester.

Cunningham would state, 'It was a stupendous victory – just six months after the Allies had landed in North Africa, and three years after Italy had entered the war and the first fighting in the Western Desert. It is not for a sailor to express his opinions on fighting ashore; but the end in Tunisia was a fitting culmination to the victorious advance of the Eighth Army from El Alamein, and the stubborn fighting of the First Army – British, American and French – in the gaunt mountains and morasses of thick mud in the valleys of Tunisia. Even in the later phases of the war I doubt if such achievements were ever surpassed.'[13]

On 12 May, some 250,000 German and Italian troops surrendered. Alexander recorded, 'It was an astonishing sight to see long lines of Germans driving themselves in their own transport or in commandeered horse carts westwards in search of prisoner-of-war cages.' That day the general sent this message to the prime minister: 'It is my duty to report that the Tunisian campaign is over. All enemy resistance has ceased. We are masters of the North African shores.' A number of German generals were captured but Rommel, the Desert Fox, was not among them. He had gone to Germany in March, 'earnestly desiring to save his own skin', as Eisenhower put it, and never returned to Africa.[14] Churchill compared the Tunis victory to the

Soviet defeat of the German army at Stalingrad. He noted that it had lifted spirits in Britain for the first time in the war.

For Eisenhower, one of the greatest results of the victory was the 'welding of Allied unity and the establishment of a command team that was already showing the effects of growing confidence and trust among all its members'.[15] A victory parade was held in Tunis, but those commanders were already busy looking ahead to the next campaign – Operation *Husky*.

A key task after the surrender was clearing minefields from the Mediterranean. On 17 May, a convoy sailed from Gibraltar and arrived at Alexandria nine days later without loss; the first to do so since 1941. Another convoy reached Malta. The route to the Middle East was open. For Ramsay, this would be a major help in getting his task force to Sicily.

CHAPTER 26

Onwards to Sicily

Taking the decision at the Casablanca conference to invade Sicily, with a view to using the island as a base for operations against southern Europe, was the easy part, as events turned out. All the key military leaders set to be involved in Operation *Husky* were still committed to the North African campaign and, in the early stages, they could not devote enough time to their new task. Planning for *Husky* would prove a major challenge, with differing views and revisions seemingly at every turn. Cunningham would reflect, 'I do not criticise the overhead plan for Husky as eventually carried out. I am perfectly confident that any of the alternative plans would have succeeded. What I do maintain is that the three months delay in the production of the final overhead plan for the operation should never, and need never, have occurred.'[1]

The joint planning staff in London had produced the first outline plan, and amendments were made in Casablanca. These proposals went to General Alexander's new headquarters at Bouzaréah, near Algiers. Major General Charles Gairdner headed the planning staff at Bouzaréah. But there was a problem. As the war in North Africa was still raging, it would not be known what resources were available for *Husky* until it ended. The Combined Chiefs of Staff had wanted the invasion to take place in the June but eventually settled on 10 July.

Alexander noted that Sicily was compared to 'a jagged arrowhead with the broken point to the west', a mountainous island of about 10,000 square miles, with a coastline of some 600 miles. The planning staff had listed more than 90 stretches of beaches. The main ports were Messina in the north-east, Palermo in the north-west, and Catania and Syracuse on the east coast. There were 19 known airfields, but this figure would rise to more than 30 by the time of the invasion. Most of the defenders were Italian, and it was initially estimated that there were three regular infantry divisions and five inferior coastal divisions. Alexander acknowledged that 'all the commanders concerned agreed that if

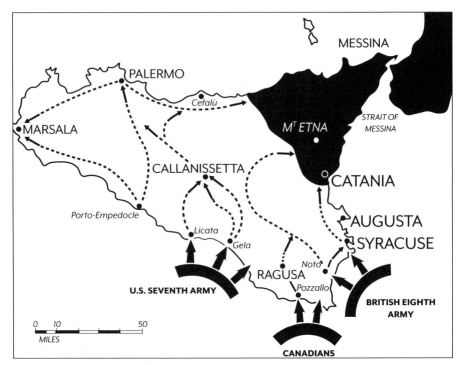

Operation *Husky*, the invasion of Sicily. How the Allies pushed German and Italian forces towards the north-east of the island from 10 to 31 July 1943.

the Italians should be reinforced with substantial well-equipped German forces before the attack the chances of success would be considerably reduced'.[2]

The initial plan envisaged a two-pronged attack in the west and south-east. Ramsay would land his British Eastern Task Force at Avola, Pachino, Pozzallo and Gela, which would consist of three infantry divisions and two tank battalions. Four parachute battalions also would be involved. The capture of the ports of Syracuse and Augusta, as well as several airfields, was the aim. There would be a simultaneous landing by the American Western Task Force at Sciacca and Marinella, with a later main strike in the Palermo area. Three days later the Eastern Task Force would make another landing, this time in the Catania area.

Ramsay was not impressed when he saw the plan, and he would later comment, 'In the early stages of planning for Husky too little importance and attention was paid to the operational aspect whilst too much was paid to the administrative, with the result that the outline plan given to the commanders of the Eastern Task Force was operationally unacceptable.'[3]

In early April, Montgomery, who would play a key role in *Husky*, was still largely in the dark about the operation. Ramsay wrote to him on 7 April, saying 'you cannot be left uninformed any longer and Dempsey is setting off tomorrow to visit you'. The admiral went on, 'It is now over a fortnight since we left Algiers and the plan is in exactly the same state, in so far as it is known to us, as on the day on which we left. As you know, we considered the original plan was based too much on mathematical factors and too little on operational or realistic ones. The new plan concedes a little in the latter direction but insufficiently to make it anywhere near being acceptable.

'You will, I hope, have observed in the foregoing that I have freely used the word "we". On the other hand, I have observed, with some disapproval and not without amusement, that in your messages to Dempsey you have been in the habit of issuing unilateral edicts on matters which require joint agreement.

'The location of the Eighth Army HQ is of course a matter for your decision alone, but it is not for you alone to dictate the location of the command HQ for the Eastern Task Force.'[4] Ramsay was based in Cairo and Montgomery wished to remain in Tripoli. The admiral stressed that they and their staffs needed to be in the same place as it was necessary to work closely on a daily basis.

Ramsay added, 'As Naval Commander Eastern Task Force I have considerable responsibility for its success and intend to have my say in the framing of the plan. Incidentally my directive states that I am in executive control of the force until the army is firmly established ashore. I do not for one moment suggest that you would contest any of the above, but I think it just as well that there should be a clear understanding between us, my mind having been somewhat disturbed by the edicts which you have issued of late with your customary clarity.'[5]

Montgomery replied five days later, 'I have your letter of 7 April, brought me by Dempsey. It is magnificent! I am having it framed!!'[6] The general decided to send his chief of staff, Major General Francis de Guingand, known as Freddie, and his advanced base commander, Major General Brian Robertson, to Cairo to work with Ramsay. Montgomery pointed out, 'If they agree, you can take it that I agree – and carry on. I will come in myself as soon as I can.'[7]

Planning groups in London and Washington were pulling in different directions, and Ramsay was further exasperated when he found that Cunningham supported the latest proposals. He protested and Cunningham agreed that he could consult with Montgomery on changes. The general was only too happy to come on board, although he remained unclear about what exactly was being proposed, such was the 'dog's breakfast'. The overall plan aside, Ramsay still had to focus on an extensive training programme for sailors and soldiers involving landing craft, beach parties and supply dumps. The training faced a number of difficulties. Both task forces had to establish bases in captured ports that had been wrecked – Sfax, Sousse, Bizerta and Tunis. 'Great credit is due to all concerned that those difficulties were ably surmounted in the time available,' Cunningham recorded. Ramsay's force was also given the task of capturing Pantellaria, 'but the task was taken in its stride and successfully accomplished without prejudice to Husky, of which operation indeed it was an essential preliminary.'[8]

On 19 April, Montgomery flew to Algiers in his recently acquired Flying Fortress (a 'gift' from Eisenhower) to see Alexander and discuss the way ahead. He admitted, 'I myself, and my army HQ staff, know very little about the operation as a whole, and nothing whatever about the detailed planning that is going on.' And he complained, 'Detailed planning is being carried out by staff officers who are not in touch with battle requirements. There is no responsible senior commander thoroughly versed in what happens in battle who is devoting his sole attention to the Husky operation.'[9] The general predicted a disaster if this carried on, and he made a series of recommendations. When de Guingand was appointed Montgomery's chief of staff, he revealed that already there had been seven plans for *Husky*.

Then Plan No 8 appeared. Montgomery went to Cairo and quickly rejected it after consulting Ramsay and his corps commanders for *Husky*, Lieutenant General Dempsey and Major General Oliver Leese. In a message to Alexander, he said he would put forward his own plan for the Eighth Army, warning that the planners were dispersing the invasion force too widely and assuming that Sicily would be captured easily. 'Never was there a greater error,' he stressed. 'Germans and Italians are fighting well in Tunisia and will repeat the process in Sicily … We must plan for fierce resistance, by the Germans at any rate, and for a real dog fight battle to follow the initial assault.'[10]

Montgomery's Plan No 9 would have the Eighth Army concentrating on an area between Syracuse and the Pachino peninsula, with subsequent operations to take airfields and ports. The general stated, 'Admiral Ramsay is in complete agreement with me and together we are prepared to launch the operation and win.'[11] Montgomery had his own ideas about the American landings but decided to hold back – for the moment.

It was Ramsay who ended up on the receiving end of 'a proper stinker' from Cunningham. Ramsay was rather upset, but Montgomery consoled him and they had 'a good laugh over it'. They agreed that Montgomery should send another message to Alexander. It read, 'I hear that Cunningham and Tedder have told you they disagree completely with our proposed plan for the Eighth Army assault on Sicily. I wish to state emphatically that if we carry out the suggested existing plan it will fail. I state on whatever reputation I may have that the plan put forward by me and Ramsay will succeed. Would you like us both to come over and explain our plan? Meanwhile work is continuing on our plan as time is short.'[12]

It was not long before Montgomery decided to tell the Americans that they were going to land in the wrong places. In Algiers, he went to see Eisenhower's chief of staff, Brigadier Walter Bedell Smith, who was 'not in his office and I eventually ran him to ground in the lavatory. So we discussed the problems then and there.' Montgomery said American landings near Palermo should be cancelled and instead the forces should be placed on the south coast between Gela and west of the Pachino peninsula. The Eighth Army and Patton's Seventh Army would then be close, 'giving cohesion to the whole invasion'.[13]

Montgomery persuaded Bedell Smith to hold a staff conference at which he outlined his plans. Ramsay also went to Algiers, later telling his wife, 'Monty has thrown a spanner of considerable size into the works. It requires all the tact I can gather to deal with him, though he and I are on the best possible terms. I've got him just where I want him as regards the navy, and there is complete understanding between us. I can, however, foresee that he will forever be putting me in difficult circumstances with ABC, which I would prefer to avoid. It's a great pity, for Monty is a great general.'[14]

Montgomery returned to his operational HQ in Tunisia. He said that at midnight on 3 May he received a signal from Alexander saying that Eisenhower had approved his proposals. 'Having been woken up and given the signal, I went to sleep again feeling that fighting the Germans was easy compared with fighting for the vital issues on which everything depended.'[15]

In his official report on Operation *Husky*, Alexander stated that he decided to recast the whole plan on 3 May, and it was approved by the Combined Chiefs of Staff on 12 May.

Ramsay was satisfied that the best plan available had been adopted. He was happy to return to Cairo, telling his wife, 'ABC was charming as ever, but the air was a bit tense owing to certain major modifications suggested by us and my army friends. I had to fly over and see Monty at his HQ and stayed the night in a caravan in an olive grove. Life was healthy but crude, and I enjoyed it. We managed to get our way, however, in Algiers, which has simplified things though causing us and everyone else an immense amount of work.

'I've been travelling about lately and seeing a lot of a very nice general called Oliver Leese, an ex-guardsman; we went many miles by air and road to Algiers and to Monty's HQ in Tunisia. The country was green and a mass of wild flowers and poppies. Some of the caravans that the generals live in are beautifully fitted up, but the one I had was barely furnished and had no wash-place or looking glass. A bath, of course, was quite out of the question. It was all the more lovely when we got back to civilisation to have one. But how I dislike this air travel, owing to the discomfort of it. Fancy sitting for hours either on boards or on a hard seat or a bench. It becomes excruciating after a while. Very, very occasionally I get a passenger plane with proper seats, but only very occasionally.'[16] Perhaps Montgomery travelled in greater comfort in his Flying Fortress.

A few days later, in another letter to his wife, Ramsay paid tribute to Montgomery. 'Monty is streets ahead of all other generals in fighting ability and I predict that he will be regarded in years to come as the outstanding master of his profession on the Allied side,' he wrote. 'He and I get on famously as I can tell him home truths in a way that none of his own profession could attempt. He is due here tonight, and about time too, as we've been having most difficult times, owing to the distances which separate the various authorities. ABC and I have been disagreeing rather seriously the last week or so, mostly due to misunderstanding and the lag of communications.'[17]

Ramsay revealed that one of his flag officers, Vice Admiral Ronald Hallifax, had been killed in an air crash. Hallifax was Flag Officer Commanding Red Sea and Canal Area, and the crash occurred at the Egyptian village of Sollum (Sallum), about 90 miles from Tobruk. 'Such a fine chap,' Ramsay wrote. 'He was on his way to see me. Philip Vian [Rear Admiral Sir Philip Vian] has taken his place and that was why he was here. I am very lucky in my admirals and chiefs of staff. They are all first class. I also like my generals so much. My staff also is excellent but is proving too small and some members are grossly overworked. Compared to Monty's staff mine are in the proportion of about one to eight.'[18]

Shortly afterwards Ramsay was able to report that relations with Cunningham had improved. It was an extremely busy time and 'the wires are red hot'. On 11 May, Montgomery was in Cairo and met Ramsay for lunch. 'Anything I ask for is done at once,' the admiral noted. 'I try and do the same by him and only hope that when it comes to action I can produce the requisite results in the quickest time.'[19] He found the general a tired man and badly in need of a rest. On 16 May, with the North Africa campaign over, Montgomery set off from Tripoli in his Flying Fortress for a holiday in England.

In late May, after visiting Roosevelt in Washington, Churchill and his party, including General Brooke, flew to Algiers. The prime minister was already looking beyond the attack on Sicily. He wanted a commitment to invade Italy. In this he was supported by Alexander, Cunningham and Tedder and later by Montgomery after his return from England. But Eisenhower was 'very reserved' and Marshall 'remained up till almost the last moment silent or cryptic'.[20] Although the British had much greater forces in the theatre than the Americans – three times as many troops, four times as many warships and almost equal air power – it was still accepted that Eisenhower was the supreme commander and that it was important to preserve the appearance of a US-led operation. Eventually, the Americans were won over. Italy would be the focus after Sicily.[21]

In the meantime, another target had gained the attention of the Allies, the island of Pantelleria, lying between Sicily and the north-east coast of Tunisia. It had an airfield, which would be invaluable for the invasion of Sicily. But the island was a natural fortress, with a rocky coastline and only one suitable landing spot – a small harbour. Its terrain ruled out a drop by paratroopers. There were an estimated 10,000 Italian troops on the island, with more than 100 gun emplacements and a large number of machine-gun positions. The Italians likened Pantelleria to Gibraltar.

Eisenhower recalled, 'Many of our experienced commanders and staff officers strongly advised against attempting this operation, since any failure would have a disheartening effect on the troops to be committed against the Sicilian shore. However, Admiral Cunningham, in particular, agreed with me that the place could be taken at slight cost. We based our conviction upon the assumption that most Italians had had a stomachful of fighting and were looking for any good excuse to quit.'[22]

Operation *Corkscrew* saw a massive air and naval bombardment, which began on 18 May and continued until 11 June. At one stage, Eisenhower and Cunningham boarded the cruiser HMS *Aurora* and went to see the progress of the attack. The admiral pointed out that the area was mined apart from a channel that had been swept. The general asked if there were any floating mines, and Cunningham replied, 'Oh yes, but at this speed the bow wave will throw them away from the ship. It would be just bad luck if we should strike one.'[23]

Churchill, at that time visiting North Africa, had wanted to go on the reconnaissance, and Cunningham recalled, 'We had some difficulty with Mr Churchill who was most anxious to come with us. He remained unconvinced by our argument that his life was far too valuable to the Allied cause to be risked in this unnecessary way. He finally left for home on 5 June … but I think he still holds it against us that he was not allowed to prolong his visit to see some action, for which he was always a glutton.'[24]

On the morning of 11 June, the battered Italians ran up the white flag as British troops were poised to make an amphibious landing. The only British casualty after landing was reportedly a soldier bitten by a donkey. The Italians claimed that they were forced to surrender because of a lack of water, but Eisenhower and Cunningham had been correct in believing that they had no stomach for further fighting after the defeat in Tunisia. The next day, the Italian garrisons on the nearby islands of Lampedusa and Linosa surrendered without a fight.

Sicily, of course, was a much tougher prospect. It was estimated that the enemy forces on the island numbered 315,000 Italians and 50,000 Germans. Reinforcements after the invasion would take the German numbers to 90,000. The Allied invasion force initially would be around 150,000, involving some 3,000 ships and landing craft and 4,000 aircraft.

As Churchill looked to the conquest of southern Italy, Ramsay and his American counterpart, Hewitt, were grappling with perhaps the most complicated assembly of ships and troops ever staged. They were coming from all over the southern and eastern shores of the Mediterranean, as well as from Britain and the US. Cunningham pointed out, 'Very detailed orders were issued regarding the routes and timing of the approach, backed up by track charts and the inevitable "Mickey Mouse" diagrams which are in my view essential to the clear understanding of a problem of this nature. Even so, everything depended, as always, on the seamanship and good sense of individual commanding officers and on the smooth working of the berthing and fuelling organisations of the several ports concerned.'[25]

It was not just ships and men who were spread around, as Alexander explained, 'My headquarters was originally near Algiers and later at La Marsa, near Carthage, with a small tactical headquarters on Malta. Seventh Army headquarters was near Oran for the planning stage, subsequently moving to Bizerta. Eighth Army headquarters was originally in Cairo and moved to Malta for the assault. Admiral Cunningham established his headquarters also in Malta, and Mediterranean air command headquarters and the headquarters of the tactical and strategic air forces were all grouped around Carthage, adjacent to my main headquarters.'[26]

A naval force of four battleships, two aircraft carriers, four cruisers and some 18 destroyers would support the troop convoys. The warships would be in the Ionian Sea by 9 July, well placed to meet any threat from the Italian navy based at Taranto and La Spezia. Another Allied force of two battleships, two cruisers and six destroyers was in reserve at Algiers.

Ramsay based himself in Malta on 2 July. There was still much to do for the admiral and his staff, including the allocation of landing craft to flotillas and briefings for all the vessels. The invasion of Sicily was still set for 10 July, and on the previous day, the admiral set sail in the forward operations ship HMS *Antwerp*, joining four main convoys south of Malta. The Eastern Task Force was now under his operational control. By early evening 'a nasty sea was running', with Ramsay recording, 'The effect of these conditions on the landing craft and at the beaches caused me some anxiety but postponement did not seriously enter my mind.' Vessels sailed on without any lights and in radio silence. The wind and sea started to drop after midnight, and in darkness landing craft embarked troops. The Eighth Army landed on beaches south of Syracuse and, on the left flank, Canadian troops went ashore near Pachino.

'The defences were taken generally by surprise when the assaulting formations landed and there was little organised resistance on the beaches,' Ramsay reported. 'It is understood that a proportion of the coast defences were not, in fact, manned on that night; those that were manned were, in the majority of cases, not stoutly fought.'[27] At first light, there was some shelling from shore batteries, but the naval force returned effective fire. Few landing craft were hit but some were lost because of poor seamanship.

That night German planes attacked and sank the hospital ship *Talamba*, fully illuminated and with Red Cross markings, as it embarked casualties. One of the survivors, junior engineer Stan Fernando, who had been in his bunk, recalled, 'I must have just fallen asleep when there was a terrific bang and whoosh. A great splash of water hit the boat deck. I was out of my bunk in a flash and put on a boiler suit. In a trice I was outside my cabin at the same time as everyone else. There appeared to be no sign of any damage but the boat deck was awash. We heard the screech of a plane race past with machine guns blasting away and there came a booming voice saying "Put those lights out". No one on a hospital ship is prepared for a situation like this. The best I could do was to take out a shoe and try to bash in some of the bulkhead lights but this was a futile attempt. In a matter of minutes the vessel was sinking quite quickly.'[28] Most of the crew, medical staff and patients were saved. The hospital ships *Aba* and *Dorsetshire*, both fully illuminated, were also attacked.

For Ramsay it was a painful reminder of the attacks on hospital ships during the Dunkirk evacuation. After the sinking of *Talamba*, he recommended that hospital ships should be kept darkened when at anchorages during the night.

The American landings, on beaches between Licata and Gela and beyond, were also successful, despite a heavy surf. All the landings had been preceded by an airborne assault but this did not go according to plan. Some of the pilots of transport planes and gliders had problems with navigation, and a wind of some 40 miles an hour took many of the paratroopers off course. Of

134 British gliders, nearly 50 came down in the sea, 75 landed somewhere in south-east Sicily and only 12 found the correct dropping zone. Ships rescued some of the paratroopers in the sea. US paratroopers were scattered in small groups over an area of 50 miles from Licata to Noto. Despite these setbacks, 'the effect on the nerves of the none too steady Italian troops of the descent of these airborne forces all over southeast Sicily was of the utmost value to the assault. Small isolated units of parachutists seized vital points, attacked roads and created widespread panic which undoubtedly disorganised all plans for defence'. By 2100 on 10 July, British troops had entered Syracuse, 'a particularly fine feat of arms'. Montgomery's Eighth Army had yet to make contact with German troops or any of the Italian mobile divisions. The men of the coastal divisions quickly surrendered. Patton's Seventh Army easily seized its objectives – Licata, Gela, Scoglitti and Marina di Ragusa.[29]

The next day the Eighth Army moved up the east coast towards Catania. The heat was intense. Contact was made with one of the Italian mobile divisions. The Americans encountered a battle group of the Hermann Goering Division, and fierce fighting broke out at Gela, lasting most of the day. With the help of naval gunfire, the German attack was repulsed. Cunningham, in the minelayer HMS *Abdiel*, was checking on the beaches, and Patton told him that the situation had been 'ticklish'.

Ramsay wrote to his wife that day, 'It was almost unreal to find oneself off Sicily with Etna looking down on the scene of the landings. Hundreds of ships of the largest size down to the smallest vessel were massed off the coast, which looked so sleepy and peaceful, and one had to pinch oneself to make sure it wasn't a dream. The opposition was surprisingly poor, but there was just sufficient to make it clear that we really were undertaking a warlike operation. Had there been stern opposition our losses would have been severe. As it was we got off extraordinarily lightly, and I never saw an enemy aircraft all day. They were about, but not in any number and they didn't wait.

'I visited all the landings in my area, and everywhere things were going well. Philip Vian [Commanding Amphibious Force] was with the Canadians, who did extremely well. The Americans did well too as they had worse weather than we had. Latest reports are to the effect that the Italians are putting up little resistance and have no heart in fighting. The Germans are only just coming into contact with us, and things will then be different, but they cannot do more than delay the capture of the whole island.'[30]

Ramsay was busy making sure that ships unloaded vehicles and supplies and sailed again. Tragedy struck on 13 July, the day that Augusta was captured, when a number of troop-carrying aircraft were shot down by Allied ships, despite the fact that warning signals had been sent. Ramsay explained, 'It is not certain that they did in fact reach all the merchantmen, and by unfortunate chance a small number of enemy aircraft was in the vicinity at the time our aircraft were approaching. As might be expected, firing which started spasmodically soon became general, and it is hard to blame ships for engaging low-flying aircraft which appeared to be menacing them during an air raid. It is considered that in only very exceptional circumstances should ships be deprived of their right to open fire at low-flying aircraft approaching them. The solution must be always to route transport aircraft clear of our shipping.'[31]

Over the next few days, cruisers and destroyers were busy bombarding enemy positions. Cunningham's former flagship, HMS *Warspite*, shelled Catania with its 15in guns. The admiral signalled the World War I veteran, which still had a turn of speed, 'Operation well carried out. There is no doubt that when the old lady lifts her skirts she can run.'[32] MTBs made night raids in the Strait of Messina, often battling E-boats. Italian and German U-boats suffered, with a total of 13 destroyed between 11 July and 22 August.

Patton, always in a hurry, headed to the north coast, and Palermo was captured on 22 July. The Seventh Army then turned east towards Messina, but progress was difficult because retreating Germans had demolished parts of the coastal cliff road. But the tactic of landing troops behind enemy lines paid dividends.

The Eighth Army also had a tough time, and there was stubborn resistance at Catania. Cunningham commented, 'The terrain, dominated by the great bastion of Mount Etna in the background, was undoubtedly most difficult, though I thought at the time we might have lessened our difficulties and hastened the advance if we had taken a leaf out of the American book and used our sea power to land troops behind the enemy lines. We had the ships ready at Augusta with commando troops embarked for just such operations, and I was sure that with Rear Admiral [Rhoderick] McGrigor, full of fire and energy, in charge, operations of this sort would have been no less successful than those on the north coast.'[33]

Ramsay's command of the Eastern Task Force came to an end on 22 July, as did Hewitt's corresponding role. The Commander-in-Chief, Mediterranean, took responsibility for supplying the troops in Sicily. Catania did not fall until 5 August. On 17 August, Patton's men entered Messina a few hours before Montgomery's troops, no doubt to the British general's annoyance. But the Germans and Italians had already decided that the island was lost. They began evacuating troops, guns and vehicles across the Strait of Messina to mainland Italy on 11 August, using ferries and other vessels, and this continued until

17 August. It was the Axis equivalent of Dunkirk, with more than 100,000 troops escaping. The narrow strait was heavily defended and the Allies were unable to prevent the withdrawal.

Eisenhower was pleased that the Allies had worked well together. 'One of the valuable outcomes of the campaign was the continued growth and development of the spirit of comradeship between British and American troops in action,' he recorded. 'The Seventh Army, in its first campaign, had established a reputation that gained the deep respect of the veteran British Eighth, while on the American side there was sincere enthusiasm for the fighting qualities of their British and Canadian partners.'[34]

After Ramsay's command ended, he returned to England. Fed up with uncomfortable planes, he decided to travel in the *Cameronia*; a liner that had been requisitioned as a troopship. During the voyage he wrote to his wife, once again singing Montgomery's praises, 'I am convinced that had we not had a general as skilful as Monty we should have taken some very nasty knocks ere now. He is streets ahead of any other general that I know of and an asset that is priceless to us. After all, we have got to win battles and he is the only one who wins them for us. And yet there are people who would like to see him take a toss. It is pleasant to come home knowing that one's job has been successfully accomplished, and it will be interesting to see what comes next.'[35]

In his memoirs Montgomery pointed out that malarial mosquitos had caused almost as many casualties as the enemy. It was so hot and humid that soldiers in the rear areas shed most of their clothing. The general recalled seeing an army lorry with the driver apparently wearing only a silk top hat. 'As the lorry passed me, the driver leant out from his cab and took off his hat to me with a sweeping and gallant gesture. I just roared with laughter. However, while I was not particular about dress so long as the soldiers fought well and we won battles, I at once decided there were limits. When I got back to my headquarters I issued the only order I ever issued about dress in the Eighth Army. It read as follows: "Top hats will not be worn in the Eighth Army".'[36]

CHAPTER 27

Neptune's Call

When Ramsay returned to Britain, he was able to spend some time with his family in Berwickshire. Riding and shooting, or simply enjoying the peace of the garden at Bughtrig, were other welcome distractions from the war; a world away from the heat and stark landscape of Sicily.

His friend, Montgomery, was still on the island and experiencing further frustration when it came to the way ahead. The general and the admiral had become exasperated over the various plans for the invasion of Sicily. A key aim had been to knock Italy out of the war, but as Montgomery would point out, 'As a first step we were to capture Sicily but there was no plan for operations beyond. There should have been a master plan which embraced the capture of Sicily and the use of that island as a springboard for getting quickly across to Italy and exploiting success.'[1]

The Italian dictator Benito Mussolini was no longer in the picture. Military defeats aside, Allied bombing of factories, food shortages and strikes had added to widespread discontent in the country. King Victor Emanuel dismissed Mussolini from office on 24 July and the dictator suffered the indignity of being arrested by the carabinieri. Behind the scenes, his successor, Marshal Pietro Badoglio, was involved in negotiations with the Allies. An armistice was signed on 3 September; the day that the Eighth Army crossed the Strait of Messina to the mainland. Montgomery had been given a plan. The British troops encountered little resistance and Reggio Calabria was soon taken.

In a cable to Churchill on 6 September, Alexander observed, 'While in Reggio this morning there was not a warning sound to be heard or a hostile plane to be seen. On the contrary, on this lovely summer day naval craft of all types were plying backwards and forwards between Sicily and the mainland, carrying men, stores and munitions. In this lively setting it was more like a regatta in peacetime than a serious operation of war.'

Reality would soon take over, as the American Fifth Army under Lieutenant General Mark Clark discovered days later, when it landed at Salerno, southeast of Naples, meeting fierce German opposition. The Germans had some 20 divisions in Italy and the Allied campaign on the ground would prove increasingly hard.

That month saw Ramsay back in London. No doubt he would have been as pleased as Cunningham at the surrender of the Italian battle fleet, which was ordered to sail to Malta. German planes attacked the ships on the way and bombs destroyed the battleship *Roma* with heavy loss of life. As the Italians neared the island, British warships including *Warspite* went to escort them. On board the destroyer HMS *Hambledon* were Cunningham and Eisenhower. The admiral of the fleet would record, 'To me it was a most moving and thrilling sight. To see my wildest hopes of years back brought to fruition, and my former flagship the *Warspite*, which had struck the first blow against the Italians three years before, leading her erstwhile opponents into captivity, filled me with the deepest emotion and lives with me still. I can never forget it. I made a signal congratulating the *Warspite* on her proud and rightful position at the head of the line.'[2]

The liberation of Europe had started, and Ramsay was about to play a major part. At a gathering in London, Mountbatten told him he was likely to be appointed the Naval Allied Commander-in-Chief for the invasion of Normandy. The First Sea Lord, Dudley Pound, had resigned because of ill health and Cunningham was chosen to replace him. 'One of my first tasks was to select the Naval Allied Commander-in-Chief for the invasion,' Cunningham recalled. 'One name stood out above all others for his ability, character and experience, that of Admiral Sir Bertram Ramsay. The prime minister cordially accepted the choice.'[3] The Americans agreed and Ramsay's appointment was confirmed on 25 October. He would be responsible for Operation *Neptune*.

Ramsay received many messages of congratulation, including one from the former Archbishop of Canterbury Lord Lang, who wrote, 'I am glad to think that a task of such mingled inspiration and responsibility has been entrusted to you, and I pray that God may give you the strength, courage and wisdom to fulfil it.'[4] And there was another honour for the admiral, the KBE (Knight Commander of the British Empire), for his services in Sicily.

While Ramsay was busy focusing on the invasions of North Africa and Sicily, planning for the assault on north-west Europe, now known as Operation *Overlord*, continued in London under the direction of the British Army's Lieutenant General Frederick Morgan, who had been given the title

Chief of Staff to the Supreme Allied Commander (COSSAC). But, at that time, there was no Supreme Allied Commander for *Overlord*. Originally it had been proposed that this would be a British post, and Churchill favoured General Brooke. At the Quebec conference in August 1943, however, the prime minister suggested that because of the huge US troop commitment an American could take the role provided Britain had supreme command of the Mediterranean. Roosevelt agreed but he was in no hurry to take a decision 'for domestic reasons connected with high personages'. Brooke was told of the change and 'bore the great disappointment with soldierly dignity'.[5] The conference examined Morgan's outline plan for *Overlord* and gave its approval, with a target date of 1 May 1944. One problem for the *Overlord* planners was the proposed simultaneous assault on southern France, Operation *Anvil*, with a similar demand on resources.

In November 1943, Roosevelt's chief of staff, Admiral William Leahy, sent a telegram to General Brooke suggesting that General Marshall should be the supreme commander of the European and North African theatres. Brooke described the proposal as 'ridiculous', and Churchill supported him.[6] On 4 December, Brooke was asked to dine alone with Churchill and he was informed that Roosevelt had decided that Eisenhower would command *Overlord*. 'The selection of Eisenhower rather than Marshall was a good one,' Brooke noted. 'Eisenhower had now a certain amount of experience as a commander and was beginning to find his feet … Marshall had never commanded anything in war except, I believe, a company in the First World War.' Brooke would have the consolation of promotion to field marshal.[7]

Eisenhower took up his new post in January 1944, with Air Chief Marshal Tedder as his deputy. Montgomery was given command of the 21st Army Group, made up mainly of the British Second Army and the First Canadian Army. He would also be responsible for American ground forces in the first phase of *Overlord*. Ramsay and Montgomery would once again be involved in a combined operation.

Eisenhower decided to retain his chief of staff, Bedell Smith. Morgan, who had done so much of the planning, was offered a command in Italy but, not surprisingly, opted to remain with *Overlord* and became one of Bedell Smith's deputies. Eisenhower did not want to be based in the centre of London and, seeking some country air, chose Bushy Park, south-west of the capital, where Camp Griffiss, European headquarters of the United States Army Air Forces, was located. The base became Supreme Headquarters, Allied Expeditionary Force (SHAEF).

The Combined Chiefs of Staff had given Eisenhower a simple order: 'You will enter the continent of Europe and, in conjunction with other Allied nations, undertake operations aimed at the heart of Germany and the destruction of her armed forces.' It was a masterpiece of understatement.

As Ramsay pointed out, the invasion involved the greatest amphibious operation in history, with more than 6,000 ships and craft. 'From the outset of detailed planning it was clear that success would be largely dependent upon the ability to exercise close and continuous control of the thousands of ships and craft taking part. This overall control would have to embrace control of loading of all types of shipping and craft, control of convoy sailing, control of tugs, and control of ship repairs. Without it time would inevitably be lost and the best use could not be made of the great resources given to the operation to establish our forces ashore and then to reinforce them as quickly as possible.'[8]

Such was the complexity that four separate organisations were set up within Operation *Neptune*. They were TURCO (Turn Round Control Organisation), BUCO (Build-up Control Organisation), COREP (Control Repair Organisation) and COTUG (Control Tug Organisation).

On Saturday 1 January, Ramsay went to spend the weekend with Rear Admiral Sir Philip Vian and his family at their home in Hampshire. Vian had experienced an eventful war, which included the *Altmark* incident, the *Bismarck* action and the invasion of Sicily. He had been awarded the Distinguished Service Order and two Bars. Vian would play a key role in *Neptune*. Ramsay had chosen him to command Force J for the landing on Juno beach, one of five areas that would be attacked. The two admirals would not always get on. But that weekend all was well.

Ramsay told his wife Margaret, 'They have a nice little house near Liphook and have two girls aged about 12 and nine. We sawed wood, played card games with the children and talked business in turn, and had an excellent tea and dinner. Sunday morning Philip and I played 18 holes of golf and the girls carried our clubs.

'I returned in time to go to Claridge's [the hotel in Mayfair, London] and meet Monty. Found him in great form in a private suite with his chief of staff, ADC and another. The people in Claridge's behave so badly, treating Monty like a beast at the zoo, to be pointed out and stared at. We had a full and free discussion of things and found ourselves in complete agreement.'

Soon afterwards Ramsay sent another letter to his wife, saying that life was hectic and exhausting. 'As anticipated, Monty has struck out a new line of action and it is my part to keep him within bounds.' It was a clear reminder of the problems with Operation *Husky*.

Montgomery had said goodbye to the Eighth Army in Italy, flying to Marrakesh on 31 December on his way to Britain. Churchill was at the

Moroccan city convalescing from an illness, and he had a copy of the plan for *Overlord*, which he asked the general to read and to give his opinion. That evening Churchill held a dinner party, and Montgomery, always keen to go to bed early and fearing lengthy New Year celebrations, asked to leave soon after the meal so that he could read the *Overlord* plan. This he did and, with his usual efficiency, he had his notes typed before breakfast. He remarked that it was the first time he had seen the plan and he had not been able to consult Ramsay or any experienced air officer – 'therefore these initial comments can have little value'. But he went on to stress that the proposed landing area was too narrow for so many divisions, and this would lead to appalling confusion. 'My first impression is that the present plan is impracticable.'[9] He then made a number of suggestions.

Montgomery recorded, 'The prime minister was intensely interested. He said he had always known there was something wrong in the proposed plan, but that the Chiefs of Staff had agreed with it and that left him powerless. Now a battlefield commander had analysed it for him and had given him the information he needed – and he was grateful.'[10]

On his return to England, Montgomery set up the headquarters of the 21st Army Group at St Paul's School in Hammersmith, west London, where he had been a pupil. The general was not popular with local residents. The area was being bombed and they blamed his presence. Montgomery insisted there was no evidence to support the claim. He moved into a block of flats near the school – Latymer Court. Ramsay and his chief of staff, Rear Admiral George Creasy, also took up residence. 'We were a most cheery party,' Montgomery recalled, 'and at dinner each evening the conversation roamed over a wide field. Discussion often ended in bets being laid. I suggested we should keep a betting book in which all bets would be entered and signed by both sides.' Ramsay bet Montgomery an even £5 that the war with Germany would be over by 1 January 1945.[11]

Montgomery's chief of staff, Major General de Guingand, observed, 'Of the top commanders of the other services, I think he got on best with that lovable little sailor Admiral Ramsay and with Air Chief Marshal Leigh-Mallory.'[12]

January 1944 saw the *Overlord* plan undergoing several changes, usually at Montgomery's request. He wanted a five-division assault instead of the proposed three divisions. There were tensions. During a meeting at St Paul's with the general and Leigh-Mallory, Ramsay 'put the naval case forcibly but as usual Monty was only interested in so far as I said I would or would not do a thing. This is quite wrong because he should acknowledge and weigh up the reasons which lead up to my conclusions. On this occasion I was not prepared to give a considered reply to any question.'[13]

Another meeting at the school, with British and American army and air force officers, was staged, in Ramsay's view, to give the impression that Montgomery was the supreme commander and the admiral and Leigh-Mallory were 'subsidiary to him which was absurd as we are all on the same level. We adjusted this by changing places.'[14] Perhaps Montgomery felt it necessary to assert himself at St Paul's where, as a boy, he had been a prefect and captain of the 1st XV. The general later apologised.

Ramsay had two task forces under his command, one British, the other American. On his recommendation, Rear Admiral Vian was appointed Naval Commander, Eastern Task Force, giving up his Force J role. Ramsay suggested that Vian should be given the rank of acting vice admiral but Cunningham refused. Rear Admiral Alan Kirk of the US Navy was given command of the Western Task Force.

But there was still no final decision on the *Overlord* plan. Eisenhower had been in the United States and on his return to Britain Ramsay went to see him. The admiral stressed the importance of increasing the invasion forces and suggested cancelling Operation *Anvil* because of the shortage of landing craft. Eisenhower remained keen on *Anvil* and, in Ramsay's view, 'wants to have his cake and eat it'.[15]

On 20 January, Ramsay marked his 61st birthday. 'Feeling no older,' he wrote in his diary. 'Ike is holding a commanders' meeting tomorrow to hear the Overlord plan demonstrated and hear the commanders views on it. I have now prepared my remarks upon Monty's revised five-division assault version of it. Ike must definitely arrive at a final decision tomorrow as to what line he is to take as we must have finality and a firm plan and date without any more waffling. I will do my utmost to make it easier for him to do so. The five-division assault must stand and Anvil must be cancelled in order to make it possible to mount it.'[16]

The meeting the next day was long but it agreed on the five-division proposal, with the necessary increase in naval forces. Washington needed to be consulted and the 'waffling' continued for some time. Eventually, the Combined Chiefs of Staff backed the plan for an extended front of 50 miles, although the Admiralty and the Americans thought that Ramsay's demands were excessive. But the admiral and Montgomery were convinced that overwhelming naval and air power was needed to establish a bridgehead and build up the invasion forces quickly.

Ramsay still had a dislike of personal publicity. At a press conference on 1 February, he faced nearly an hour of 'frightful' photographs. 'There must have been 70 press photographers in the room and the snapping and flashing was continuous. The results, when seen in the evening papers, were dreadful.'[17] The next day, he had a more pleasant experience when the king presented him with the KBE.

On 11 February, Ramsay's wife travelled from Scotland to London by train to see her husband. Margaret arrived late at King's Cross station because of an air raid and there was only a brief reunion before Ramsay had to dash off to the coastal town of Swanage in Dorset, where an invasion exercise was being held. The king, Montgomery and Leigh-Mallory were among the onlookers. Afterwards, Ramsay was able to join his wife at Claridge's.

There was interest in the couple in the United States, and the British Information Services in New York issued a press release about them. The admiral was 'working the accustomed long hours that have earned him the soubriquet "Dynamo Ramsay", planning the Allied naval strategy for the European front'. Lady Ramsay was described as 'a tall and graceful brunette with hazel eyes and a low and attractive voice'.[18]

For those curious about how she filled her time, the release explained, 'Besides looking after her house and her sons, Lady Ramsay is county secretary for the WVS [Women's Voluntary Service]. Three days a week she works at their office in Duns. In the book drive last summer, Berwickshire, which is fairly sparsely populated (about 27,000), they aimed to get 57,000 books for the forces but beat that target with 72,000 books. Her two boys do their bit by collecting national savings – "more or less without protest", as their mother said.

'When she is in London, Lady Ramsay is very much aware of the concentration with which the organisers of the European front are working. With her ready humour she will counter any question on this with, "My husband only tells me what I may know. He is a very discreet man."'

The press release ended with a poignant remark from her, 'After the war we shall all go home. We shall all be together, again.'[19]

Despite his major role in *Overlord*, Ramsay was still on the retired list, and Churchill was among those who found this odd. He suggested that the admiral should be placed back on the active list. It seemed a simple request. But at this crucial stage of the war, bureaucratic wrangling took over. It was at a Downing Street dinner on 16 February that the prime minister told Ramsay he had made the active list request to Cunningham and the First Lord of the Admiralty, A. V. Alexander. Ramsay wrote in his diary, 'Very good and I think proper that the Allied Naval C-in-C should be on the active list.'[20] Alexander, however, was still agonising over the proposal in April, and it is worth quoting the letter he sent to Churchill:

'When the First Sea Lord and I discussed the question of Admiral Ramsay's appointment you expressed the view that the duties he had to perform were so important that it was desirable that he should return to the active list and you asked us to consider the means by which this could be achieved.

'We told you that we felt that it was most undesirable that Admiral Ramsay's reinstatement on the active list should have the effect of blocking the promotion of younger men and that the only way in which this could be avoided would be to make the appointment a supernumerary one. As you accepted our view we proceeded accordingly.

'The Admiralty have been having some correspondence with the Treasury to fix the details and the Treasury say they understand that you accepted Admiral Ramsay's return to the active list as supernumerary only for the period of his present appointment and that on the cessation of his present appointment if we wished to retain him on the active list he would count towards the authorised establishment of admirals.

'Neither the First Sea Lord nor I have any recollection of your making such a stipulation at the time when we discussed the matter. A stipulation of this kind would tie the hands of the Board [of Admiralty] in so far as Admiral Ramsay will have to revert to the retired list when his present duties come to an end even though we should wish to give him further employment. Had we felt that such a qualification would be made neither the First Lord nor I would have supported the proposal to replace Admiral Ramsay on the active list.

'We should be glad to have your ruling on this point which so much affects the future of Admiral Ramsay and we trust that you will feel able to agree that so long as Admiral Ramsay is employed on active service he should remain on the active list and supernumerary to the establishment of admirals.'[21]

Although Alexander emphasised the involvement of Cunningham, the First Sea Lord was probably not that concerned. He admired Ramsay and, in any case, he was known to have little enthusiasm for administrative matters. Cunningham did not mention the issue in his memoirs. And Churchill was unlikely to have been impressed by Alexander's treatment of a national hero. The prime minister was quick to respond to the First Lord's letter. Ramsay, who had retired as a vice admiral, was placed on the active list in that rank. And the next day, he was promoted full admiral on the active list.

By 2 March, the naval plan for the invasion had been completed, and Ramsay paid tribute to his staff and especially the work of Commander George

Rowell and Commander Robert Harland. That day he had a meeting with the Vice Chief of Naval Staff, Vice Admiral Sir Edward Syfret, who handed him a pencil. 'I was overjoyed as I had not any notion where I'd lost it and this pencil is my mascot.'[22]

The next day Ramsay announced that he had appointed Rear Admiral James Rivett-Carnac as Flag Officer, British Assault Area. He was critical of two of his senior officers, Rear Admiral William Tennant, who had played such a key role in the Dunkirk evacuation, and Rear Admiral Vian. Tennant, who was in charge of the invasion's Mulberry harbours, had been keen to get the flag officer post. Ramsay's view: 'Bill T is too flashy for it and too inclined to act independently of instead of with me. Also he is prone to think too much of Tennant and too little of his C-in-C. He has a clear job to carry out and that is what is wanted of him, not what he wants for himself. Went and saw P Vian and had a long discussion with him about his functions. He strikes me as being a little helpless and requires to be given so much guidance on matters which I feel he could work out for himself. In fact I feel that I am organising his part of the show as well as my own which gives me additional work. I don't think he uses his staff enough.'[23]

On 7 March, Ramsay decided that the naval force to bombard enemy coastal positions needed increasing by one battleship, seven cruisers and 14 destroyers. This would bring the total to six battleships, 25 cruisers and 56 destroyers. He also wanted an additional 24 minesweepers. The Royal Navy would be unable to 'meet the bill', with its commitments in the Atlantic, Mediterranean and Indian Ocean, and it was only 'right and proper' that the US should provide the extra ships.

There was welcome news on 25 March when Ramsay learned that Operation *Anvil* had finally been postponed. 'Now things can happen which we have been long been waiting for. It only shows how cumbersome is the machine which wields the power. All here have known for six weeks that Anvil would have to be off but it has taken till now to get the decision.'[24]

There were a number of training exercises for *Neptune* and *Overlord*, and early on 27 April, Ramsay and Montgomery travelled to Devon to watch one of them at Slapton Sands. This was a landing by American troops and the spot was chosen because it was similar to Omaha beach, their eventual target. The exercise, involving live ammunition, was delayed for one hour but some of the landing craft did not receive the signal and troops reached the beach during a bombardment, resulting in friendly fire deaths. But worse was to come. In the early hours of 28 April, German E-boats attacked a convoy of eight LSTs [tank landing ships]. Two of the ships were sunk, with an official total death toll of 749 US soldiers and sailors, though speculation remains that more died. Survivors were sworn to secrecy. Ramsay and Montgomery had left Slapton Sands on the afternoon of 27 April. In his diary, Ramsay referred to the one-hour delay as a 'fatal error', but strangely he did not mention the greater tragedy of the LSTs.

Friendly fire was not confined to Slapton Sands. On 4 May, Ramsay recorded, 'Our MTBs were shot up by our Beaufighters and many casualties inflicted.'[25] By this time the admiral was working from Southwick House; a Georgian mansion some five miles north of Portsmouth, which had become the advance post of the Supreme Headquarters, Allied Expeditionary Force.

Two days later Ramsay received two 'hysterical' letters from Kirk, the American rear admiral in command of the Western Task Force. In one of the letters, Kirk expressed concern about the E-boat threat to his task force in the wake of the Slapton Sands attack. He wanted an air and naval bombardment of E-boat bases before D-Day. 'He has quite lost his sense of proportion besides being rather offensively rude,' Ramsay recorded. 'My opinion of him decreases steadily. He is not a big enough man to hold the position he does.'[26]

The following day, Kirk attended a meeting of naval commanders, and he annoyed Ramsay with his 'pomp and stupidity. I somewhat lost patience with him. He is forever trying to save face and clear his yardarm in the event of trouble. A poor fish.'[27]

At another meeting, Eisenhower brought up the question of the E-boats, apparently prompted by Kirk's 'hysterical' letter on the subject. Ramsay said the matter was under consideration. 'Pressed further I said that it was, certainly, a serious menace, but it would be a mistake to overestimate it. That it was impossible to ensure security but everything would be done to destroy E-boats prior to D-Day, but that a naval bombardment of Cherbourg was not included as it was ineffective and risky. Pressed further on this I said that I would not order a naval bombardment unless I received a direct order from him to do so. He then asked Kirk what he thought of what I'd said which was a very wrong thing to do, seeing that I was his naval adviser and Kirk my subordinate. However, nothing came of it. It was a bad meeting altogether and made me cross.'[28] Ramsay was reluctant to bomb the E-boat base at Cherbourg in case it alerted the Germans to the planned invasion beaches. His staff produced a paper countering Kirk's concerns. A few days later, Kirk rang Ramsay and told him there were reports of major new obstacles off Omaha beach. This was bad news as it once again affected the timing of the landings – H-Hour. Ramsay slept badly that night 'dreaming absurd situations regarding landings', only to discover later that Kirk had exaggerated the obstacle problem.

On 15 May, the king, Churchill, the British Chiefs of Staff, and Eisenhower and his key commanders went to St Paul's School for a final presentation of the invasion plans. As Cunningham observed, 'Never in all my long experience have I seen a conference chamber more crowded with officers and others of high rank. The meeting had naturally been kept a dead secret, but I found myself wondering what might happen if the Germans made a daylight raid in force and landed a bomb on the building.' Ramsay spoke for 30 minutes on *Neptune*, 'which I think was quite good'. Once again Kirk annoyed him. In conversation with Churchill, the American 'tried to make out that part of my orders were not clear. He is getting me amazed by his wilful stupidity which, I know, is only face saving.'[29]

Field Marshal Brooke was not impressed with Eisenhower, and he had some telling observations on the other speakers: 'Monty made excellent speech. Bertie Ramsay indifferent, and overwhelmed by all his own difficulties. Spaatz [US Lieutenant General Carl Spaatz, commander of Strategic Air Forces] read every word of a poor statement. Bert Harris [Air Chief Marshal Sir Arthur Harris, Bomber Command] told us how well he might have won this war if it had not been for the handicap imposed by the existence of the other two Services!!'[30]

On 1 June, Ramsay went to the Cabinet Office to see the prime minister and was surprised to find the king there. He was even more surprised when both men said they wished to go over with the assault forces. Already under intense pressure, 'joyriders' were the last thing he needed. Ramsay said the risk was unacceptable. Perhaps the king could go when it was safer. The king agreed but Churchill said the 'ban' did not apply to him, although he agreed to think it over.

The next day, Cunningham and the First Lord, Alexander, visited the prime minister and they found themselves facing the same dilemma, as the admiral of the fleet amusingly recorded: 'Once there he blithely informed us that he had arranged with Sir Bertram Ramsay to embark in the *Belfast* with Rear Admiral Dalrymple-Hamilton for Overlord, and that he would be seriously angry with anyone who tried to prevent him. I do not know if he was really in earnest, but remembering his obstinate efforts to witness the bombardment of Pantelleria a year earlier, I replied that I would risk his wrath and said outright that it was absolutely wrong for him to go. He grunted and glared at me. Apparently he had approached Eisenhower on the same subject, and his request had been refused. To that Mr Churchill had retorted that while Eisenhower was the Supreme Commander, he was not in administrative control of the Royal Navy, and there was nothing to prevent Winston Spencer Churchill being enrolled as a genuine member of some ship's company. The intransigence, thank goodness, was finally settled by His Majesty, who wrote telling the prime minister that if he went, he, the King, was equally entitled to go as the head of all three Services. That finished the argument, though I have no doubt Mr Churchill was bitterly disappointed.'[31]

The following evening Ramsay had supper with Cunningham and they had a long talk. After several delays, the invasion was set for 5 June but the weather forecast was not good. 'For the first time I noticed signs of strain in Ramsay,' Cunningham recorded. 'He was extremely anxious about the operation, though he really need not have been. Though the responsibility lay heavily on his shoulders his organisation and planning were as nearly perfect as they could be, and I had no doubt that with the average conditions of weather he would put the army ashore in the right place at the right time.'[32]

CHAPTER 28

We're Going!

Eisenhower and his commanders met at Southwick House at 0400 on 4 June for the final conference on whether to launch the invasion the next day. The weather forecast was still bad, with low clouds, high winds and strong waves predicted. Ramsay thought the sea conditions were 'unpromising but not prohibitive'. But the meeting heard that air support would be impossible and naval gunfire was unlikely to be effective against enemy defences. The admiral recorded, 'I pointed out we had only accepted a daylight assault on the understanding that overwhelming air and naval bombardment would be available to overcome the enemy coast and beach defences.' According to Montgomery, Ramsay 'would not commit himself one way or the other'. The general wanted the invasion to go ahead on 5 June. Tedder disagreed. Eisenhower felt he had no choice but to postpone D-Day. Vessels with troops already at sea were ordered to head to ports. Another conference was held that evening but the outlook remained bleak.[1]

In the early hours of 5 June, Eisenhower experienced a wind of 'almost hurricane proportions' and rain that 'seemed to be travelling in horizontal streaks' as he made his way to Southwick House from his nearby quarters. It was not good news when Group Captain James Stagg of the RAF and his team of meteorologists began their briefing, suggesting that if the invasion had gone ahead that day 'a major disaster would almost surely have resulted'. But then came Stagg's 'astonishing' prediction. The following morning would see relatively good weather, probably lasting for 36 hours. This was promising news but the commanders had to consider the possibility of a successful initial attack being compromised by an unsuccessful build-up of forces. Eisenhower decided it was a risk worth taking. D-Day would be 6 June. He recorded, 'No one present disagreed and there was a definite brightening of faces as, without a further word, each went off to his respective post of duty to flash out to his command the messages that would set the whole host in motion.' Ramsay wrote in his diary, 'We shall require all the help that God can give us and I cannot believe that this will not be forthcoming.' Montgomery recorded, 'We were all glad. This conference did not last more than fifteen minutes. Eisenhower was in good form and made his decision quickly.'[2]

That day Ramsay wrote to his wife, saying that her letters were a great comfort. He told her, 'We've been having a particularly anxious and trying time the last two or three days owing to the weather having turned sour and we've had to make some difficult decisions and accept considerable risks or rather take them. I can only pray that they may prove justified for the lives of hundreds of thousands are at stake.' But his thoughts quickly switched to life in Berwickshire, as his next sentence showed, 'How maddening for you that your bicycle tyre should burst and spoil your lovely excursion to the beach.'[3]

The Germans were expecting an invasion, but the Allies had spent some time deceiving them as to the time and the place. Coastal defences were stretched in northern France, and the enemy were led to believe that Pas de Calais was the likely target. The RAF frequently bombed the area to encourage this belief. As a result, Pas de Calais was heavily fortified. Another fictitious target was Norway.

Instead, the Allies planned a five-pronged assault on a stretch of coast west of Le Havre in this order: Sword beach (3rd British Infantry Division); Juno beach (3rd Canadian Infantry Division); Gold beach (50th British Infantry Division); Omaha beach (1st US Infantry Division); and Utah beach (4th US Infantry Division). Airborne drops would precede the amphibious landings.

With such a large invasion fleet, one of Ramsay's greatest fears was enemy minelaying. In the six weeks before D-Day, the Germans intensified minelaying off the south coast of England, using aircraft on a scale that had not been seen for more than two years. The admiral noted, 'This minelaying was confined to moonless periods. Had D-Day been in such a period it is doubtful whether the Portsmouth channels could have been cleared in time. As it was, no interruption was caused to the rehearsals nor to the assembly of our forces and it is considered that the enemy missed a great opportunity in not still further extending this form of attack.'[4] Ramsay's vessels, from ports along the south coast, were using ten approach channels, and a massive minesweeping operation was carried out. The bad weather did not help. Tidal conditions

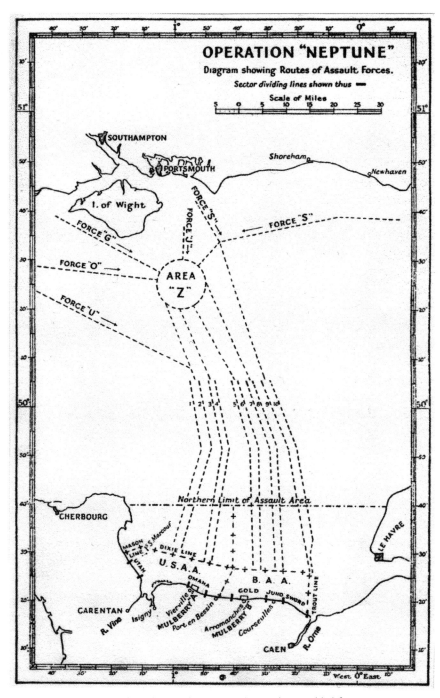

An Admiralty chart showing how Ramsay's armada assembled for D-Day.

were another concern because of beach obstacles that might remain hidden and wreck landing craft.

As *Neptune's* vessels approached the French coast in the early hours it dawned on Ramsay that tactical surprise had been achieved, 'an astonishing feat'. This was down to several factors – the miscalculations of the enemy, Allied air superiority, which reduced the Luftwaffe's reconnaissance, the bad weather, which led to the withdrawal of E-boat patrols, and radio counter measures.[5]

More than 2,000 British, American and Canadian planes began bombing Normandy soon after midnight on 6 June. Low cloud, however, hampered the attack on the defences at Omaha beach, which would prove costly when the American troops landed. In the early hours, there were significant drops of British and American airborne troops inland. Then came the naval bombardment. The battleships *Warspite* and *Ramillies*, and the monitor HMS *Roberts*, with their 15in guns, along with five cruisers and 15 destroyers, opened fire on the defences covering Sword beach. A 'half-hearted' attack was made by four E-boats and some armed trawlers from Le Havre. The big ships evaded the torpedoes, but the Norwegian destroyer *Svenner* was hit, breaking in two and sinking quickly. Fire from enemy batteries was largely ineffective. Ramsay believed that much of the success of the naval bombardment was down to fighter spotters, who carried out their tasks 'tirelessly and gallantly'.[6]

Two X-craft were used to guide in the assault forces for Sword and Juno beaches. These four-crew, cramped, midget submarines took up position off the enemy coast in rough seas on the morning of Sunday 4 June after negotiating minefields.

Lieutenant George Honour commanded *X23*, which went to a spot 1.25 miles from Ouistreham for Sword beach. 'We marked our position through the periscope and sat on the bottom until nightfall,' Honour recalled. 'We surfaced, dropped our anchor, hoisted our radio mast and we got a signal that the invasion had been postponed, so we had to retreat to the bottom again and wait till the Monday night. We received a message that the invasion was on. So once again we went down and sat on the bottom. At about 4.40am on Tuesday, 6 June we surfaced, put up all our navigational aids, 18ft telescopic mast with a light shinning to seaward, a radio beacon and an echo sounder tapping out a message below the surface.

'The main tension was the postponement because we were on oxygen from air bottles and when we had the postponement it didn't say how long it was for and so we had this awful problem, would we have enough oxygen. On the Sunday we did a periscope reconnaissance and one of the main things we saw was a lorry load of Germans arriving and they started playing beach ball and swimming. I thought I hope they don't have any Olympic swimmers and find out where we were.'[7]

Honour, who was awarded the Distinguished Service Cross, added, 'Our operation was called Gambit, and when we had this codename given us we looked it up in the dictionary and much to our horror it said the pawn you throw away before a big move in chess, which didn't encourage us too much.'[8]

Both X-craft returned safely to Britain. Ramsay paid tribute: 'It is considered that great skill and endurance was shown by the crews of *X20* and *X23*. Their reports of proceedings, which were a masterpiece of understatement, read like the deck log of a surface ship in peacetime, and not of a very small and vulnerable submarine carrying out a hazardous operation in time of war.'[9]

Leading waves of the 3rd Infantry Division, supported by British and French commandos, landed on Sword beach, a five-mile front, at about 0730. They met only moderate opposition. The division's main objective was the capture of Caen, but this would turn out to be a much tougher task than originally thought. By 1300 on 6 June, commandos led by Lord Lovat had linked up with airborne troops at bridges over the Orne waterways.

The frigate HMS *Lawford* was the command ship for the Juno beach landing by the Canadian 3rd Infantry Division. Recalling the early hours of 6 June, Colin Madden, the frigate's navigating officer, said, 'As dawn came round we saw masses of ships all around. They were more or less in their right positions. Everybody was having trouble with speed because of the rough weather, so we retarded H-Hour [0630] by ten minutes. The rocket craft fired approximately at H minus ten, a little early but their fire was effective. The destroyers closed right in to the beach and provided the most excellent close support. We had trouble launching our DD tanks [Duplex Drive tanks, which could float] because the commanding officer quite rightly realised they would never last in the rough weather, the 7,000 yards they were meant to go, and he closed right to the beach to about 1,500 yards to launch them. They got ashore and did a good job.'[10]

Natural obstacles, such as reefs and shoals, hampered the landing craft, and mines took a heavy toll. The first wave of troops encountered withering fire, but by mid-morning, the town of Bernières had been taken. Two days later *Lawford* sank after an air attack, with the loss of 37 of the crew.

Ramsay noted that the Gold beach landings, between Le Hamel and Arromanches, were 'dead on time', but DD tanks were not launched because of the weather and had to be beached later. Again, beach obstacles and mines damaged a large number of landing craft. One sector of the beach close to Le Hamel experienced considerable difficulty because it was being enfiladed by two strong points. It took until 1600 to silence the enemy. As well as gun emplacements, there were pillboxes and heavily fortified houses along the front.

The 1st Battalion Hampshire Regiment played a key role. The troops had spent five days aboard ship in cramped conditions 'without even a glass of beer'. Despite taking seasickness pills, many were ill. Then the time came to board their landing craft.

The commanding officer was Lieutenant Colonel Harold Nelson Smith, who recalled, 'When about four miles away, the coast could be seen dimly through the haze and morale was raised by the roar of naval guns in support. Heavy concentrations of fire by Royal Navy ships and RAF bombers had been planned before the landings. However, due to bad visibility, all this bombardment overshot and enemy positions escaped untouched, including those of Le Hamel, as we were soon to find out.

'Several landing craft encountered sandbars, on which they grounded. Thinking this was the beach proper our naval crews lowered the ramps and the leading troops jumped into six feet of water. In their heavy equipment they sank like stones. Others struggling on the surface were run over by their own craft, which surged forward with their lightened load. So the first casualties occurred before the landing.' Nelson Smith added, 'There was no warning by the navy that these sandbanks existed. That was an unpleasant surprise.'[11]

Another problem soon became apparent. Support in the form of artillery and DD tanks and flail tanks to clear mines failed to arrive, and the infantry 'were on their own'. All the planning 'went to hell' because of the rough sea.

Soon after landing on Gold beach, Nelson Smith was hit by a mortar round. As a soldier tried to drag him to safety, he was wounded again. Evacuated that night, he spent the next five months being treated and having shrapnel removed from much of his body, stretching from his right foot to his right shoulder.

By the end of the day, the battalion had achieved its objectives. Arromanches was cleared. In 12 hours, the battalion's casualties amounted to 60 dead and 120 wounded.[12]

Trooper Frederick Gooding of the 4th/7th Royal Dragoon Guards was the 20-year-old driver of one of the tanks that failed to reach Gold beach. His Valentine tank was the first to roll down a landing craft ramp but it stopped soon after entering the water. The Valentine was not one of the DD tanks.

'I was wondering what the devil to do and I felt my legs floating,' Gooding said. 'I looked down and water was coming into the tank. The engine had stopped and I thought I'd better get out.' Because of the pressure of water outside, he was unable to open his hatch, which had a spring-loaded bolt. 'I was on the roof of the tank trying to get the last bit of air when suddenly the hatch opened and I saw a hand, which I grabbed.'[13] An officer riding on the tank pulled him out.

As Gooding looked around, he saw all the other tanks meeting the same fate. 'They went straight to the bottom,' he said. 'We were out too far. The worst part was we were sat up there for two or three hours to see the other tanks coming off the LCTs with infantry on the back and some of them were falling off and drowning because of the weight of their equipment. It was terrible seeing them washed in and out on the waves.'[14]

Ramsay also acknowledged that the American attack on Omaha beach faced 'considerable difficulty'. He recorded, 'Assault craft on their way inshore had a bad time, a number of craft were swamped and the assaulting infantry in the remainder in general arrived on the beach in rather poor shape. DD tanks were launched three miles offshore as planned on the left flank but regrettably all but two or three foundered. Thus the initial attack here had to be carried out with little tank support. On the right flank DD tanks were landed directly and successfully on to the beach, but were quickly put out of action by enemy fire.'[15]

Troops who landed were pinned down for two hours and only small groups were able to push forward. 'All naval personnel who witnessed the battle were unanimous in paying tribute to their determination and gallantry,' Ramsay pointed out. 'The supporting destroyers and gun support craft stood in close inshore during the period of fiercest fighting on the beach and rendered great support to the troops.'[16]

John Tarbit was a Royal Navy coxswain taking 35 Rangers to Omaha beach. His landing craft was one of six, but that number reduced to five after a collision. Soon afterwards, two other craft were swamped in rough seas and sank. 'When I got to them, all the Americans were floating upside down,' Tarbit said. 'Because they had so much equipment round their necks the only place they could put their lifebelts was around the waist. They hung on to their equipment and of course they were top heavy. There were 35 in each craft so there were 70 backsides floating in the water. The only survivors were the crews. That left three of us to go in to Omaha beach. About 100 yards from the beach the Germans started shelling us with mortars. We were hit in the engine room.'[17]

Eisenhower admitted later that he and Lieutenant General Omar Bradley, commander of the US First Army, had feared stiff resistance at Omaha beach. The defences had been boosted by the 352nd Division, which included many veterans of the Eastern Front.

Admiral King pointed out that the heavy ships had no trouble putting the major shore batteries out of action. 'Our chief difficulties came from the light artillery and machine guns which the enemy had sited to fire up and down the beach instead of out to sea. These guns, which were very difficult to detect, waited for our troops to land before opening fire. Specially trained navy shore fire control parties attached to army units were put ashore early in the assault to inform our ships by radio of the location of such targets, but many of them were unable to set up their radio equipment because of casualties and enemy fire. At this juncture eight United States and three British destroyers closed the beach and took many enemy positions under fire. This unplanned bombardment deserves great credit.'[18]

Of all the beaches, Omaha had the highest number of casualties, with some 2,000 killed, wounded or missing. US airborne troops also had a high casualty rate.

Almost complete surprise was achieved at Utah beach, and opposition was light. DD tanks were landed successfully. The attack was supported by airborne troops. The main objective was to secure a beachhead on the Cotentin Peninsula, with the important target of Cherbourg. Ramsay noted, 'There was less sea at Utah than elsewhere and very good progress was made in landing troops and vehicles throughout the day.'[19]

Despite the unfavourable weather, Ramsay noted that the plan for *Neptune* had been carried out 'as written'. Tactical surprise, which was not expected, had been achieved at four of the beaches – the exception being Omaha. There were only minor attacks on shipping by the Luftwaffe because of Allied air superiority. In 24 hours, the Allies flew more than 14,600 sorties. Ramsay reported, 'By the end of D-Day immediate anxiety was felt on only one count – whether the weather would improve sufficiently quickly to enable the build-up to start as planned.'[20]

Churchill found it remarkable that the enemy had been taken by surprise. But the German high command was led to believe that the weather would be too rough for an amphibious landing, and it had no worthwhile reconnaissance reports of the massive build-up of shipping along the English coast. On the night before D-Day, rocket-firing planes destroyed many of the radar stations in northern France. Rommel, who spent a great deal of time improving the defences, had gone to visit Hitler at Berchtesgaden on

5 June, and the enemy remained confused for some time, believing that the landings were only a diversionary attack.

On the morning of 7 June, Ramsay and Eisenhower sailed from Portsmouth in the minelayer HMS *Apollo* to the invasion area. Off Omaha beach, there was a scene of 'great confusion'. Blockships had arrived to be sunk as shelters off the beachhead, but they were 'hanging about awaiting someone to tell them what to do'. No large landing ships were unloading. The beach was littered with stranded craft. Ramsay had talks with Rear Admiral Kirk and Bradley but 'they did nothing to relieve my anxiety'. The bridgehead was still very shallow. *Apollo* went on to Gold and Juno beaches, where operations were going more smoothly. Montgomery, who had sailed from Portsmouth in another ship, went on board *Apollo* and gave 'a quite cheerful description' of the land battle. *Apollo* later ran over a sandbar, badly damaging both propellors. Ramsay was not impressed, believing the captain was at fault.[21]

The build-up of troops and supplies began that day with the arrival of eight convoys, but poor weather hampered unloading. Nine large personnel ships sailed from the Thames, the first such vessels to pass through the Strait of Dover for four years. Smoke screens were laid for this and subsequent convoys. Although one ship was sunk after coastal batteries opened fire, Ramsay decided that the risk of a daylight passage must be accepted.

Mines remained a problem and a number of ships were sunk or damaged on 7 June. In some cases, vessels had not used swept channels. A major threat was a U-boat offensive. The enemy had increased its submarine force at Bay of Biscay ports in readiness for an invasion. The Commander-in-Chief, Plymouth, took measures, and Coastal Command flooded the western approaches to the English Channel with aircraft. On the night of 6 June, 11 U-boats were spotted, six of which were attacked. But during that month, submarines had little success, in spite of the high number of targets.

Allied ships opened fire on Dakota aircraft carrying airborne reinforcements on the night of 6 June, and at least one plane was shot down. 'This most unfortunate incident, which was a repetition, though happily on a small scale, of our experiences in Operation Husky, emphasises the danger of routeing our own aircraft over our naval forces,' Ramsay stated. 'This had been pointed out repeatedly during the planning but the naval objections had to give way to the demands of the air force plan.'[22]

The Allies did not have use of a French port, and there was an important development on 8 June, with the arrival of sections of Mulberry harbours, which were crucial for the rapid unloading of cargo. There were plans for two artificial harbours, Mulberry A at Omaha beach and Mulberry B at Gold beach.

Ramsay told his wife, 'One can honestly say that the naval side of this great operation, so far as it has gone, has been very successful, and for this I am most grateful to providence, to my staff for their excellent planning and meticulous care of details, and to all those to whom the actual carrying out of my orders was entrusted. It will certainly go down in history as a very great achievement and I have reason to be proud at being the head of it. We have broken the crust only, however, and have a very long way to go before one can feel any sense of complacency. We are certain to have setbacks and will have some big jobs to undertake and overcome, but provided we are blessed by providence the end is not in doubt.'[23]

Back in England, Ramsay paid a visit to Southampton to see how that port was operating. He was not happy with what he saw. Ramsay met the flag officer in command, Vice Admiral James Pipon, 'whose main idea seemed to be to get home, which he soon did'. Tank landing ships were being loaded but there was little supervision. 'Not surprising seeing that James Pipon is in command,' Ramsay wrote in his diary. 'I should like to turf him out and put Eric Fullerton [Admiral Sir Eric Fullerton] in instead. He would soon get a move on. Returned in a rage and rang up C-in-C Portsmouth and told him of my experience and views.'[24]

On 10 June, Montgomery was able to report that the Allies held an area 60 miles long and eight to 12 miles deep. 'There had been considerable cause for alarm on Omaha beach in the early stages, but that situation was put right by the gallantry of the American soldiers, by good supporting naval fire, and by brave work by fighter-bomber aircraft.'[25]

Churchill soon got his wish to see some of the action. Along with Field Marshal Brooke and Field Marshal Jan Smuts, he sailed across the Channel in the destroyer HMS *Kelvin*. General Marshall and Admiral King, who had flown to Britain from the United States, also made the trip to Normandy, though in an American destroyer. Churchill and his party were taken to Montgomery's headquarters, in the grounds of a chateau about five miles inland. The area around the chateau had been heavily bombed the previous night. Before returning to Portsmouth in *Kelvin*, Rear Admiral Vian asked Churchill if he would like to see battleships and cruisers bombarding German positions. The answer, of course, was yes. The fire was 'leisurely and continuous', and the prime minister suggested that they might 'have a plug at them ourselves'. Vian replied, 'Certainly.' *Kelvin* moved closer to the coast and opened up. It was fortunate that the enemy did not reply.[26]

Ramsay was told of a shortage of 15in and 16in guns for battleships, and he sent a signal to Vian that *Rodney* and *Nelson*, mounting 16in guns, were to be used only if there were worthwhile targets. On 15 June, he recorded in his diary, 'Vian sent two most stupid and childish signals protesting against some instructions I'd given him in regard to employment of battleships and to movement of cruisers. He is temperamental and at times a great annoyance and trial to me as I feel he is always apt to work against rather than with me.' But there was 'magnificent' news that day. Ramsay had asked for a Bomber Command strike on the naval base at Le Havre. Ten E-boats were sunk and five badly damaged.

Ramsay was not the only one concerned about the use of battleships. Cunningham told Vian that the Admiralty was 'quite horrified' at the enormous expenditure of ammunition. He stressed that battleships should only fire when it was essential.[27]

It was not long before the king went to Normandy, sailing from Portsmouth in the cruiser *Arethusa*, with Ramsay and Cunningham in his party. Montgomery met the king on Juno beach and they went to his chateau headquarters. Ramsay thought the general was under considerable strain. The king returned to Portsmouth that evening, apparently having not made a Churchillian request for *Arethusa* to 'plug' the enemy.

Ramsay told his wife about the king's visit and revealed that 'a fully armed German soldier' had been hiding in a wood next to Montgomery's headquarters for several days. 'He finally gave himself up, never having discovered the chance he had of shooting the British Army C-in-C whose caravan was within 25 yards of the edge of the wood.' Ramsay acknowledged that the king's visit was a morale boost for naval personnel, but official visitors were becoming a problem, as he pointed out: 'The number of persons of greater or lesser importance who produced good reasons for proceeding there was alarming, observing that, during their stay, of necessity they occupied the time and attention of officers who should have been engaged in other more useful work.'[28]

The admiral was still concerned about Vian's 'peculiar behaviour', telling his diary on 17 June, 'I think he is not quite normal at times. Because I wanted certain things done in my own way, which did not happen to coincide with his, he goes into a fit and wants to come out of NCETF [Naval Commander Eastern Task Force] long before it is ripe to do so. So this morning I made a policy signal to him as to future events and trust it will settle the manner. He is to stay until the situation is stabilised.' The next day Ramsay was back in France. Omaha beach was of particular interest. He inspected German defences, and was impressed with the 'great progress' made by the Americans.

The weather had not been kind to the Allies and a north-east gale on 19 June played havoc with work off and on the beaches. The next day, the wind prevented all sailings to the assault areas. Large numbers of craft were beached. By 21 June, it was apparent that the high seas had seriously damaged the Mulberry harbours. The worst affected was Mulberry A at Omaha beach, which had to be abandoned. Hundreds of craft were left damaged. One estimate suggested that over several days the gale had prevented the unloading of 140,000 tons of stores and 20,000 vehicles. Fortunately, Ramsay's repair organisation, COREP, was soon at work on vessels.

The admiral also was under pressure to release vessels for the planned invasion of southern France, Operation *Anvil* (later *Dragoon*). He was in no hurry to do so: 'Previous experience in this war had shown the danger of withdrawing ships from an area before an operation had fully succeeded, and I was careful not to agree to the release of ships before I was really satisfied that they could be spared.'[29]

With the help of naval attacks, American troops captured Cherbourg on 27 June. The Germans had made a thorough job of sabotaging the docks, and the harbour was heavily mined, with many sunken ships. Ramsay saw the damage, which he described as 'unbelievable'. It would take 90 days to clear the port.

Unexpected praise for Ramsay came from his World War I 'foe', Roger Keyes, who now held the rank of admiral of the fleet and had been given a peerage. Keyes wrote, 'As you know it has been a great pleasure to me to watch you go from one success to the next, and that it should have been given to you to organise both the evacuation of Dunkirk and the return invasion to France. I must send you my warmest congratulations on the tremendous success the navy has achieved during these last days, under your guidance. It has indeed been a wonderful display of excellent staff work and good organisation and I should like to congratulate all concerned.'[30]

By the end of June, it was time for Rear Admiral Vian and Rear Admiral Kirk to relinquish their assault force commands. Rear Admiral James Rivett-Carnac was appointed Flag Officer British Assault Area and set up his headquarters ashore. Rear Admiral John Wilkes of the US Navy took a similar role in the American sector. Of Kirk, Ramsay observed, 'He has done fairly well but I think others could have done better.'[31]

And Ramsay's role? His headquarters was still at Southwick House, near Portsmouth, but he had been travelling to and from Normandy for nearly a month. He wrote in his diary, 'I want now to clear up my affairs on this side and get over to France where my main responsibilities exist.'[32]

CHAPTER 29

Breaking Out

Although Ramsay was keen to move his headquarters to France, he remained at Southwick House for several weeks. There were still many convoys to be sent from English ports. Poor weather continued to be a factor. But over ten months, 2.5 million men, 500,000 vehicles and four million tons of supplies would pass through the Mulberry B harbour at Arromanches. The Pluto pipeline in the Channel, running from the south coast to Cherbourg, was the partial answer to the fuel supply question.

On 8 July, the battleship *Rodney* bombarded German armour on the outskirts of Caen, firing at ranges of up to 32,000 yards. The next day, the ship returned to Portsmouth, much to Ramsay's relief. It had been feared that it might strike a mine because of its great draught. That afternoon, the admiral went to play golf at Swinley Forest in Berkshire, afterwards having tea with the Earl and Countess of Portarlington. 'Lady P very kindly offered me one of her litter of Labradors, a nice looking dog,' he wrote in his diary. 'I must find out whether I can get a good keeper to train him and whether Mag will take him.' (Ramsay collected the puppy later and it was called Shaef; the same name as Eisenhower's cat.) Returning to Southwick House, he had a busy evening 'squaring things up'. It was thought that Caen was now in Allied hands, but ferocious resistance continued and it was not until 20 July that the city fell, much of it reduced to rubble by naval and air strikes.

Churchill recorded that by the middle of July, 30 Allied divisions were ashore. There were 27 German divisions, but the enemy had suffered a high number of casualties.

The Germans were firing V-1 flying bombs, known as doodlebugs, at south-east England from sites along the French and Dutch coasts, and one night, Ramsay was kept awake when some flew close to Southwick House.

In Ramsay's view, the flow of supplies to Normandy was going well, and he was annoyed when the US Army transport chief, Major General Frank Ross, sent 'a hysterical signal' giving 'a totally false picture'. Ross backed down, admitting that he had been seeking to build a large reserve for the winter.

The admiral continued to make trips to France and he took another look at Cherbourg where American soldiers were busy trying to get the port operational. Only small numbers of coasters could berth. There was an Allied plan, Operation *Hands Up*, to seize the Quiberon Bay area of Brittany. Ramsay thought the capture of Brest was an essential first step, but he did not think much of *Hands Up* anyway, viewing it as 'tactically a nasty one and it is only to be undertaken if the advantages are clear and good, which to me they are not'.[1] He had lost considerable forces to Operation *Anvil* and was set to lose more to Russian convoys. To his relief, *Hands Up* was abandoned.

On 18 July, he learned that Churchill wanted to make another visit to northern France, not a day trip but a stay of several nights. He was not pleased: 'This will give me and all a lot of extra work and is a great nuisance.'[2] Strangely, Ramsay made no further mention of this visit in his diary. On 20 July, the prime minister flew to the Cotentin Peninsula in a US Army Dakota. He was taken to see the 'shocking' damage at the port of Cherbourg, later going on to Utah beach and Arromanches, where he boarded the cruiser HMS *Enterprise*, remaining in the ship for three days. Churchill took a great interest in the working of the Mulberry B harbour 'on which all the armies now almost entirely depended'.[3] On the last day of his visit, he went to Montgomery's headquarters, and the general took him to see the ruins of Caen.

It was at this time that news filtered through of the abortive attempt on Hitler's life by Colonel Claus von Stauffenberg and other conspirators at the dictator's Wolf's Lair headquarters in east Prussia. Ramsay thought the Germans were 'cracking'. He was told of a U-boat that had been scuttled, 'a most significant incident as she was not being attacked and it is just a case of unconditional surrender'. The admiral also learned that two Messerschmitt fighters had landed at RAF Manston in Kent, the pilots giving themselves up. 'Every little helps,' he observed.[4]

Lieutenant General Bradley, commander of the US First Army, was desperate to break out from the Cotentin Peninsula. His troops had found it difficult to make progress through the bocage – fields with thick hedgerows, which were ideal hiding places for the enemy. He devised Operation *Cobra*, which began with the carpet bombing of the Saint-Lô area on 25 July. Over the next six days, the Germans suffered heavy losses and Avranches, the gateway to Brittany, was taken.

'Good reports of progress in France,' Ramsay wrote in his diary on 31 July. 'Americans have reached Avranches and have little in front of them. Second Army met with stiffer resistance but have gained useful ground, which promises further advances. Altogether our situation is good and that of Germans approaching critical. With no immediate reserves they will quickly need to decide whether to stay and be rounded up or to get out. Either would be a desperate course. Surely the end of the war is in sight.'

Lieutenant General Patton's US Third Army was soon in action to clear the Brittany peninsula and move south and eastwards. On 8 August, Montgomery ordered the Allied armies to encircle the Germans in the salient from Falaise to Mortain. The battle of the Falaise Pocket would prove decisive in liberating Normandy.

Ramsay was keen to take a break with his family, and on 2 August, he flew to RAF Charterhall on the Scottish Borders. Significantly, as events would turn out, the pilot was Lieutenant Commander Sir George Lewis of the Fleet Air Arm and the plane was a Lockheed Hudson for coastal reconnaissance. The admiral took Lewis to lunch at Bughtrig and later, with his two sons, accompanied him back to the airfield. Before taking off, the pilot showed the boys the plane. 'It is lovely to be home,' Ramsay recorded. 'Shaef made a good passage and settled down well.'[5]

Soon there was unwelcome news. He received a message that Churchill wanted him to return for a meeting to discuss a major change concerning Operation *Anvil*. 'What a nuisance,' Ramsay recorded. On 5 August, he was back at RAF Charterhall, where a Beaufighter was waiting to fly him south. At a meeting that afternoon, it emerged that the prime minister wanted to cancel *Anvil* and instead land forces near the Atlantic port of St Nazaire. Eisenhower, reflecting the views of the Joint Chiefs of Staff in Washington, was firmly opposed to the switch and Ramsay supported him. Cunningham backed Churchill, who eventually lost the argument.

The prime minister had made some uncomplimentary remarks about Ramsay being on leave and Cunningham's advice was not to return to Berwickshire. Ramsay was fuming: 'Spent busy evening getting up to date with correspondence and events but I am filled with disgust at having been brought back so unnecessarily, solely due to the wildcat scheme of the PM! I really needed the change and now I don't see much chance of getting it.'[6]

On 14 August, he visited Eisenhower, who had set up his French headquarters near Tournieres, ten miles west of Bayeux. Ramsay also needed an advance HQ and he had been offered a villa at Granville, some 60 miles south of Cherbourg. After an inspection, he decided the villa was 'poor' and demanded a chateau outside the town. There were reports that the huge number of Germans trapped in the Falaise Pocket lacked petrol, ammunition and food, and supplies were being brought in by vehicles bearing Red Cross symbols and by a hospital train. 'Horrible brutes,' the admiral seethed. Operation *Anvil*, renamed *Dragoon*, a largely American assault, was successfully launched in southern France on 15 August.

Ramsay was still longing to have a break, admitting that his mind 'is nothing like as clear as it generally is'.[7] On 19 August, Lewis, who became his personal pilot, flew him to RAF Charterhall in the Hudson. Once again, Lewis had lunch at Bughtrig, before heading back to his base at Lee-on-the-Solent, west of Portsmouth. Despite the pleasure of being back with his family, Ramsay felt 'extraordinarily tired'. He admitted, 'I suppose the reaction after weeks of strain and suddenly coming home. Anyhow my legs ached and I felt as if I had not a spark of energy in my body. Went to bed early and took two Soneryls [sleeping tablets].'[8] He remained tired for several days and was told by the family doctor that he needed 'a good mental rest'. Nearly a week later, he headed to London 'ready for anything'.[9] It was fortunate that he felt better because he found 'many problems awaiting settlement'.

The Germans surrendered Paris on 25 August. Allied troops would soon be crossing the Seine at many points, and 30 August marked the end of Operation *Overlord*. Churchill commented, 'There has been criticism of slowness on the British front in Normandy, and the splendid American advances of the later stages seemed to indicate greater success on their part than on ours. It is therefore necessary to emphasise again that the whole plan of campaign was to pivot on the British front and draw the enemy's reserves in that direction in order to help the American turning movement.'[10]

On 1 September, Eisenhower took over direct command of the land forces in northern France from Montgomery. There were now some 37 divisions, made up of Montgomery's 21st Army Group and Bradley's 12th Army Group. Montgomery had one consolation, promotion to the five-star rank of field marshal. This did not please Ramsay, who saw it as 'most offensive' to Eisenhower, who was a four-star general. Churchill was behind the decision. Montgomery was, after all, a national hero. The prime minister was no doubt aware that Montgomery would not outrank the American for long. There were moves in Washington to give Eisenhower the US Army's highest rank, the five stars of General of the Army.

Plans to shape Germany after its total surrender were already in train, and Cunningham left Ramsay in despair after suggesting that his task after the war would be to take charge of the German navy and disarm it, a Berlin posting.

'Nothing could displease me so much,' Ramsay wrote. 'I have now been over five years away from my family and from home and am getting on in years. I have so looked forward to return home more than I can say and I cannot bear the thought of a further period of separation.'[11]

On 8 September, he went to Paris. After a ceremony at Hôtel des Invalides, General Pierre Koenig's headquarters, he accompanied Eisenhower to the Arc de Triomphe, where there was a wreath-laying ceremony at the Tomb of the Unknown Soldier. He told his wife, 'We then went back to the Invalides, where we were given a vin d'honneur and some excellent champagne. Versailles and Paris and the Bois de Boulogne were looking lovely and completely peacetime like.'[12]

Later that day, Ramsay travelled to his new headquarters. He did indeed get a chateau, which he found very cold because surrounding trees shut out the sun. 'But it is quite nice inside thanks to a great deal of hard work by my retinue of servants, the number of whom I am ashamed to give you. Madame St Pierre, the owner, is a widow without children, aged about 50, and a very nice woman. She's had Germans living there most of the time, then some Americans for a short time and now us. She works like a slave at her garden, chickens, cows, geese, turkeys etc, and she rides as she said for distraction. Unfortunately she has only one horse.'[13]

Ramsay's offices were in an old barracks. He added, 'I now have all my staff with me but we are a much smaller party. The Wrens are all very excited at being in France and are putting up with physical discomforts quite cheerfully. Their officers' dress is most attractive, as they wear a blue battledress jacket with shoulder straps and a blue beret with a badge on the side. I have some anxiety over the Wren ratings, as I see them walking hand in hand with American soldiers and it is difficult to keep much control over them.'[14]

But Ramsay had a greater worry than romantic Wrens. Getting supplies to the advancing Allied armies was continuing to be a challenge. Although key Channel ports, including Le Havre and Calais, had been captured, the Germans before retreating made sure there was little left of the dock facilities, repeating the destructive efficiency shown at Cherbourg. The exception was the Belgian port of Antwerp, which was taken almost intact by the British Second Army. But Ramsay and Cunningham had to point out to army commanders that the port, some 60 miles up the River Scheldt, could not be used. There were minefields in the approaches to the Scheldt and the Germans had strong defences on the banks of the estuary. South Beveland and Walcheren were two of the main obstacles. The defences had to be eliminated before minesweeping could begin. As Cunningham recorded, 'For the time being one of the finest ports in Europe was of no more use to us than an oasis in the Sahara desert.'[15]

Eisenhower was made aware of the problem, but he thought that clearing the defences would be a tough and time-consuming operation. It was tempting to continue 'our eastward plunge against the still retreating enemy with the idea of securing a possible bridgehead across the Rhine in proximity to the Ruhr'. And Montgomery was convinced that his 21st Army Group, properly supplied, could continue its dash towards Berlin 'and end the war'. Eisenhower would reflect, 'I am certain that Field Marshal Montgomery, in the light of later events, would agree that this view was a mistaken one.' The plan was Operation *Market Garden*, an airborne assault to seize key bridges in the Netherlands and then advance into northern Germany. It was launched on 17 September and most famously failed at Arnhem. Montgomery would insist that Eisenhower was fully behind the plan and had not seen the use of Antwerp as the priority. Ramsay was left frustrated at the 'lack of zeal' to free up the port.[16]

On 19 September, Ramsay inspected the harbour at Dieppe, which was helping to ease the supply problem, though the facilities were limited. There were 17 coasters, 'a full house'. The French dockers were on strike, demanding 13 francs an hour instead of ten. The admiral shrugged this off, thinking more of the Canadian and British lives that had been lost there on 19 August 1942. 'I was struck by the absurdity of ever having contemplated, much less carried out, the Dieppe Raid, which was just a tragedy.' Later he flew over Le Havre, seeing 'the terrible devastation caused by our bombing and the demolition caused by the Germans'.[17] It would be a long time before that port was operating.

Two days later, he visited Antwerp and inspected the docks. 'I was most impressed by the vast extent of them. Numberless cranes, all undamaged.' The Germans had planned to destroy the docks, but the Allied advance was too swift. Ramsay was on the move and the next day he went to his new home, Château St Léger, near St Germain-en-Laye, 12 miles west of the centre of Paris. He was not impressed. 'A frightful house, all salons and no comfort, smells of Hun. My steward has done well and got the place going and won round the madame who was caretaker. Nice grounds and good view. Went on to inspect my HQ at Chateau Hennemont. Found great confusion but work going ahead fast. My office a vast apartment with great gilt chairs, mirrors etc. The place filthy.' Ramsay attended a meeting of service chiefs called by Eisenhower, who had moved his headquarters to Versailles. The importance of using Antwerp was stressed, and Eisenhower agreed. But, of course, he had delayed that action by committing himself to the Arnhem operation.[18]

Ramsay met Major General Robert Laycock, Chief of Combined Operations, on 1 October and they discussed plans to attack the approaches to the Scheldt. The admiral had 'great anxiety' about them, believing that 'the army are not taking this operation sufficiently seriously and I see I shall have to do something to make them'.[19] Canadian troops had been chosen to play a major role. Operation *Infatuate* was the planned assault on the heavily defended island of Walcheren.

Cunningham also was concerned about the plans and asked Ramsay to fly to London to discuss them. On the way, Ramsay stopped in Ghent to confer with the Canadian commander. 'I pointed out that the army had decided to stage the landing at the worst possible spot from a naval point of view and required an agreed joint outline plan not an army one.'[20] The worst possible spot was Westkapelle, on the westernmost tip of Walcheren, where there was a fortress.

On 5 October, Eisenhower held a high-level meeting. Ramsay joined Brooke, Tedder, Leigh-Mallory and Bradley. 'Monty made the startling announcement that we could take the Ruhr without Antwerp,' Ramsay recalled. 'This afforded me the cue I needed to lambast him for not having made the capture of Antwerp the immediate objective at highest priority and I let fly with all my guns at the faulty strategy we had allowed. Our large forces were now practically grounded for lack of supply and had we now got Antwerp and not the corridor [salient running north-east from the Dutch border with Belgium to the Rhine] we should be in a far better position for launching the knockout blow.'[21]

Ramsay had support. 'During the whole discussion one fact stood out clearly, that Antwerp must be captured with the least possible delay,' Brooke recalled. 'I feel that Monty's strategy for once is at fault. Instead of carrying out the advance on Arnhem he ought to have made certain of Antwerp in the first place. Ramsay brought this out well in discussion and criticised Monty freely. Ike nobly took all the blame on himself as he had approved Monty's suggestion to operate on Arnhem.'[22] And Montgomery's view: 'I remain Market Garden's unrepentant advocate.'[23]

Ramsay had a 90-minute meeting with Eisenhower on 21 October. There was concern about ammunition, with expenditure far exceeding supply. Once again, the admiral raised the importance of Antwerp and learned that Montgomery was 'at last fully alive to it'. The Second Army would attack westward to help the Canadians and two US divisions had been offered in support. Ramsay recorded, 'I reminded him that I'd warned him three weeks ago that the army were underestimating the difficulty of taking Walcheren, South Beveland and the south shore and that Monty was six weeks late in taking the action he was now doing. I told him that the latest date for the assault on Walcheren was 14 November and that I was pointing out the seriousness of the delay to Canadian Army HQ.'[24]

The next day Ramsay approved a new plan for Operation *Infatuate*. Walcheren would see 48 hours of heavy bombing and then simultaneous amphibious landings at Flushing and Westkapelle 'before the Hun can recover'.[25] He thought there were 'reasonable' prospects of success. Later, Montgomery complained that Ramsay had been dealing directly with the Canadian army.

The battle of the Scheldt, involving the First Canadian Army, as well as British and Polish troops, had been raging for several weeks. It involved fierce fighting to clear the area north of Antwerp, the Breskens Pocket and South Beveland. The final phase was *Infatuate*. Royal Marine commandos played a decisive part at Westkapelle on 1 November, supported by the heavy guns of *Warspite* and the monitors *Erebus* and *Roberts*. Eight days later, the island was finally in Allied hands. A massive minesweeping operation to clear the Scheldt was quickly under way.

On 16 November, Ramsay learned that an aircraft carrying Leigh-Mallory was missing. The commander of the Allied air forces had been appointed to a similar post in south-east Asia. Leigh-Mallory was on the first leg of the journey east when his plane disappeared over the French Alps in bad weather. 'This is a terrible tragedy unless they turn up unexpectedly,' Ramsay recorded.[26] It was confirmed that the plane had crashed and all on board were killed – the air chief marshal, his wife and eight crew.

Later that month, Ramsay had a scare when his plane was caught in a strong crosswind near a Brussels airfield and 'threw us about and on landing we were tilted over, necessitating immediate decision to take off again'.[27] The plane, slightly damaged, landed safely at the second attempt. Lieutenant Commander Lewis was not the pilot. Ramsay went on to inspect the port of Antwerp, where the first supply ships had arrived.

Major General Sir Francis de Guingand, Chief of General Staff, 21st Army Group, told Ramsay he was not happy with the course of the war. The Allies were no nearer knocking out Germany. De Guingand was fiercely critical of Eisenhower and SHAEF plans, and in Ramsay he found an ally. The admiral wrote in his diary, 'I said that there was no prospect of Ike getting any wiser and that the only course of action seemed to be a change of supreme commander. He agreed. I said the US would never accept Monty and he agreed. I said there was no suitable American to take his place and that Alan Brooke appeared to me the only suitable candidate. He agreed. He said that the American leadership had been bad, the generals being too inexperienced. They did not know how to combine artillery with infantry, put all divisions in line and had no supports to leapfrog and make headway. That they were everywhere too weak to break through and that they had utterly failed to reach their objective – the Rhine. This was all very depressing but not a surprise to me.'[28]

In contrast, Eisenhower had a high opinion of de Guingand. After noting Montgomery's 'eccentricities', he said the chief of staff had 'an enviable reputation and standing in the entire Allied force. He lived the code of the Allies and his tremendous capacity, ability and energy were always devoted to the coordination of plan and detail that was absolutely essential to victory.'[29]

On 16 December, the Allies were taken completely by surprise. The Germans launched a massive counter offensive through the forested Ardennes region, the enemy's last throw of the dice. The aim was to split the Allied lines and block the use of Antwerp. That day, Ramsay observed that 'the situation is in hand and the results may in the end benefit us more than the Hun'. Three days later, he was not so optimistic, noting that the enemy had penetrated the American First Army front with 'such ease'.[30]

On 20 December, he recorded, 'The news of the German offensive is less reassuring than before and it is evident that little opposition confronts the German Panzer forces who have broken through. Doubtless they will have replenished their tanks from US dumps and obtained a fresh lease of life. I cannot understand why our intelligence did not give warning of what was impending.' The Germans did not locate the American dumps and their tanks began running low on fuel soon afterwards. Montgomery was attacking from the north and Patton from the south. On Christmas Eve, Ramsay expressed his concern: 'This offensive has most unpleasant possibilities unless it is speedily taken a firm grip of. There is no sign yet that this is so.'[31]

On Christmas Day, Ramsay attended a church service after a staff meeting. There were presents from his wife and children, and Lewis, his pilot, gave him a scarf. Lewis was one of the guests at lunch. Afterwards, the admiral played table tennis and then spent the rest of the afternoon 'in front of the fire'. In the evening there was a 'very jolly party' with the staff of HMS *Royal Henry* – the official name of his headquarters.[32]

Two days later, Ramsay learned that the Germans were 'in a bit of a fix'. The tide had turned, but the battle of the Bulge, as it became known, would carry on into January, with Americans and Germans suffering high numbers of casualties.

As 1944 neared its end, Ramsay admitted that the past three years had been particularly strenuous 'because I have been dealing with matters for which little or no precedent existed and for which everything – staffs, complements, material both afloat and ashore, planning memoranda – had to be thought out and created'.[33]

CHAPTER 30

The Last Flight

On New Year's Eve 1944, Ramsay wrote to his wife. It would be his last letter
to her. Over the war years, he had written many times, and this letter began,
as usual, Darling Mag. He was full of hope.

'May 1945 bring nothing but good things to you and to me and best of all
bring us under the same roof again for keeps,' he wrote. 'It's been a successful
year for me and I have a great deal to be grateful for, both for my own sake
and the nation's, and we are in a far more hopeful position as regards peace
than we expected to be in June.'[1]

Margaret had written about Christmas Day with their sons, David and
Charles, and Ramsay commented, 'I'm so glad that Xmas went so well and
that food has abounded and everybody replete without ill results. It is quite
wonderful to me how you manage to produce so many presents for them and
give them such a wonderful time. It was touching of Charles to give you five
shillings, quite unique I should say, but very generous minded and shows the
right spirit. David's report is, as you say, very good and very satisfactory and
evidently he has worked.

'I had started to make plans to come home this week, possibly the 2nd,
but events have made this impossible and I have to go up to Belgium and
Holland tomorrow, possibly till Friday or Saturday. I will then review the
situation again with the hope of coming home on Sunday or Monday the
7th or 8th. It's beginning to thaw here but it is still very cold and I have to
sit in my office with my Lammy coat on always. The German offensive has
definitely halted but the situation is not yet stable and future developments
remain to be seen. I think that on the whole the advantage is with the Allies
rather than the Boche.'[2]

He touched again on his proposed visit to Bughtrig and suggested he might
fly up with Lewis. But he would return to London on the night train. He
expressed concern about cloud conditions.

The letter closed, 'Tons of love, darling Mag, and may 1945 allow us to see very much more of each other than 1944. Go on as you are doing, and not allow black moods to take root for a moment, however difficult. I am so awfully grateful for all your love and warm feelings and the way you have faced so many difficulties so bravely. My best 1945 blessing on you. Bert.'[3] He had been concerned that his wife was living in social isolation and that was the reason for his reference to 'black moods'.

Earlier that month, they had spent a few days in London together. Ramsay confided in his diary, 'Sad to part again and I am worried at her lack of spirits and obvious tiredness. But alas without company at home and without servants there is no society except with she herself. I know that at the bottom of it lies the feeling that she is out of it at Bughtrig and that she is becoming dull and stagnant. I only hope that this war will soon end and that at last we can be more together.'[4]

Ramsay had sent a cheque for £5 to Montgomery after losing his bet that the war would be over by 1 January 1945. The field marshal replied thanking him, saying the payment had been recorded in his betting book. He added, 'I won't give you my views on the present situation. I might say things I should not!'[5]

On New Year's Day, Ramsay worked on Scheldt defence plans that he wanted to discuss with Montgomery, and he arranged to go to the field marshal's headquarters near Brussels the following day. The trip involved a flight from an airfield at Toussus-le-Noble, near Versailles and about ten miles from Ramsay's base. The US Army Air Force was responsible for the airfield, known as AAF Station 46 or A-46. The admiral arrived at about 1100 on 2 January, and the Hudson and Lewis were waiting for him. A film crew happened to be at the airfield and Ramsay was pictured putting on a flying jacket before boarding the plane. Three others went aboard, Commander George Rowell, a staff officer, Lieutenant Derek Henderson, Ramsay's flag lieutenant, and Petty Officer Airman David Morgan.

The Hudson taxied to the runway and was cleared for take-off. The plane had barely got off the ground when it attempted to turn to port and then spiralled out of control, crashing in flames. It was about 1115. Ramsay, Lewis and Rowell were killed instantly. Henderson and Morgan were pulled from the wreckage alive but died shortly afterwards. Bertram Ramsay was 61.

The Admiralty was informed in the afternoon that the five men had died on war service. The Lords Commissioners sent a letter to Lady Ramsay expressing their profound sympathy and pointing out that they were 'deeply sensible of the loss which the Royal Navy has sustained in the passing of an officer and leader of transcendent quality. They recall especially in a lifetime of devoted and distinguished service, Sir Bertram Ramsay's achievement in the organisation of the evacuation from Dunkirk and of the landings of successive expeditionary forces in North Africa and Sicily, and finally the great service which he rendered as Allied Naval Commander of the Expeditionary Force which has carried the army of liberation to western Europe.'[6]

Lady Ramsay received nearly 400 letters, 30 telegrams and many other messages. The king and the queen offered their 'heartfelt sympathy in your great sorrow'. Cunningham said he had lost a friend of many years, 'a man of the highest integrity with great personal charm of manner'.[7]

Montgomery told Lady Ramsay of his sadness and how 'very fond' he was of Bertie. He sent her a copy of a tribute he had written for *The Times*, which also mentioned his 'other great friend', Trafford Leigh-Mallory. It ended: 'They were not to live to see the fruits of their labours, but when this business is all over, and the world is once more at peace, we must not forget the part that was played by Bertie Ramsay and Leigh-Mallory – a great sailor and a great airman, both great friends of the army, and both great English gentlemen.'[8]

Roosevelt and Eisenhower also paid tribute, with the general describing Ramsay as his 'warm personal friend'. And people from all walks of life sent Lady Ramsay poignant messages. Major Walter Garnier of the Royal Marines told how he and the admiral were shipmates in the cruiser *Hyacinth* in 1903 and had remained great friends ever since. The major wrote, 'Although I am a completely obscure person, he was one of those who could walk with kings and keep the common touch. He will go down in history as one of our greatest admirals, and the country has suffered a staggering blow in his loss.'[9]

On 8 January, a cold day with snow on the ground, Ramsay was buried with full naval honours in the cemetery at St Germain-en-Laye, close to his headquarters. The other victims of the crash were also buried there. Eisenhower, Cunningham, the military governor of Paris, General Koenig, and the British ambassador, Duff Cooper, were among the mourners. In London that day, there was a memorial service at Westminster Abbey, which Lady Ramsay attended.

CHAPTER 31

Mystery of the Crash

The crash of the Hudson was baffling, and Lady Ramsay was desperate to find answers. A board of inquiry was set up, but a family friend, Admiral Sir Geoffrey Arbuthnot, told her that its findings would be kept secret.

'I am sorry but there is no chance of you being able to get extracts from the board of inquiry as the regulations are very strict in that the members of a board are forbidden to divulge their findings,' Arbuthnot wrote. He added, 'I think, however, I can tell you the main facts as given to me from various sources. The engines of the machine were brought to this country dismantled. They were in good working order. The pilot's take-off was not good. The people on the airfield at the time commented on this fact. It was noted that he did not have his machine moving fast enough. One dislikes saying it but I gather that the view held is that the pilot made an error of judgement. He banked his machine in a turn when he was very low and not travelling fast.'[1]

Lady Ramsay was also in contact with her husband's chief of staff, Commodore Maurice Mansergh, who told her that the Hudson went into a spin after climbing only about 100 feet. 'There has been a most searching examination of what is left of it and, so far, the experts have been unable to discover any technical fault,' he wrote. 'George Lewis was a most experienced pilot and very careful, which makes the accident all the more inexplicable. I don't think we shall ever know what caused it. The aeroplane did catch fire, but it was so close to the airfield when it crashed that both Derek Henderson and the petty officer airman were taken out alive. There is no doubt, however, that the admiral and the other two were killed at once by the crash. I have questioned Surgeon Captain Miller on this point and he assures me that it must have been so. I wish I could tell you more, but there is really nothing more that I know.'[2]

Mansergh had worked with Ramsay for the past 15 months and he missed him 'terribly'. On the practical side, the commodore pointed out that the admiral's mess bills had been paid with money found in his safe. What remained of the admiral's wine stock had been taken over by his successor, Vice Admiral Sir Harold Burrough, 'who has I think already written to you about it'.[3]

Mansergh ended his letter, 'I am so very, very sorry for you and I hope that in time your grief will be healed. You will always have the proudest memories of your husband and I am so glad you have your two boys, who are old enough to know what a great and splendid man their father was.'[4]

The Fleet Air Arm carried out a preliminary investigation into the crash of Hudson AM 550 and found no signs of mechanical failure. But attention was drawn to photographs that appeared to show frost patches on the aircraft. And there was evidence of 'bad airmanship amounting to negligence' on the part of the pilot, Lewis.[5]

The Royal Aircraft Establishment at Farnborough, Hampshire, was consulted about the dangers of frost on aircraft, and the expert view was that it could markedly contribute to stalling.[6]

It emerged that the commanding officer of 781 Naval Air Squadron, Lieutenant Commander W. B. Caldwell, had serious reservations about Lewis's handling of the Hudson. Caldwell had been a passenger on a short flight and 'felt rather uncomfortable' at the lack of speed on take-off. He did not mention this to Lewis because 'I thought he was doing it deliberately to "bait" me – knowing my intense dislike of flying as a passenger'.[7]

But another officer, Lieutenant Commander A. B. Cunningham, did speak to Lewis after a demonstration to trainee pilots on the take-off procedure for the Beaufighter II. This followed a complaint that Lewis climbed the aircraft at 80mph when the safety speed before climbing should have been 160mph. Cunningham noted, 'I asked Lieutenant Commander Lewis if he knew what the definition of safety speed was. This he did not know. He endeavoured to reassure me that that 80 to 85mph was quite a safe speed at which to climb a Beaufighter II aircraft.'[8]

Vice Admiral Burrough ordered the naval board of inquiry, appointing Captain Charles Keighley-Peach as its president. The inquiry opened at the *Royal Henry* headquarters on 26 February 1945. One of the witnesses was a French navy pilot, Lieutenant Albert Bret, who was in charge of a small unit looking after planes at the Toussus-le-Noble airfield, including the Hudson. He had been at the airfield on 2 January and he was asked about ice on the Hudson. Bret said men had been working since about 0830 clearing snow and ice from the plane. 'I am satisfied that the leading edges were clean, and in my own mind I am satisfied that the remaining ice was taken off as far as possible, and that whatever was left was blown off during the taxiing. In other words ice was not fixed to the skin of the aeroplane.'[9]

Bret watched the Hudson on the runway and did not like what he saw. When the plane should have been doing 70mph it was 'only something like 40 miles, and it went on accelerating still extremely slowly in tail down position, and got off the ground, I should say just at the end of the runway'.[10]

He had seen Lewis take off before and noticed that the engines were not giving full power. He was so concerned that he approached him later and asked if there had been a problem with the engines. Lewis insisted he had given 'full boost and full revs'. Several US Army Air Force officers also gave statements that the Hudson's take-off on 2 January had been too slow.

Petty Officer William Stokes told the inquiry that six or seven men had been working to clear snow and ice from the Hudson, using brooms and rags. Asked if the pilot had checked that the plane was clear, Stokes replied, 'Not to me and I haven't heard that he mentioned it to anyone else.'[11]

Another witness was Lieutenant Robert Horan, a photographic officer at the Royal Naval Air Station, Lee-on-the-Solent, who was asked about the pictures showing white patches on the wings of the Hudson. Horan suggested that it could have been loose snow or frost blowing from the wings. Or it might have been wet patches caught by the light. 'Another possibility is that there would be a very fine powdering of frost, which was exaggerated by an under-exposed film.' Horan, who had 35 years' experience of photography, said he would be reluctant to give sworn evidence that the white marks were hoar frost or snow. The inquiry decided that the photographs were unreliable evidence, and accepted that de-icing had been carried out to the satisfaction of supervising officers.

The Hudson had taken off in favourable weather conditions. After some difficulty, the plane became airborne about 200 yards from the end of the runway. It climbed to a height of 200 feet and slowly turned, the port wing dipping. Then the Hudson stalled and started to spin, crashing into a field some 650 yards from the end of the runway.

The board of inquiry blamed the pilot for the crash, noting that Lewis's take-off technique for the Hudson was at fault. The board was also critical of the fact that he had not checked that the plane was clear of ice or snow. The Hudson had a flight authorisation sheet (A700), which the ground crew completed, but Lewis failed to sign it in a number of places, as he was required to do.

Sir George Lewis, who inherited his title, was a London lawyer who joined the Royal Naval Volunteer Reserve at the outbreak of war. He had a civil pilot's licence and soon acquired his 'wings' in the Fleet Air Arm, which was expanding rapidly.

The inquiry examined Lewis's flying logbook and discovered that he had not received proper instruction on the Hudson. But he had a qualifying certificate for the plane – which he had signed himself. This was against the spirit of the relevant regulations. At the time, he was commanding 781 Naval Air Squadron.

The inquiry stated, 'It is recommended, therefore, that pilots, and in particular communication pilots who are called upon to fly a new type of multi-engined aircraft with passengers, should receive a comprehensive course in its characteristics before embarking on regular flights.'[12]

It was a sign of the times that the inquiry did not touch on one aspect that would be seen as important today: alcohol and flying. In those war years, it was not uncommon for pilots to drink. The RAF fighter ace James 'Johnnie' Johnson, for example, carried a silver hip flask. *King's Regulations* had no restrictions on pilots drinking before flying.

Today, with aircraft a lot more sophisticated, the picture is completely different. There are upper and lower limits for RAF and Fleet Air Arm crew. Pilots must comply with the lower limit, which is effectively zero. The Armed Forces Act 2016 gives a commanding officer the power to order alcohol testing after an accident. Restrictions on alcohol and drug use were further tightened in January 2019. In the event of a fatal accident, a pathologist carrying out a post-mortem examination would be required to test for alcohol consumption.

Returning to the morning of 2 January 1945, the question arises: was Lewis's poor take-off technique further affected by alcohol? There is no indication that he was teetotal. With the end of the war in sight, the New Year celebrations would have been prolonged. French cellars had been liberated, and the RAF was even using empty bomb racks to transport barrels of beer.

Unfortunately, there is no Ramsay diary entry for New Year's Eve, though the admiral had recorded having 'a very jolly party' at his headquarters on Christmas night. His pilot was one of the guests.

Lewis, who had enjoyed the hospitality of Bughtrig, would have been well aware how desperate his VIP passenger was to return to his wife and sons at the family home in Berwickshire. Yet Admiral Sir Bertram Ramsay would remain forever in a foreign land.

Ramsay's Legacy

In the post-war years, a number of military and political leaders produced memoirs of the great struggle, notably Sir Winston Churchill, General Eisenhower, Admiral of the Fleet Viscount Cunningham of Hyndhope, Field Marshal Viscount Montgomery of Alamein and Marshal of the Royal Air Force Lord Tedder. These books certainly raised their public profile, with Churchill's six-volume *The Second World War* winning the 1953 Nobel Prize in Literature.

Field Marshal Viscount Alanbrooke of Brookeborough did not write his memoirs, but during World War II, he had kept a detailed diary, which was often highly critical of some of the key figures, especially Churchill, Eisenhower and General Marshall. Originally, he had intended to keep the diary private. But he changed his mind in the fifties after deciding that the Chiefs of Staff had not been given enough credit in Churchill's memoirs. Publication followed, though some of the scathing remarks were not included.

Which brings us to the question, would Admiral Sir Bertram Ramsay have been tempted to produce his memoirs? In the closing days of 1944, he was looking forward to the end of the war and retirement from the navy. When Cunningham suggested a posting to Berlin after Germany's surrender, he was appalled. Ramsay wanted to return home to his family and the life he had once enjoyed in Berwickshire. He no longer wanted to be in the public eye. In any case, the admiral had an intense dislike of personal publicity, so he may not have been tempted to put pen to paper. Sadly, fate intervened on 2 January 1945.

To a large extent Ramsay became a forgotten hero of World War II. Until now, comparatively little has been written about him. In 1959, there was a biography, *Full Cycle*, by Rear Admiral W. S. Chalmers, but it was limited in scope. Fortunately, Ramsay left a wealth of material in the form of letters to his wife, diaries and other papers, which are now held at the Churchill Archives

Centre, Cambridge. Unfortunately for Chalmers, he was unable to use some of this material because it was too sensitive at the time. Like Alanbrooke, Ramsay could be highly critical of his contemporaries.

With some irony, Alanbrooke provided a foreword for *Full Cycle*. He stressed how important Ramsay had been to the war effort: 'Providence had favoured us in placing Ramsay at the critical point during the evacuation of Dunkirk, and Providence again served our cause by placing Ramsay as a counterpart at sea to Montgomery on land, both for the invasion of Sicily and for the liberation of Normandy. It would have been hard to find more ideal commanders for combined operations of such magnitude …'

Indeed, Ramsay's mastery of the Dunkirk evacuation cannot be underestimated. Churchill admitted at the time that he thought only 20,000 to 30,000 troops might be saved. The most optimistic estimate was 50,000. In the end more than 338,000 were brought to Britain. Though battered, the country still had the nucleus of an army that would fight another day. In Dover, Ramsay remained on the front line as fears grew of a German invasion.

It took time for the tide to turn. In November 1942, Britain, along with the United States, was ready to go on the offensive, with the invasion of French North Africa. Ramsay proved a mastermind of the amphibious operation. He repeated this feat the following July with the invasion of Sicily. And then came his immense planning for the greatest sea invasion, Operation *Neptune*, which led to ultimate victory.

After the war ended, Ramsay's achievements surely ranked alongside those of Churchill, Eisenhower, Cunningham, Montgomery and Tedder, yet he never received the public recognition he deserved.

Ramsay's Career

Cadet (January 1898)
Britannia Royal Naval College
Crescent (cruiser), May 1899

Midshipman (September 1899)
Crescent

Sub Lieutenant (September 1902)
Crescent
Hyacinth (cruiser), October 1903

Lieutenant (December 1904)
Hyacinth
Good Hope (cruiser), April 1905
Terrible (cruiser), September 1905
Renown (battleship), July 1906
Dreadnought (battleship), September 1906
Victory, Portsmouth, signals course, February 1909
Albemarle (battleship), August 1909
Bacchante (cruiser), September 1910
Victory, signals instructor, June 1912

Lieutenant Commander (December 1912)
Victory, war staff course, February 1913
Orion (battleship), January 1914
Dreadnought, July 1914
President, signals appointment, February 1915
M25 (monitor), in command, August 1915

Commander (June 1916)
M25
Broke (destroyer) in command, October 1917
President, special service, January 1919
New Zealand (battlecruiser), February 1919
Emperor of India (battleship), November 1920
Benbow (battleship), April 1921
Victory, unemployed time and technical course, May 1923

Captain (June 1923)
Victory
President, senior officers' war course, March 1924
Weymouth (cruiser), in command, October 1924
Danae (cruiser), in command, March 1925
Royal Naval College, Greenwich, instructor on senior officers' war course, May 1927
Kent (cruiser), in command and flag captain and chief of staff to Commander-in-Chief, China Station, July 1929
Imperial Defence College, instructor, July 1931
Royal Sovereign (battleship), in command, November 1933

Rear Admiral (May 1935)
Chief of staff to Commander-in-Chief, Home Fleet, August 1935
Victory, technical course, January 1937
No subsequent appointments until nominated Flag Officer in Charge at Dover in the event of war shortly before being placed on retired list

Vice Admiral (retired list January 1939)
Flag Officer, Dover, August 1939
Vice Admiral, Dover

Acting Admiral (retired list July 1942)
Naval Commander-in-Chief, Expeditionary Force, July 1942
Deputy Naval Commander-in-Chief, Expeditionary Force, November 1942
Operation *Torch*
Operation *Husky*

Admiral (active list April 1944)
Allied Naval Commander-in-Chief, Expeditionary Force July 1943
Operation *Neptune*

Ramsay's Awards

Africa General Service Medal bar Somaliland 1902–4
1914–15 Star
British War Medal 1914–20
Victory Medal 1914–19 with Mention in Despatches
Crown of Italy (Officer) 1917
Member of the Royal Victorian Order 1918
French Legion of Honour (Chevalier) 1918
Belgian Croix de Guerre 1919
Companion of the Bath (Military) 1936
Knight Commander of the Bath (Military) 1940
Knight Commander of the Order of the British Empire 1943
Soviet Union Order of Ushakov 1st Class 1944
US Legion of Merit (Commander) 1945
French Croix de Guerre with Palme 1945

Admiral Ramsay also would have been entitled to campaign medals for World War II.

British Vessels in Operation *Dynamo*

	Total	Lost	Troops landed
Cruiser	1	–	1,856
Destroyers	41	6	96,197
Corvettes	6	–	1,100
Sloop	1	–	436
Gunboats	2	1	3,512
Minesweepers	36	6	46,434
Trawlers	52	12	5,396
Drifters	61	5	12,370
Special service vessels	3	1	4,408
MTBs, MA/SBs	13	–	99
Armed boarding vessels	3	1	4,848
Skoots	40	4	22,698
Yachts	26	3	4,681
Personnel vessels	45	8	87,810
Hospital ships	8	1	3,006
Naval motorboats	12	6	96
Tugs	40	3	3,164
Landing craft	13	8	118
War Department motor launches	8	–	579
Dockyard lighters	8	2	418
Barges	40	10	4,308

RNLI lifeboats	19	1	323
Motorboats, launches	202	78	5,031
Blockships	6	2	–
Seaplane tenders	6	3	–
Ships' lifeboats	56	39	–
Dinghies, etc.	16	16	–
Totals	764	216	308,888

Figures listed in W. J. R. Gardner (ed), *The Evacuation from Dunkirk: 'Operation Dynamo', 26 May–4 June 1940* (Naval Historical Branch, Ministry of Defence. Naval Staff Histories).

Key Vessels Lost During Operation *Dynamo*

ROYAL NAVY

Destroyers
Basilisk
Grafton
Grenade
Havant
Keith
Wakeful

Gunboat
Mosquito

Minesweepers
Brighton Belle
Brighton Queen
Devonia
Gracie Fields
Skipjack
Waverley

Trawlers
Argyllshire
Blackburn Rovers

Calvi
Comfort
Nautilus
Ocean Reward
Polly Johnson
St Achilleus
Stella Dorado
Thomas Bartlett
Thurringia
Westella

Drifters
Boy Roy
Fair Breeze
Girl Pamela
Lord Cavan
Paxton

Special Service Vessel
Crested Eagle

Armed Boarding Vessel
King Orry

MERCHANT NAVY

Personnel Ships
Clan Macalister
Fenella
Lorina
Mona's Queen
Normania
Queen of the Channel
Scotia
Sequacity

Hospital Ship
Paris

French Destroyers
Bourrasque
Foudroyant
Siroco

French Cargo Ships
Donaissien
St Camille

Names listed in W. J. R. Gardner (ed), *The Evacuation from Dunkirk: 'Operation Dynamo', 26 May–4 June 1940* (Naval Historical Branch, Ministry of Defence. Naval Staff Histories).

Warships in Operation *Neptune*

	Eastern Task Force	Western Task Force
Battleships	2	3
Monitors	1	1
Cruisers	13 (1 Polish)	10 (3 US, 2 French)
Gunboats	2 (1 Dutch)	1 (Dutch)
Fleet destroyers	30 (2 Norwegian)	30 (US)
Hunt class destroyers	14 (2 Polish, 1 Norwegian, 1 French)	5
Sloops	5	–
Fleet minesweepers	42	56 (9 US)
Other minesweepers and danlayers	87	62 (16 US)
Frigates and destroyer escorts	19 (2 French)	12 (6 US, 2 French)
Corvettes	17 (2 Greek)	4 (2 French)
Patrol craft	–	18 (US)
A/S trawlers	21	9
Minelayers	2	–
Coastal craft	90 (30 US)	113 (81 US)
Seaplane carrier	1	–
Midget submarines	2	–

Other warships, including a battleship, destroyers, frigates and corvettes, were available, making a total of 1,213.

Bibliography

Admiral Ramsay's letters, diaries and other papers are held at the Churchill Archives Centre, Churchill College, Cambridge. Admiralty, War Office and Royal Air Force reports, along with Cabinet papers, are held at The National Archives, Kew, in southwest London.

Beevor, Antony. *D-Day, The Battle for Normandy* (Viking, 2009)

Blackwell, Ian. *Battle for Sicily, Stepping Stone to Victory* (Pen & Sword Military, 2008)

Boyd, Douglas. *Normandy in the Time of Darkness, Everyday Life and Death in the French Channel Ports 1940–45* (Ian Allan, 2013)

Brodhurst, Robin. *Churchill's Anchor, The Biography of Admiral of the Fleet Sir Dudley Pound* (Leo Cooper, 2000)

Chalmers, Rear Admiral W. S. *Full Cycle, The Biography of Admiral Sir Bertram Home Ramsay* (Hodder & Stoughton, 1959)

Chatfield, Admiral of the Fleet Lord. *The Navy and Defence* (William Heinemann, 1942)

Churchill, Winston S. *The Second World War*, six volumes (Cassell, 1948 onwards)

Coad, Jonathan. *Dover Castle, A Frontline Fortress and its Wartime Tunnels* (English Heritage, 2011)

Crossley, Jim. *Monitors of the Royal Navy, How the Fleet Brought the Great Guns to Bear* (Pen & Sword Maritime, 2013)

Cunningham, Admiral of the Fleet Viscount. *A Sailor's Odyssey: The Autobiography of Admiral of the Fleet Viscount Cunningham of Hyndhope* (Hutchinson, 1951)

Danchev, Alex and Todman, Daniel, (eds). *War Diaries 1939–1945, Field Marshal Lord Alanbrooke* (Weidenfeld & Nicolson, 2001)

David, Saul. *After Dunkirk, Churchill's Sacrifice of the Highland Division* (Brassey's, 1994)

Dildy, Douglas C. *Dunkirk 1940, Operation Dynamo* (Osprey, 2010)

Divine, A. D. *Dunkirk* (Faber & Faber, 1945)

Divine, David. *The Nine Days of Dunkirk* (Faber & Faber, 1959)

Eisenhower, Dwight D. *Crusade in Europe* (Doubleday, 1948)

Ellis, Major L. F. *The War in France and Flanders* (The Naval & Military Press, 2004 reprint)

Fenby, Jonathan. *The Sinking of the Lancastria, Britain's Greatest Maritime Disaster and Churchill's Cover-Up* (Simon & Schuster, 2005)

Fraser, David. *Alanbrooke* (William Collins, 1982)

Gardner, W. J. R. (ed.). *The Evacuation from Dunkirk, 'Operation Dynamo', 26 May–4 June 1940* (Routledge, 2000)

Grehan, John and Mace, Martin, (eds). *Operations in North Africa and the Middle East 1939–1942, Tobruk, Crete, Syria and East Africa*, commanding officers' reports (Pen & Sword Military, 2015)

Grehan, John and Mace, Martin eds). *Operations in North Africa and the Middle East 1942–1944, El Alamein, Tunisia, Algeria and Operation Torch*, commanding officers' reports (Pen & Sword Military, 2015)

Herder, Brian Lane. *Operation Torch, The Invasion of French North Africa* (Osprey, 2017)

James, Admiral Sir William. *The Sky Was Always Blue* (Methuen, 1951)

Karslake, Basil. *1940 The Last Act, The Story of the British Forces in France After Dunkirk* (Leo Cooper, 1979)

King, Fleet Admiral Ernest J. *US Navy at War 1941–1945* (US Navy Department, 1946)

King, Ernest J. and Whitehill, Walter Muir. *Fleet Admiral King* (Eyre & Spottiswoode, 1953)

Lord, Walter. *The Miracle of Dunkirk* (Viking, 1982)

Love, Robert W. and Major, John (eds). *The Year of D-Day, The 1944 Diary of Admiral Sir Bertram Ramsay* (The University of Hull Press, 1994)

Mace, Martin (ed). *The Royal Navy at Dunkirk, Commanding Officers' Reports of British Warships in Action During Operation Dynamo* (Frontline, 2017)

Masefield, John. *The Nine Days Wonder* (William Heinemann, 1941)

Middlebrook, Martin and Mahoney, Patrick. *Battleship, The Loss of the Prince of Wales and the Repulse* (Penguin, 1979)

Montgomery, Field Marshal Viscount. *The Memoirs* (Collins, 1958)

Moore, Robert J. and Rodgaard, John A. *A Hard Fought Ship, The Story of HMS Venomous* (Holywell House, 2010)

Napier, W. E. P., *History of the War in the Peninsula and in the South of France, From the Year 1807 to the Year 1814*, Volume five (Constable, 1993, originally published in 1836)

Pound, Reginald. *Evans of the Broke, A Biography of Admiral Lord Mountevans* (Oxford University Press, 1963)

Roskill, Captain S. W. *The War at Sea 1939–1945*, three volumes (Her Majesty's Stationery Office, 1950s)

Roskill, Stephen. *Churchill & the Admirals* (Collins, 1977)

Schofield, Vice Admiral B. B. *Operation Neptune, The Inside Story of Naval Operations for the Normandy Landings 1944* (Pen & Sword Military, 2008, first published by Ian Allen, 1974)

Sebag-Montefiore, Hugh. *Dunkirk, Fight to the Last Man* (Viking, 2006)

Simpson, Michael (ed). *The Somerville Papers, Selections from the Private and Official Correspondence of Admiral of the Fleet Sir James Somerville* (Scolar Press for the Navy Records Society, 1995)

Stasi, Jean-Claude. *Dunkirk 1940, Operation Dynamo* (Heimdal, 2017)

Stephen, Martin. *The Fighting Admirals, British Admirals of the Second World War* (Leo Cooper, 1991)

Sutton, Terry and Leach, Derek. *Dover in the Second World War* (Phillimore, 2010)

Taffrail, *Endless Story, Destroyer Operations in the Great War* (Seaforth, 2016)

Vian, Admiral of the Fleet Sir Philip. *Action This Day*, memoirs (Frederick Muller, 1960)

Vince, Charles, *Storm on the Waters, The Story of the Lifeboat Service in the War of 1939–1945* (Hodder & Stoughton, 1946)

Winton, John. *Cunningham, The Greatest Admiral Since Nelson* (John Murray, 1998)

Woodward, David. *Ramsay at War, The Fighting Life of Admiral Sir Bertram Ramsay* (William Kimber, 1957)

Wukovits, John. *Eisenhower* (Palgrave Macmillan, 2006)

Zaloga, Steven J. *Sicily 1943, The Debut of Allied Joint Operations* (Osprey, 2013)

Endnotes

Chapter 1

1 Whitworth's letter dated 6 July 1937.
2 Tyrwhitt's letter dated 13 November 1938.
3 Cunningham's letter dated 3 November 1938. Other letters sent that month.
4 Notes on how to keep a ship clean, Ramsay, captain of HMS *Danae*, 14 May 1925.
5 Comment by James Rivett-Carne, who was HMS *Kent's* executive officer in 1929 when stationed at Wei-hai-wei.
6 *Picture Post*, 18 September 1943.
7 Letter sent by Admiral Fisher, dated 5 November 1936.
8 Letter Ramsay wrote to his wife, 27 May 1939.
9 Letter Ramsay wrote to his wife, 5 September 1939.

Chapter 2

1 Biographical notes by G. B. Creasy. *Eastern Daily Press*, 10 March 1903. *Gloucestershire Echo*, 18 March 1933. *Cheltenham Chronicle*, 25 March 1933.
2 *Dictionary of National Biography 1885–1900*, Volume 47, Ernest Marsh Lloyd. W. E. P. Napier, *History of the War in the Peninsula*.
3 Letter from John Masefield to Ramsay, dated 3 September 1940.
4 *The Gunner* magazine, date unknown.
5 *Dictionary of National Biography 1885–1900*, Volume 47, Ernest Marsh Lloyd. *The Gunner* magazine, date unknown.
6 Information from Trevor Hearn, president of the Old Colcestrian Society, who has written a history of the school. He pointed out: 'Rather embarrassingly, the school somehow managed to miss Ramsay off its war memorial window (probably because of his short tenure at the school). A student made this startling discovery and it has now been rectified.'
7 Ramsay's service record.
8 Letters dated 28 October 1901 (HMS *Crescent*) and 7 December 1901 (*Crescent*).
9 Letter dated 24 November 1902 (HMS *Hyacinth*).
10 Letter dated 3 November 1903 (SS *Arabia*).
11 Ramsay's service record.
12 Rear Admiral W. S. Chalmers, *Full Cycle*, Chapter 1.

Chapter 3

1 16 August 1914.
2 Rear Admiral W. S. Chalmers, *Full Cycle*, Chapter 2.
3 Ibid.

4   Ramsay's service record. Diary entries for August 1914.
5   Ramsay's diary entry for 23 August.
6   *The Times*, 26 November 1914.
7   Ramsay's report was headed, 'Some remarks on the state of HMS *Broke* when I assumed command of her in October 1917.'
8   Rear Admiral W. S. Chalmers, *Full Cycle*, Chapter 2.
9   Ramsay's wife made the comments to Rear Admiral W. S. Chalmers in 1967.
10 Taffrail, *Endless Story, Destroyer Operations in the Great War*, Chapter 15.
11 Rear Admiral W. S. Chalmers, *Full Cycle*, Chapter 2.
12 Inquiry report dated 1 July 1918. Commodore A. F. Davidson headed the inquiry.
13 Keyes's report was dated 5 July.
14 Admiralty letter dated 2 August.
15 Inquiry letter dated 7 November.
16 Ibid.
17 Admiralty letter to Keyes dated 10 December.
18 Ramsay's wife made the comments to Rear Admiral W. S. Chalmers in 1967.

Chapter 4

1   Ramsay's diary for 5 and 18 January 1919. Service record.
2   Rear Admiral W. S. Chalmers, *Full Cycle*, Chapter 3.
3   Ibid.
4   Rear Admiral W. S. Chalmers, *Full Cycle*, Chapter 3. National Centre of Biography at the Australian National University.
5   Dictionary of New Zealand Biography.
6   Ramsay's service record.
7   Kelly's inspection report, dated 22 January 1923.
8   Rear Admiral W. S. Chalmers, *Full Cycle*, Chapter 3.
9   Report to Commander-in-Chief, Mediterranean Fleet.
10 Report to the Admiralty, sent from Hong Kong and dated 27 December 1924.
11 Rear Admiral W. S. Chalmers, *Full Cycle*, Chapter 4.
12 Waistell's comments dated 30 May 1925 (HMS *Barham*).
13 Keyes's comments dated 4 July 1925 (HMS *Queen Elizabeth* at Gibraltar).
14 Notes on how to keep a ship clean, Ramsay, captain of HMS *Danae*, 14 May 1925.
15 Ibid.
16 Ibid.
17 Ramsay's diary entry for 11 July 1925.
18 Report sent to the Commander-in-Chief of the Mediterranean Fleet on 7 January 1927.
19 Rear Admiral W. S. Chalmers, *Full Cycle*, Chapter 4.
20 Jellicoe's notes on Ramsay's lecture paper.
21 Rear Admiral W. S. Chalmers, *Full Cycle*, Chapter 4.
22 Ramsay's service record.
23 Family notes written by Margaret, undated.
24 Letter written at the United Services Club, Pall Mall, London, on 7 September 1925.
25 Written comments by Lady Ramsay, undated but probably circa 1958.
26 Ibid.

Chapter 5

1 Service record. Ramsay's comments to his wife, December 1933.
2 Letter from Backhouse dated 6 January 1935, marked personal and sent from a London address.
3 Letter from Backhouse dated 23 January 1935.
4 Service record.
5 Memorandum by Ramsay, undated, based on much correspondence.
6 Ibid.
7 Ibid.
8 Letter to his wife dated 8 September 1935.
9 Letters to his wife dated 17 and 19 September 1935.
10 Letter to his wife dated 30 September 1935.
11 Memorandum by Ramsay, undated, based on much correspondence.
12 Ibid.
13 Ibid.
14 Ibid.
15 Ibid.
16 Ibid.
17 Letter to Admiral Arbuthnot dated 6 November 1935.
18 Letter dated 21 November 1935.
19 Memorandum by Ramsay, undated, based on much correspondence.
20 Ibid.
21 Ibid.
22 Ibid.
23 Royle's letter dated 5 December 1935.
24 Memorandum by Ramsay, undated, based on much correspondence.
25 It is not clear when Ramsay sent his letter but Chatfield's reply was dated 6 January 1936.
26 Ibid.
27 Memorandum by Ramsay, undated, based on much correspondence.
28 Royle's letter dated 18 March 1936.
29 Memorandum by Ramsay, undated, based on much correspondence.
30 Ibid.
31 Royle's letter dated 20 May 1936.
32 Royle's letter dated 8 June 1936.
33 Ramsay's letter dated 22 March 1937.
34 Royle's letter dated 28 April 1937.

Chapter 6

1 Letter Ramsay wrote to his wife, 5 September 1939.
2 Information from English Heritage.
3 Terry Sutton and Derek Leach, *Dover in the Second World War*, chapter on 1940.
4 Letter dated 25 September 1939.
5 Ibid.
6 Letter dated 30 September 1939.
7 Letter dated 17 October 1939.
8 Letter dated 4 December 1939.
9 Ibid.

Chapter 7

1 Terry Sutton and Derek Leach, *Dover in the Second World War*, chapter on 1939. *Dover Express* 1, 8 and 15 September 1939.
2 Hugh Sebag-Montefiore, *Dunkirk*, Part 1, Chapter 2.
3 Letter to Ramsay's wife dated 13 January 1940.
4 Letter dated 17 March 1940.
5 Letter to Ramsay's wife dated 27 February 1940.
6 Letter dated 26 April 1940.
7 Letter to Ramsay's wife dated 16 May 1940.
8 Letter to Ramsay's wife dated 21 May 1940.
9 Robert J. Moore and John A. Rodgaard, *A Hard Fought Ship*, Chapter 4.
10 Report on the operations of the 2nd Battalion Irish Guards in the Boulogne area from Tuesday 21 May 1940 to Thursday 23 May 1940.
11 20 Brigade's Boulogne War Diary.
12 Letter to Ramsay's wife dated 23 May 1940.
13 Letter to Ramsay's wife dated 25 May 1940.
14 Somerville's notes on the evacuation of Dunkirk and Calais, 24–28 May 1940.
15 Ibid.
16 Ibid.
17 Winston S. Churchill, *The Second World War, Their Finest Hour*, Chapter 4.
18 *Hansard*, 4 June 1940.

Chapter 8

1 Ramsay's report on the Dunkirk evacuation, 18 June 1940.
2 Duggan's report, as quoted in A. D. Divine, *Dunkirk*, Chapter 7.
3 Hill's report, as quoted in A. D. Divine, *Dunkirk*, Chapter 7.
4 Ramsay's report on the Dunkirk evacuation, 18 June 1940.
5 Report by Tennant, 7 June 1940.
6 Imperial War Museum interview, 7 September 1983.
7 Ramsay's report on the Dunkirk evacuation, 18 June 1940.
8 Ibid.
9 Letter dated 27 May 1940.

Chapter 9

1 Winston S. Churchill, *The Second World War, Their Finest Hour*, Chapter 4.
2 *Hansard*, 28 May 1940.
3 *Hansard*, 4 June 1940.
4 Report by Tennant, 7 June 1940.
5 Imperial War Museum interview, 6 February 2015.
6 Ibid.
7 Ramsay's report on the Dunkirk evacuation, 18 June 1940.

Chapter 10

1 Report by Commander Fisher, 30 May 1940.
2 Ibid.
3 Ibid.

4   Report by Lieutenant McRea, 3 June 1940.
5   Ibid.
6   Hughes's report, as quoted in A. D. Divine, *Dunkirk*, Chapter 10.
7   Ramsay's report on the Dunkirk evacuation, 18 June 1940.
8   Ibid.
9   Report by Tennant, 7 June 1940.
10 Ramsay's report on the Dunkirk evacuation, 18 June 1940.
11 Mackie's report, as quoted in A. D. Divine, *Dunkirk*, Chapter 10.
12 Cubbon's report, as quoted in A. D. Divine, *Dunkirk*, Chapter 10.
13 Report by Lieutenant Commander Hine, 1 June 1940.
14 Ibid.
15 Report by Commander Byle, 11 June 1940.
16 Ibid.
17 Comments by Corporal Turner, *The Royal Navy at Dunkirk*, reports compiled by Martin Mace, Chapter 3.
18 Report by Commander Boyle, 11 June 1940.
19 Report by Lieutenant Commander Booth, 31 May 1940.
20 Report by Lieutenant Eric Jones.
21 Ramsay's report on the Dunkirk evacuation, 18 June 1940.
22 Report by Wake-Walker.
23 Message sent on 29 May 1940.
24 Report by Wake-Walker.
25 Ibid.
26 Ramsay's report on the Dunkirk evacuation, 18 June 1940.
27 Ramsay's letter dated 29 May 1940.
28 Letter dated 29 May 1940.

Chapter 11

1   Report by Tennant, 7 June 1940.
2   Report by Elliott, 4 June 1940.
3   Report by Lieutenant Commander Parish, 12 June 1940.
4   Report by Tennant, 7 June 1940.
5   Report by Wake-Walker.
6   Ramsay's report on the Dunkirk evacuation, 18 June 1940.
7   Ibid
8   Report by Wake-Walker.
9   Report by Berthon, 16 June 1940.
10 Ibid.
11 Ibid.
12 Ibid.
13 Ibid.
14 Winston S. Churchill, *The Second World War, Their Finest Hour*, Chapter 5.
15 Report by Wells.
16 Report by Vavasour, 7 June 1940.
17 Imperial War Museum interview, 22 June 1983.
18 Report by Lieutenant Arthur Gadd, 7 June 1940. Gadd replaced Commander Apps, who had been injured.

19 Imperial War Museum interview, 8 August 1983.
20 Report by Maund.
21 Ibid.
22 Report by Thew, 5 June 1940.
23 Letter dated 30 May 1940.
24 www.bbc.co.uk/news/uk-england-norfolk-10795088.
25 Ramsay's letter dated 30 May 1940.

Chapter 12

1   Report by Tennant, 7 June 1940.
2   Ibid.
3   Report by Wake-Walker.
4   *Daily Express*, 31 May 1940.
5   Information from the Association of Little Ships.
6   Imperial War Museum interview, 23 November 1989.
7   Imperial War Museum interview, 10 April 2007.
8   Imperial War Museum interview, 27 February 1989.
9   Dench's report, as quoted in A. D. Divine, *Dunkirk*, Chapter 12.
10 Imperial War Museum interview, 28 June 1990.
11 Imperial War Museum interview, 22 June 1983.
12 Hutchins's report, as quoted A. D. Divine, *Dunkirk*, Chapter 12.
13 Ibid.
14 Ibid.
15 Report by Wake-Walker.
16 Ibid.
17 Ibid.
18 Ibid.
19 Report by Tennant, 7 June 1940.
20 Winston S. Churchill, *The Second World War, Their Finest Hour*, Chapter 5.

Chapter 13

1   *Dunkirk* by A. D. Divine, Chapter 13.
2   Report by Wake-Walker.
3   Ibid.
4   Ibid.
5   Report by Commander Philip Hadow, 3 June 1940.
6   Report by Wake-Walker.
7   Reports by Wake-Walker and Captain Edward Berthon, 15 June 1940.
8   Imperial War Museum interview, November 2001.
9   Report by Burnell-Nugent, 5 June 1940.
10 Report by Richmond, 2 June 1940.
11 Hughes's report, as quoted in A. D. Divine, *Dunkirk*, Chapter 13.
12 Ibid.
13 Report by Braithwaite, 11 June 1940.
14 Report by Wake-Walker.
15 Ibid.
16 Ibid.

17 Lightoller's report, as quoted in A. D. Divine, *Dunkirk*, Chapter 13.
18 Ibid.
19 Ibid.
20 Report by Wake-Walker.
21 Ibid.
22 Ibid.
23 Ramsay's report on the Dunkirk evacuation, 18 June 1940.

Chapter 14

1   Imperial War Museum interview, 28 July 1989.
2   Report by Condor.
3   Ramsay's report on the Dunkirk evacuation, 18 June 1940.
4   Report by Wake-Walker.
5   Ibid.
6   Ibid.
7   Report by Munton, as quoted in A. D. Divine, *Dunkirk*, Chapter 14.
8   Report by Biles, as quoted in A. D. Divine, *Dunkirk*, Chapter 14.
9   Ramsay's report on the Dunkirk evacuation, 18 June 1940.
10 A. D. Divine, *Dunkirk*, Chapter 14.
11 Report by Wake, 4 June 1940.
12 Ibid.
13 Report by Wake-Walker.
14 Imperial War Museum interview, 1983.

Chapter 15

1   Report by Wake-Walker.
2   Ibid.
3   Ramsay's report on the Dunkirk evacuation, 18 June 1940.
4   Ibid.
5   Report by Wake-Walker.
6   Imperial War Museum interview, 24 August 1983.
7   Imperial War Museum interview, 15 August 1983.
8   Report by Wake-Walker.
9   Report by Wise, 7 June 1940.

Chapter 16

1   Report by Troup.
2   Report by Clarke, as quoted in A. D. Divine, *Dunkirk*, Chapter 15.
3   BBC archive WW2 People's War.
4   Report by Dean, 8 June 1940.
5   Imperial War Museum interview, 3 March 1987, and article in *The Naval Review*, October 1995.
6   Ibid.
7   Ibid.
8   Report by Wake-Walker.
9   Letter to Ramsay, 17 June 1940.
10 Admiralty message, 4 June 1940.

11 Letter to Ramsay, 2 June 1940.
12 Letter dated 12 June 1940.
13 *Hansard.*
14 Ramsay's report on the Dunkirk evacuation, 18 June 1940.
15 Ibid.
16 Ibid.
17 Ibid.
18 Ibid.
19 Ibid.
20 Letter dated 5 June 1940 and written at the United Services Club, Pall Mall, London.
21 Letter dated 7 June 1940.
22 Ibid.

Chapter 17

1 Karslake's report on operations in France 23 May to 13 June 1940.
2 Brooke's diary entries for early June 1940.
3 Ibid.
4 Ibid.
5 Ibid.
6 Letter dated 9 June 1940.
7 Ramsay's letter to his wife dated 9 June 1940.
8 Awards for Dunkirk appeared in *The London Gazette* for several months after the evacuation.
9 Ramsay's letter to his wife dated 9 June 1940.
10 James's report on Operation *Cycle*, 18 June 1940.
11 Ibid.
12 Ibid.
13 Ibid.
14 Diary of Major James Grant, 12 June 1940.
15 Lovett-Cameron's report, 13 June 1940.
16 Admiral Sir William James, *The Sky Was Always Blue*, Chapter 16.
17 Report by Tower.
18 Brooke diary entry for 12 June 1940.
19 Brooke diary entry for 13 June 1940.
20 Brooke's diary entries for 12–19 June 1940.
21 Brooke diary entry for 15 June 1940.
22 Ibid.
23 James's report on Operation *Aerial*, 19 June 1940.
24 War Office figures confirmed by historians in October 1949.

Chapter 18

1 www.steam-packet.com/information/aboutus
2 Ramsay's report, 18 June 1940.
3 Qaultrough quoted in Ramsay's report.
4 Report by the officer in charge, No 3 party, RN barracks, Chatham, dated 6 June 1940.
5 Company letter dated 6 June 1940.
6 Granville's letter dated 2 September 1940.
7 Little's reply dated 7 September 1940.

8   Ibid.
9   Letters dated 11 June and 27 November 1940.
10 Ibid.
11 Ramsay's report, 18 June 1940.
12 Letter dated 8 June 1940.
13 Letter dated 7 June 1940.
14 Mallory sent two letters of explanation to the principal sea transport officer at Southampton, dated 2 and 11 June 1940.
15 RNLI records of service 1939–45, *The Dover Express and East Kent News*, 28 June 1940.
16 Ibid.
17 Report by Maud, 10 June 1940.
18 Ramsay's letter dated 20 March 1941.
19 Report by Jones covered 27–30 May.
20 Ibid.
21 Temple's report dated 7 June 1940.
22 BBC news report, 27 May 2010.
23 Ibid.
24 by J. L. S. Coulter, Official History of the Second World War, *The Royal Navy Medical Service*, page 328.

Chapter 19

1   Message dated 4 June 1940.
2   Winston S. Churchill, *The Second World War, Their Finest Hour*, Chapter 13.
3   Diary entry 20 July 1940.
4   Ibid.
5   Diary entry for 22 July 1940.
6   Letter dated 12 July 1940.
7   Ibid.
8   Diary entry 26 July 1940.
9   Terry Sutton and Derek Leach, *Dover in the Second World War*, Chapter on 1940.
10 Winston S. Churchill, *The Second World War, Their Finest Hour*, Chapter 13.
11 Letter dated 8 August 1940.
12 Letter dated 20 August 1940.
13 Letter dated 8 September 1940.
14 Rear Admiral W. S. Chalmers, *Full Cycle*, Chapter 11.
15 Letter dated 9 September 1940.
16 Rear Admiral W. S. Chalmers, *Full Cycle*, Chapter 11.
17 Letter dated 29 September 1940
18 Admiral Sir William James, *The Sky Was Always Blue*, Chapter 16.
19 Somerville report covering 30 June to 4 July 1940.
20 Winston S. Churchill, *The Second World War, Their Finest Hour*, Chapter 11.
21 Letter to wife dated 29 September 1940.
22 Report by Ramsay to Admiralty dated 3 August 1940 and report by Surgeon Lieutenant Garmany dated 17 August 1940.
23 Ibid.
24 Ibid.

Chapter 20

1 Diary entry for 10 January 1941.
2 Rear Admiral W. S. Chalmers, *Full Cycle*, Chapter 12.
3 Terry Sutton and Derek Leach, *Dover in the Second World War*, Chapter on 1941.
4 Letter to his wife, dated 28 April 1941.
5 Diary entry for 17 June 1941.
6 Brooke diary entry for 17 June 1941 and his foreword to Rear Admiral W. S. Chalmers, *Full Cycle*.
7 Diary entry for 22 June 1941.
8 BBC broadcast by Churchill on 22 June 1941.
9 Letter to his wife, dated 13 December 1941.
10 Ibid.
11 Captain W. S. Roskill, *The War at Sea*, Volume 1, Chapter 26.
12 M. Middlebrook and P. Mahoney, *Battleship, The Loss of the Prince of Wales and the Repulse*, Chapter 9.
13 Letter to his wife, dated 13 December 1941.
14 Letter to his wife, dated 11 December 1941.
15 Letter dated 21 December 1941.
16 Winston S. Churchill, *The Second World War, Their Finest Hour*, Volume 3, Chapter 32.

Chapter 21

1 Ramsay's report on the escape of the German warships, dated 16 February 1942. Report of the Board of Enquiry (sic), dated 2 March 1942.
2 Ibid.
3 Ibid.
4 Reports by Sub Lieutenant Lee and the intelligence officer at RAF Manston.
5 Ramsay's report on the escape of the German warships, dated 16 February 1942. Report of the Board of Enquiry (sic), dated 2 March 1942.
6 Pumphrey's evidence to inquiry.
7 Report of the Board of Enquiry (sic), dated 2 March 1942.
8 Ramsay's report on the escape of the German warships, dated 16 February 1942. Report of the Board of Enquiry (sic), dated 2 March 1942.
9 Report by Captain Pizey, dated 16 February 1942, which quoted Captain Wright.
10 Ibid.
11 Ramsay's report on the escape of the German warships, dated 16 February 1942.
12 *The Times*, 14 February 1942.
13 Message sent by Air Vice Marshal Norman Bottomley, 13 February 1942.
14 Report of the Board of Enquiry (sic), dated 2 March 1942.
15 Ibid.
16 Ibid.
17 Memo dated 17 February 1942.
18 Obituary of Sub Lieutenant Lee, *The Daily Telegraph*, 17 November 2009.
19 Ramsay's evidence to inquiry.
20 Ibid.
21 Ibid.
22 *Hansard*, 17 February 1942.
23 Admiralty and Air Ministry joint communiqué, 3 May 1942.

Chapter 22

1 Letter from Roosevelt to Churchill, dated 3 April 1942.
2 Brooke diary entries for 14–15 April 1942.
3 Brooke diary entry for 14 April 1942.
4 Ibid.
5 Letter quoted in Rear Admiral W. S. Chalmers, *Full Cycle*, Chapter 14.
6 Message dated 25 June 1942.
7 Admiralty letter dated 9 July 1942.
8 Letter quoted in Rear Admiral W. S. Chalmers, *Full Cycle*, Chapter 14.
9 Letter to wife dated 11 July 1942.
10 Brooke diary entry for 17 July 1942.
11 Ibid.
12 John Wukovits, *Eisenhower*, Chapter 6.
13 Brooke diary entry for 22 July 1942.
14 Winston S. Churchill, *The Second World War, The Hinge of Fate*, Volume 4, Chapter 18.
15 Letter quoted in Rear Admiral W. S. Chalmers, *Full Cycle*, Chapter 14.
16 Dwight D. Eisenhower, *Crusade in Europe*, Chapter 4.
17 Winston S. Churchill, *The Second World War, The Hinge of Fate*, Volume 4, Chapter 29.
18 Captain S. W. Roskill, *The War at Sea 1939–1945*, Volume 2, Chapter 10.

Chapter 23

1 Winston S. Churchill, *The Second World War, The Hinge of Fate*, Volume 4, Chapter 25.
2 Messages between the two leaders, 27 and 28 July 1942.
3 Dwight D. Eisenhower, *Crusade in Europe*, Chapter 4.
4 Ibid.
5 Ibid.
6 John Winton, *Cunningham*, Chapter 17.
7 Dwight D. Eisenhower, *Crusade in Europe*, Chapter 5.
8 Andrew Browne Cunningham, *A Sailor's Odyssey*, Chapter 36.
9 Ibid.
10 John Winton, *Cunningham*, Chapter 17.
11 Letter dated 8 August 1942.
12 Letter dated 14 August 1942.
13 Letter to Ramsay dated 22 August 1942.
14 Report sent 24 August 1942.
15 Message dated 26 August 1942.
16 Winston S. Churchill, *The Second World War, The Hinge of Fate*, Volume 4, Chapter 30.
17 Message dated 27 August 1942.
18 Message dated 30 August 1942.
19 Winston S. Churchill, *The Second World War, The Hinge of Fate*, Volume 4, Chapter 30.
20 Rear Admiral W. S. Chalmers, *Full Cycle*, Chapter 14.
21 *Cunningham* by John Winton, Chapter 17.
22 Andrew Browne Cunningham, *A Sailor's Odyssey*, Chapter 36.
23 Inquiry report, undated.
24 *Cunningham* by John Winton, Chapter 17.

25 Andrew Browne Cunningham, *A Sailor's Odyssey*, Chapter 37.
26 Dwight D. Eisenhower, *Crusade in Europe*, Chapter 6.
27 Andrew Browne Cunningham, *A Sailor's Odyssey*, Chapter 37.
28 Ibid.
29 Letter dated 2 November 1942.

Chapter 24

1 Cunningham's report on *Torch*, dated 30 March 1943.
2 Ibid.
3 Report by Layard, dated 11 November 1942.
4 Cunningham's report on *Torch*, dated 30 March 1943.
5 Ibid.
6 Brian Lane Herder, *Operation Torch 1942*, page 37.
7 Andrew Browne Cunningham, *A Sailor's Odyssey*, Chapter 37.
8 Cunningham's report on *Torch*, dated 30 March 1943.
9 Letter dated 9 November 1942.
10 Letter dated 12 November 1942.
11 Letter sent from Combined Operations Headquarters, 19 November 1942.
12 Dwight D. Eisenhower, *Crusade in Europe*, Chapter 6.
13 Ibid.
14 Letter dated 11 November 1942.
15 Letter dated 12 November 1942.
16 Letter to his wife dated 21 November 1942.
17 Winston S. Churchill, *The Second World War, The Hinge of Fate*, Volume 4, Chapter 36.
18 Letter dated 21 November 1942.
19 Peter Kross, Warfare History Network.
20 Winston S. Churchill, *The Second World War, The Hinge of Fate*, Volume 4, Chapter 35.

Chapter 25

1 Comments made on 9 November 1942.
2 Ibid.
3 Message to Churchill, 26 November 1942.
4 Messages from Churchill and Roosevelt, 3 December 1942.
5 Winston S. Churchill, *The Second World War, The Hinge of Fate*, Volume 4, Chapter 38.
6 Minutes of Chiefs of Staff meeting, 18 February 1943.
7 Letter dated 7 March 1943.
8 Letter to his wife dated 15 March 1943.
9 Letter to his wife dated 19 March 1943.
10 Ibid.
11 Alexander's message dated 8 May 1943.
12 John Winton, *Cunningham*, Chapter 19.
13 Andrew Browne Cunningham, *A Sailor's Odyssey*, Chapter 39.
14 *The Alexander Memoirs 1940–45*, Chapter 4.
15 Dwight D. Eisenhower, *Crusade in Europe*, Chapter 8.

Chapter 26

1 Andrew Browne Cunningham, *A Sailor's Odyssey*, Chapter 40.
2 Alexander's report on *Husky*, February 1948.
3 Ramsay's report on *Husky*, dated 1 October 1943.
4 Letter dated 7 April 1943.
5 Ibid.
6 Letter dated 12 April 1943.
7 Ibid.
8 Cunningham's report on *Husky*, dated 1 January 1944
9 *The Memoirs of Field Marshal The Viscount Montgomery of Alamein*, Chapter 11.
10 Ibid.
11 Ibid.
12 Ibid.
13 Ibid.
14 Letter dated 28 April 1943.
15 *The Memoirs of Field Marshal The Viscount Montgomery of Alamein*, Chapter 11.
16 Letter dated 6 May 1943.
17 Letter dated 10 May 1943.
18 Ibid.
19 Letter to his wife dated 11 May 1943.
20 Winston S. Churchill, *The Second World War, The Hinge of Fate*, Volume 4, Chapter 45.
21 Ibid.
22 Dwight D. Eisenhower, *Crusade in Europe*, Chapter 9.
23 Ibid.
24 Andrew Browne Cunningham, *A Sailor's Odyssey*, Chapter 40.
25 Cunningham's report on *Husky*, dated 1 January 1944
26 Alexander's report on *Husky*, February 1948.
27 *The Sunday Times* of Sri Lanka, 24 February 1980.
28 Ibid.
29 Alexander's report on *Husky*, February 1948.
30 Letter dated 11 July 1943.
31 Ramsay's report on *Husky*, dated 1 October 1943.
32 John Winton, *Cunningham*, Chapter 20.
33 Andrew Browne Cunningham, *A Sailor's Odyssey*, Chapter 41.
34 Dwight D. Eisenhower, *Crusade in Europe*, Chapter 10.
35 Letter dated 29 July 1943.
36 *The Memoirs of Field Marshal The Viscount Montgomery of Alamein*, Chapter 11.

Chapter 27

1 *The Memoirs of Field Marshal The Viscount Montgomery of Alamein*, Chapter 12.
2 Andrew Browne Cunningham, *A Sailor's Odyssey*, Chapter 41.
3 Andrew Browne Cunningham, *A Sailor's Odyssey*, Chapter 43.
4 Rear Admiral W. S. Chalmers, *Full Cycle*, Chapter 19.
5 *The Second World War, Closing the Ring* by Winston S. Churchill, Volume 5, Chapters 5 and 21.
6 Brooke diary entry, 8 November 1943.
7 Brooke diary entry, 4 December 1943.

8   Ramsay's report on *Neptune*, 16 October 1944.
9   *The Memoirs of Field Marshal The Viscount Montgomery of Alamein*, Chapter 13.
10 Ibid.
11 Ibid.
12 Rear Admiral W. S. Chalmers, *Full Cycle*, Chapter 19.
13 Ramsay diary entry, 10 January 1944.
14 Ibid.
15 Ramsay diary entry, 17 January 1944.
16 Ramsay diary entry, 20 January 1944.
17 Ramsay diary entry, 1 February 1944.
18 British Information Services press release dated 20 February 1944.
19 Ibid.
20 Ramsay diary entry, 16 February 1944.
21 Letter dated 19 April 1944.
22 Ramsay diary entry, 2 March 1944.
23 Ramsay diary entry, 3 March 1944.
24 Ramsay diary entry, 25 March 1944.
25 Ramsay diary entry, 4 March 1944.
26 Ramsay diary entry.
27 Ibid.
28 Ramsay diary entries, 6, 7 and 8 May 1944.
29 Ramsay diary entry.
30 Brooke diary entry, 15 May 1944.
31 Andrew Browne Cunningham, *A Sailor's Odyssey*, Chapter 44.
32 Ibid.

Chapter 28

1   Dwight D. Eisenhower, *Crusade in Europe*, Chapter 13. Ramsay diary entry, 4 June 1944. *The Memoirs of Field Marshal The Viscount Montgomery of Alamein*, Chapter 13.
2   Dwight D. Eisenhower, *Crusade in Europe*, Chapter 13. Ramsay's diary entry, 5 June 1944. *The Memoirs of Field Marshal The Viscount Montgomery of Alamein*, Chapter 13.
3   Letter dated 5 June 1944.
4   Ramsay's report on *Neptune*, 16 October 1944.
5   Ibid.
6   Ibid.
7   Imperial War Museum interview, 23 February 1987.
8   Ibid.
9   Ramsay's report on *Neptune*, 16 October 1944.
10 Imperial War Museum interview, 18 February 1985.
11 Imperial War Museum interview, January 1993.
12 Ibid.
13 Imperial War Museum interview, 1997.
14 Ibid.
15 Ramsay's report on *Neptune*, 16 October 1944.
16 Ibid.
17 Imperial War Museum interview, 29 April 2006.

18 *U.S. Navy at War 1941–1945, Official Reports by Fleet Admiral Ernest J. King*, Chapter 4.
19 Imperial War Museum interview, 1997.
20 Ibid.
21 Ramsay diary entry, 7 June 1944.
22 Imperial War Museum interview, 1997.
23 Letter dated 8 June 1944.
24 Diary entry.
25 *The Memoirs of Field Marshal Viscount Montgomery of Alamein*, Chapter 14.
26 Winston S. Churchill, *The Second World War, Triumph and Tragedy*, Volume 6, Chapter 1, letter to Roosevelt, 12 June 1944.
27 *Action This Day, The Memoirs of Admiral of the Fleet Sir Philip Vian*, Chapter 12.
28 Letter quoted in *Full Cycle* by Rear Admiral W. S. Chalmers, Chapter 23.
29 Ramsay's report on *Neptune*, 16 October 1944.
30 Letter dated 12 June 1944.
31 Diary entry.
32 Diary entry.

Chapter 29

1   Diary entries for 19, 20 and 21 July 1944.
2   Ibid.
3   Ibid.
4   Ibid.
5   Diary entry, 2 August 1944.
6   Diary entry, 5 August 1944.
7   Diary entry, 17 August 1944.
8   Diary entry, 19 August 1944.
9   Diary entry, 27 August 1944.
10 Winston S. Churchill, *The Second World War, Triumph and Tragedy*. Volume 6, Chapter 2.
11 Diary entry, 2 September 1944.
12 Letter dated 11 September 1944.
13 Ibid.
14 Ibid.
15 Andrew Browne Cunningham, *A Sailor's Odyssey*, Chapter 44.
16 Dwight D. Eisenhower, *Crusade in Europe*, Chapter 16. *The Memoirs of Field Marshal The Viscount Montgomery of Alamein*, Chapter 16. Ramsay's diary entry, 11 September 1944.
17 Diary entry.
18 Diary entry, 22 September 1944.
19 Diary entry.
20 Diary entry.
21 Diary entry, 5 October 1944.
22 Brooke diary entry, 5 October 1944.
23 *The Memoirs of Field Marshal The Viscount Montgomery of Alamein*, Chapter 16.
24 Diary entry.
25 Diary entry.
26 Diary entry.
27 Diary entry.
28 Diary entry, 29 November 1944.

29 Dwight D. Eisenhower, *Crusade in Europe*, Chapter 15.
30 Diary entry.
31 Diary entry.
32 Diary entry.
33 Letter to Admiral Sir Frederic Dreyer, 30 December 1944.

Chapter 30

1 Letter to his wife, 31 December 1945.
2 Ibid.
3 Ibid.
4 Diary entry, 9 December 1944.
5 Letter dated 22 December 1944.
6 Letter dated 4 January 1945.
7 Andrew Browne Cunningham, *A Sailor's Odyssey*, Chapter 46.
8 *The Times* tribute, 3 January 1945. Letter to Lady Ramsay, 5 January.
9 Letter dated 3 January 1945.

Chapter 31

1 Letter dated 29 January 1945.
2 Letter dated 21 January 1945.
3 Ibid.
4 Ibid.
5 Report by Lieutenant Commander C. G. Moore, a senior engineering officer, 5 February 1945.
6 Letter from H. B. Squire, principal scientific officer at Farnborough, dated 3 February 1945, which followed a conversation with Lieutenant Commander Moore.
7 Letter from Lieutenant Commander Caldwell to Lieutenant Commander Moore, 23 February 1945.
8 Comments to Lieutenant Commander Moore from Lieutenant Commander Cunningham, 23 February 1945.
9 Bret's evidence to inquiry into crash, The National Archives.
10 Ibid.
11 Stokes' evidence to inquiry into crash, The National Archives.
12 Inquiry into crash, The National Archives.

Index